The Antique Collector's Handbook

By the same author

EIGHTEENTH CENTURY GERMAN PORCELAIN
EIGHTEENTH CENTURY ENGLISH PORCELAIN
ART AND ANTIQUE RESTORER'S HANDBOOK
FORGERIES, FAKES AND REPRODUCTIONS ETC

The Antique Collector's Handbook

GEORGE SAVAGE

DRAWINGS BY FREDERICK CURL

Spring Books

LONDON · NEW YORK · SYDNEY · TORONTO

First published 1959 by Barrie and Rockliff (Barrie Books Ltd)
© Copyright 1959, 1968 George Savage

This new, revised edition published 1968 by
The Hamlyn Publishing Group Ltd,
London . New York . Sydney . Toronto
Astronaut House, Feltham, Middlesex, England
Seventh impression 1976

Printed and bound in Great Britain by
REDWOOD BURN LIMITED
Trowbridge & Esher

ISBN 0 600 00054 0

Contents

List of Illustrations

List of Illustrations vii

Facing page

Acknowledgments

Antique Porcelain Company, Ltd: 5
British Museum: 8, 13
Christie, Manson & Woods: 1, 2, 3, 6, 18, 21, 23
Colonial Williamsburg, Williamsburg, Va.: 10
Hove Museum and Art Gallery: 7
Kestnermuseum, Hanover: 28
Parke-Bernet Galleries, New York: 14, 16, 25, 26, 30
Sotheby and Company: 4, 11, 12, 15, 17, 19, 20, 22, 24, 29, 31, 32
Victoria and Albert Museum: 9, 27

Preface

Within the last few years collecting antiques has become not only one of the most absorbing pastimes known to civilized man, but an internationally recognized investment for the wise and farseeing. This aspect is new both in this country and in the United States, but the collecting of works of art of all kinds for this purpose has been common on the Continent, especially in France, for more than two hundred years, and antiques and works of art wisely bought have more often brought spectacular profits than losses.

Nevertheless, if the Frenchman grows up with an acute sense of values and a distrust of paper currency, this is still new in England, and there is a dearth of information of a practical kind relating to the purchase of antiques, and to the pitfalls which in this, as in every other field of endeavour, await the newcomer. The purpose of this book is to review the principal kinds likely to attract the greater number of intending collectors and investors, and to suggest lines on which further study may profitably be pursued, as well as providing essential information about buying and selling.

Although books can never be a substitute for seeing and handling the objects, neither seeing nor handling can be sufficient in themselves, and only books can provide the essential background against which purchases must be weighed. "Fools," Bismarck once said, "say they learn from experience. I prefer to learn from the experience of others." This book is the product of a good many years spent very pleasantly in buying and selling antiques, and if the experience therein recorded can help the reader to buy wisely, then there is little point in buying in a dearer market.

Undoubtedly there are many omissions. Since an enormous subject, to which the appended Bibliography amply testifies, has been compressed into a very small space, it could hardly be otherwise, but the Bibliography will suggest ways of augmenting knowledge, and the titles have been selected for their value as further reading. Many of them contain Bibliographies of less-well-known works which will enable the subject to be pursued still further.

The newcomer to antique collecting can view the objects themselves in museums, dealers' showrooms, the larger auction-rooms, and in the numerous country houses now open to the public. Of these sources, the dealer's showroom, where objects can be seen, handled, and discussed, is probably the most useful and informative, and the Victoria & Albert Museum houses the world's finest collection of most of the things which will interest the greater number of collectors. Museums abroad often contain objects which are to be found in antique shops at home, often at much lower prices than those charged by dealers in their country of origin, where the demand is greater.

My thanks are especially due to Gerald Taylor and to Penguin Books for permission to reproduce the silver marks from the author's admirable handbook to old English silver in the Pelican series. I am grateful to Kenneth Ullyett and Barrie and Rockliff for permission to reproduce the clock charts which clearly set forth the development of the English clock during the 17th and 18th centuries. I am grateful to Josiah Wedgwood & Sons Limited for the marks on old Wedgwood pottery here reproduced.

G.S.
London, 1968

How to Use This Book

The information contained herein has been set out in dictionary form for easy reference. The main subjects are treated under a single heading, subdivided into appropriate sections. For example, pottery and porcelain are included under the heading of *Ceramics*, and subdivided into such sections as English porcelain, German pottery, and so forth.

An Index Key to the Contents follows which analyses the entries into subjects, and reference to this will enable the reader to select the article likely to give the information required, or to select all the articles which have a bearing on a particular subject. For instance, under the heading *Chinese Art* will be found a note of all the entries relating to Chinese pottery, porcelain, bronzes, jades, lacquer, and so forth, as well as those which deal with styles to be seen during the various periods, and motifs of decoration.

If the desired information cannot be obtained in this way the detailed index at the back of the book should be consulted.

It has not, of course, been possible to define or explain the various terms in each section in which they are used. In such cases, therefore, the index will supply the main reference. As an example, the term rococo is quite frequently used without definition, but this has been given on p. 197 in a special note devoted to the principles of this style.

The book is intended to be a brief review of those things which can be found in the shops of good art and antique dealers. Naturally, detailed information has had to be excluded. If, therefore, the required information cannot be found in the index the reader should turn to the Bibliography. Here he will find a comprehensive selection of the more important books on the subjects discussed herein, at least one of which should provide the desired information. Books which are out of print or very scarce have been omitted if there is a recent work which would serve the purpose as well.

Most books on antiques are expensive and comparatively scarce, despite the demand for them. Standard works are worth buying if they are likely to be required for reference from time to time. Otherwise, for brief references, many of them are available in the larger reference libraries, and public libraries usually have a representative selection of the less expensive works.

If this is insufficient, the books listed can be obtained by public libraries through the National Central Library service, which rarely fails to find a copy in one of its member libraries. If this fails, the only source then becomes a good antiquarian bookseller, but the book will, obviously, be so scarce that it is likely to be highly priced.

The value of a good library on a collector's speciality cannot be too highly stressed. I have rarely purchased an expensive book which has not eventually paid for itself several times over, and the best hold their value remarkably well. It has been truly said that anyone is as good as his library, and the beginner will soon realize the value of a well-ordered collection of books on his subject.

Key to the Contents

WITH TITLES OF ARTICLES

BUYING AND SELLING
Auction (Bidding Agreements) Act, 1927
British Antique Dealers' Association
Dealers
Fashion in works of art
Investment, antiques as an
Invoices and descriptions
"Knockers"
Quality
"Runners"
Valuations for insurance
Valuations for probate
Value of works of art

CARPETS AND RUGS
Carpets:
    Chinese
    European
    Hooked rugs
    Indian
    Persia and the Middle East
    Turkey

CERAMICS
Ceramics:
    American pottery and porcelain
    Belgian pottery and porcelain
    Chinese pottery and porcelain
    English porcelain
    English pottery
    French porcelain
    French pottery
    German porcelain
    German pottery
    Holland, porcelain

Derby (Derbyshire)
Longton Hall (Staffs)
Lowestoft (Suffolk)
Nantgarw (S. Wales)
New Hall (Staffs)
Pinxton (Derby)
Plymouth (Devon)
Rockingham (Yorks)
Swansea (S. Wales)
Wedgwood (Staffs)
Worcester (Worc)

PROCESSES AND TECHNIQUES
Enamel and Enamelling
Gilding
Marquetry
Parquetry
Scagliola
Schwarzlot
Sgraffito
Tin-enamelling
Transfer printing
Veneering

REPAIRS AND RESTORATIONS

STYLES
Adam
Baroque
Gothic
Louis Seize
Neo-classical
Palladian
Régence
Regency period
Rococo
Style in works of art
Victorian period

TEXTILES
Embroidery
Tapestries

ULTRA-VIOLET RADIATION

WOOD-CARVING

Information in Alphabetical Order

ADAM STYLE, THE   The version of the NEO-CLASSICAL STYLE (*q.v.*) associated with the brothers, Adam.

James [1721–1792] and Robert Adam [1728–1792] were Scottish architects. Robert visited Italy in 1754, and became infected with the current enthusiasm for ancient art. On his return to England, in association with his brother, he introduced the neo-classical style here. One of the most characteristic examples of their work is Lansdowne House in London. The Adam style is more or less synonymous with the neo-classical in England.

ARMS AND ARMOUR   The collecting of arms and armour falls into so many different categories that it is difficult to give more than a very brief survey in the space available.

The weapons of Neolithic man were nearly always of flint, although such hardstones as obsidian and greenstone were used occasionally in some parts of the world. Spear-heads, arrow-heads, and axes were often made with great skill when the crudeness of the material and the available tools are considered, the usual method being by flaking until the desired shape had been attained. The flint dagger is probably the rarest and most prized of all weapons of this kind. The subject is a specialized one, and reference should be made to the various authorities on the period. Like most other things, flint implements have been forged, especially during the 19th century, when much interest was taken in them by collectors. The implements of "Flint Jack", a wandering workman who copied Neolithic stone implements with some exactness, are reputed to be particularly deceptive, and he made a large quantity during his lifetime.

Early bronze weapons are of much more interest, and swords especially were made with great skill and tempered by cold hammering. They have been found throughout Europe, and are often well preserved. Weapons of the Chinese Bronze Age range from the sword to the halberd head (*ko*), and are sometimes handsomely decorated. Of particular interest is the extremely rare and well-made cross-bow lock, with a trigger action and a grooved channel for the bolt, which first appears during the Han Dynasty. Bronze arrow-heads are comparatively rare in Europe and the Far East, and it can safely be assumed that flint continued to be used for such expendable objects for many years after it had been superseded by bronze for other things, since metal was scarce and valuable.

The first item of personal armour was undoubtedly the shield, at first made of wood or leather, and later of bronze. This was followed by the bronze helmet, and greaves (or shin-guards) of the same metal, the body being protected by a *cuirass* comprising both breast and back plates.

Roman armour of better quality was designed to fit the body closely, and had the addition of *tassets*, or flexible plates, to protect the belly and the lower part of the body generally.

Items of Greek and Roman arms and armour are rare, but both Greek and Roman helmets exist. The metal of surviving examples is nearly always bronze, with varying degrees of corrosion. Weapons of iron have usually rusted away completely, leaving only a deposit of iron oxide in the ground to mark the spot. A few early iron weapons have been recovered where conditions have been exceptionally favourable – in parts of northern Europe, for instance.

Most of the armour still to be found dates from after the Norman Conquest, and early specimens are extremely valuable. Up to the beginning of the 15th century most of the armour used was mail, made up of linked rings of steel. The term "mail", in fact, means armour of this kind, and the often-used "chain mail" is tautological. The date of the introduction of mail is uncertain, but it is probably referable to the early part of the present era, and may even have been known to the Romans. Certainly it was almost universally used in Europe by the 12th century, and its reinforcement by plates of steel at vital points led, eventually, to the development of the full suit of plate armour.

At the time of the Norman Conquest the most usual form of armour for the warrior of standing was a tunic (or *hauberk*) of mail for the body, and similar protection for the legs. The helmet was conical, with a projection downwards to protect the nose. The shield was either circular or in the shape of a kite.

By the 13th century the helmet was much heavier. The advance in the quality and type of weapons changed its shape first to a flat-topped variety, and later to a rounded form similar in shape to the skull. Additional protection for the hands against disabling sword-cuts was provided by mittens.

At the beginning of the 15th century the use of mail as a primary defence began to give place to the full suit of plate armour. The various parts have a special nomenclature of their own, which is given below.

The helmet is divided into the *skull*, which protected the top and the back of the head, and the *visor* (which could be raised or lowered at will) protecting the eyes and the face. The visor, when closed, was pierced at eye-level, and this is called the *sight*. The lower part of the helmet was also pierced for ventilation, and this is termed the *breath*.

The neck was protected by a *gorget*, articulated in later suits, and the shoulder by the *pauldron* or *épaulière*, the latter surviving in the *épaulettes* of some military uniforms. The plates from the shoulder to the hand were jointed to allow of arm movement, the upper arm being covered by over-lapping plates (the *rerebrace*), to which was added a circular plate protecting the armpit – the *roundel*. The articulation of the elbow was protected by the *couter* or *coudière*, whilst the forearm was covered by the *vambrace*, which terminated in an articulated *gauntlet* protecting hand, fingers, and thumb.

The *breastplate*, as the name implies, covered the chest from *gorget* to waist, and terminated in a series of articulated plates covering the belly, called the *tassets*. The back was protected by a *backplate*.

The thigh was covered by the *cuisse*, and the shin by the *greave* or *jamb*, whilst between them, over the knee-cap, came the *poleyn* or *genouillère*. Finally, the leg armour terminated in the square-toed *sabaton*, or the flexible, pointed *solleret*.

Additional protection of leather and mail was worn to

cover weak spots and joints which might be disclosed by movement, and to reduce the force of blows.

The principle behind the design of all plate armour is that of deflection. The object was not so much to resist blows as to turn them aside. A little reflection will make it obvious that a heavy blow from a sword or a club, if it landed fairly and squarely, would probably render the recipient unconscious from concussion, even if the plate resisted the blow. Armour, therefore, was designed so that blows slid off without exerting their full force. This had the useful result, more often than not, of putting the striker off-balance, and in a bad position to resist a blow at a joint in his own armour which was the weakest spot.

The lance was used by the horseman primarily to dislodge a mounted opponent, and to this end he directed the point to a part of the armour where it stood a chance of lodging. If he were fortunate, the combined impetus of man and horse was sufficient to throw down an opponent, and sometimes his horse as well. On the ground the weight of armour made a man fairly easy prey, and remounting was difficult. Armour therefore, had to deflect lances and provide the slightest possible opportunity for a lance-point to lodge.

This need can well be seen in the ridge which runs down the centre of some breastplates. It obviates the possibility of the lance catching the wearer squarely in the centre, and induces it to slide off to one side or the other. The shield served much the same purpose, and acted as a first line of defence, absorbing some of the shock of a blow, and often deflecting it altogether.

Although field-armour, and most tilting-armour, was made with due attention to these requirements, suits of plate armour intended for ceremonial purposes disregarded them to some extent. This can be seen in elaborate fluting and decoration, some of which would obviously be a disadvantage in combat.

Most combats at this time took place between horsemen, and quite obviously an unarmoured horse was a weak point to which an opponent would direct his attack. The practice of armouring horses, therefore, grew up at the same time, and became most elaborate.

With the growing use of gunpowder, armour fell into disuse, since it offered but slight protection and unduly hampered the man. The heavy plate, therefore, began to give place to lighter armour by the 16th century, and much ceremonial armour belongs to this period. The helmet and the breastplate lingered on. The former is still used today, and the latter was in use until the end of the 17th century and even beyond. The other parts fell into disuse one by one, the gauntlet, for example, being superseded by a more effective sword-guard which protected the hand almost equally well.

The arms of interest to the collector include swords, rapiers, sabres, and daggers. The earliest swords offered very poor protection for the hand, being little more than a blade with a simple cross-piece (the *quillon*), but the hilt became more elaborate as the gauntlet fell into disuse. Swords are often decorated in a variety of ways, an example being damascening, done by hammering gold wire into grooves cut into the blade. A common place for decoration is the *ricasso* – the flat, rectangular part of the blade immediately below the hilt.

The scimitar of the East fathered a number of curved European types – the cavalry sabre, the cutlass, the hanger, and the falchion. The rapier was a light sword with a straight blade which was used for its point rather than its edge, and it owed its vogue to the rise of the science of fencing. It was popular as a weapon of defence, and much used in duels. Daggers are too numerous to attempt to describe them.

Staff weapons (or pole-arms) are descended from the battle-axe, and include such things as the halberd, which combines an axe blade with a lance-point, and the partizan, which has a more or less symmetrically shaped blade based on the axe. The earliest lances were a plain shaft with a steel head, but later developed into a shaft increasing in diameter towards the hand-grip, which was recessed into it to protect the hand. A bracket to form a lance-rest was often integral with the breastplate. The mace, originally far from a ceremonial object, was a heavy club with an iron head.

Undoubtedly the masters of the long-bow during medieval times were the English, and we owe many important victories to its use. It was about 6 feet in length, and was used with a 3-foot shaft. It had an effective range of about 250 yards. Actually the cross-bow preceded it in point of time, but its use was discouraged, except against infidels, by the Lateran Council.

The cross-bow was small, but extremely powerful, and had a tiller (or stock) at right angles to the bow which was held against the shoulder. It was usually prepared for firing by a *cranequin*, a windlass fitted with a ratchet, and the bolt was discharged with great force by means of a lock. The cross-bow was taken very seriously by the armourer and his customers, and led to the introduction of a special quality, known as proof-armour, which was tested by firing a cross-bow bolt at it.

The cross-bow (or *arbalest*) was principally used during the 12th and 13th centuries, and fired a short winged shaft tipped with metal. Occasionally much larger versions were constructed for special purposes, but usually it was a light weapon. In comparison with the long-bow, it suffered from the severe disadvantage of taking much longer to prepare for discharge, but some specimens still survive today, whereas long-bows have disappeared.

The invention of gunpowder caused a complete revolution in the art of warfare. Although it had been known for centuries before its first application to implements of war – there is reference to it in A.D. 846 – gunpowder was not used to project missiles until the beginning of the 14th century.

The principle of the cannon, and of subsequent hand-guns, is simple. Into a hollow tube, closed at one end, is inserted first a charge of powder, then a wad to assist in confining the explosion, and finally a missile. The application of a detonating agent converts the charge into a gas, which expands violently, forcing the missile from the tube.

The rate at which the gas expands is of great importance. If the expansion is so rapid that the projectile cannot get clear of the barrel quickly enough the barrel bursts, usually with disastrous results to anyone near it. It is for this reason that relatively slow-burning explosives like gunpowder or cordite are used for the purpose. The so-called high- (or fast-burning) explosives, such as dynamite, TNT, or the modern RDX, are so rapid in their action that the missile would not be pushed from the barrel quickly enough to allow for expansion of the gases, and it would be shattered to fragments which would fly off at a high speed. Even gunpowder put a considerable strain on early barrels, and they not infrequently exploded if too great a charge was used.

It was, of course, necessary to provide a means of igniting the charge, and a small hole was drilled into the barrel through which fire could be introduced for this purpose. This first took the form of a slow match – wick soaked in saltpetre – or a red-hot wire, and often a pan was provided next to the touch-hole on which a small quantity of gunpowder was placed and ignited, the ignition being transferred to the charge in the barrel.

A mechanism for hand-guns was later devised to carry the slow match, and to bring it in contact with the touch-hole, and guns of this kind are referred to as match-locks. These came into use about the end of the 15th century, and were still occasionally used towards the close of the 17th. They were followed by the wheel-lock, which was devised at the beginning of the 16th century, and followed the principle of the modern cigarette-lighter. The revolution of a toothed wheel struck sparks from a fragment of pyrites, and these ignited powder in the pan near the touch-hole. The wheel-lock was uncertain in action, and misfires were common – a fact which will be apparent to anyone who uses a cigarette-lighter. It had certain definite advantages when applied to pistols and light carbines for cavalry use, and had a period of popularity, but, by the end of the 17th century, it had given place to the flint-lock. The earliest version of the flint-lock is the snap-haunce, introduced about 1575, which is much the same in principle, but with an uncovered pan. The flint-lock proper, introduced about fifty years later, had a cover to the pan which made ignition more certain, and protected the priming powder from rain. The charge in a flint-lock gun was ignited by sparks struck from a piece of flint as it snapped down on to the pan. It was more certain than the wheel-lock, but still prone to misfires, and both locks sometimes had a match-lock in addition as an alternative means of igniting the powder.

The flint-lock continued in use until the early part of the 19th century, when it was superseded by the percussion cap. This was a small copper cap containing a detonator, such as mercury fulminate, which would explode at a blow. It fitted over the touch-hole, and the trigger mechanism caused a hammer to fall on it with sufficient force to explode the detonating charge, and thence the powder. The detonating cap was later incorporated with the powder and the bullet into a cartridge, which led to the development of the modern system of projecting missiles.

The earliest guns had a smooth bore, but rifling of the bore to impart a spinning action to the bullet was first tried at the beginning of the 16th century. A rotating missile kept a much straighter course, and aiming was more precise. The difficulties of manufacture, however, were so great that rifling did not come into general use until the 19th century.

Nearly all early guns were loaded by way of the muzzle, although attempts were made to devise a method of breech-loading as early as the 15th century. The methods of manufacture in use made this difficult, since great precision is necessary if the gases are not to escape through the breech. This would not only be dangerous to the user, but would reduce the force of the missile. The first effective breech-loading hand-gun was not made until about 1810, when Colonel John Hall of Maine, in the U.S.A., took out a patent for a flint-lock of this kind.

Many attempts were made to devise a multiple-firing weapon, a musket with revolving chambers being made in Brussels in 1632, but it was not until the invention of the modern cartridge that a satisfactory mechanism could be devised. Since that time the revolver, which brings each cartridge in line with the barrel in turn by means of a rotating chamber, and the automatic pistol, rifle, and machine gun, which utilize the recoil of one cartridge to bring the next into firing position, have been brought to a high degree of efficiency.

The pistol, a firearm for discharge by one hand, was introduced during the first quarter of the 16th century. Early specimens can be found with wheel-locks, and subsequently with flint-locks. The match-lock was not used. At first it was essentially a cavalry weapon, and the butts were fitted with a heavy boss so that they could be reversed after firing and used as a club. They varied in length. Early pistols are extremely long by modern standards, eighteen inches or more being not unusual. Later, when pistols came to be used by the man on foot, the length became progressively less, and pistols which could be carried in the pocket, or thrust into the belt, were popular from about the end of the 17th century.

Many early attempts were made to convert the pistol to

multiple-firing, but an efficient weapon had to await the percussion cap and the modern cartridge. The first really effective revolver was made by Samuel Colt early in the 19th century. He improved upon earlier attempts to devise a mechanism whereby the pull on the trigger revolved the chambers to bring the next cartridge into firing position.

The breech-loading revolver, utilizing cartridges made on the modern principle, was devised by Smith and Wesson about the middle of the 19th century, and the system whereby the weapon "breaks" in the middle for easy and rapid reloading followed shortly afterwards. This was soon used extensively by Webley and by American gunsmiths. The ejector for the used cartridge-case was developed about the same time, and led to experiments in the use of recoil to effect an automatic action, the first automatic pistol coming from Germany about 1890.

The earliest guns were fitted with a straight stock and held at the side. Holding the gun to the shoulder obviously made for greater precision in aiming, but the force of the recoil made it unpleasant to use in this way. Sometime during the 15th century, therefore, the curved stock was introduced. This not only absorbed some of the recoil by deflecting it upwards but permitted the user to sight along the barrel without trouble. The V-shaped sight was also introduced at a comparatively early date.

It is difficult to give much guidance on the question of value. Complete suits of plate armour are very rare, and high prices are often given for single pieces and part-suits of fine quality. Most in demand is the helmet, and a good early helmet is a great rarity. Helmets of the 17th century have no especial value. Armour was made by the finest craftsmen and metal-workers of the period. An eye for quality can be gained by studying examples in the Wallace Collection and the Tower of London. Both places have many extremely fine specimens.

Early swords and similar weapons are in demand, and prices are often increased by association value when a specimen comes from an important source. Latterly, pistols have also been much in demand, and high prices are paid for early revolvers by Samuel Colt and others.

Prices for hand-guns are often increased by decoration,

and many pistols and the larger firearms were inlaid with silver, and embellished in other ways. Plate armour, too, was often decorated, especially when it was made for ceremonial purposes.

Forgeries and reproductions of plate armour are not un-common. Hand-guns and weapons in this category have not been forged to any noticeable extent, although the prices at present ruling suggest the possibility in the future.

AUCTION (BIDDING AGREEMENTS) ACT, 1927

This Act was passed to suppress agreements between purchasers at Auction which are directed against the vendor, and which have, for their object, the acquisition of the property offered at much below its real value. Such "rings" are usually com-posed of two, three, or more persons, of which only one bids for any particular lot, thus limiting competition. It very rarely happens that competition can be suppressed altogether. After the sale the "ring" holds another auction at which the highest bidder holds the lot, whilst the difference between the first and second selling prices is distributed in varying proportions between its members.

Although the practice still persists, the Act has not, to my knowledge, been used to prosecute persons acting in this way. It is difficult to see how a conviction could be secured, since the second auction is always held clandestinely.

This is the so-called "knock-out", magnificently de-scribed by a dealer in Government surplus as "a modified form of friendship". It now operates but rarely in the well-known salerooms, although it still continues in some country salerooms. Reputable dealers are not in favour of the practice.

There is no doubt that the practice works against the interests of an uninformed seller, although the reserve price acts as a safeguard to some extent. It is frequently urged in its favour, with truth, that some vendors take advantage of un-informed buyers by bidding for their own lots. Unless this is expressly provided for in the conditions of sale, bidding on the part of the vendor makes the sale fraudulent, but it is as difficult to prove such intervention as it is to prove the existence of a "knock-out" among dealers.

Perhaps the worst aspect of the "knock-out" is that it

encourages persons of an undesirable kind in the saleroom who have no intention of buying anything if they can avoid it, but attend for the purpose of claiming a share of any money passing as the result of such agreements.

It is very doubtful whether these practices can ever be suppressed entirely. The vendor, with the advice of the auctioneer or some other knowledgeable person, must protect his property by putting on it a suitable reserve price, and the buyer must decide in his own mind what is a fair price to pay for a lot, and then stick to it. If the vendor does not succeed in his design to bid up the price, and buys his lot in consequence, he has to pay the auctioneer's commission on it, and a few such lots thrown back at him will teach him that the practice is undesirable far more surely than Acts which cannot be made effective.

BAROQUE STYLE, THE   A style particularly prominent during the 17th and early part of the 18th centuries, giving place to the ROCOCO (*q.v.*) about 1730.

The architectural style of the Italian Renaissance was based on that of ancient Rome, but early in the 17th century the disciplines imposed by the classical models were thrown off, and greater freedom led to the emergence of the baroque style. The beginnings are often referred to the work of Giovanni Lorenzo Bernini [1598–1680], who designed the baldachin of St. Peter's in Rome, and who unsuccessfully submitted designs to Louis XIV for the Louvre.

The effect of the movement was to endow architectural design with a new vitality. It is true that this led, on occasion, to vulgarity, but its general effect was salutary, since the classical style of the Renaissance had become a meaningless intellectual exercise. The baroque architect took the straight supporting columns of Roman architecture and twisted them. He built terraces, and great flights of steps, and when he could not get the vistas he wanted naturally, he had them painted like a back-cloth. He decorated his buildings with statuary in theatrical poses. His fountains were posturing nymphs, spouting water from ample breasts, amid such creatures as dolphins and the hippocampus.

Baroque art is always dramatic. At its worst it is the art of the theatre back-cloth, but it is to be seen at its best in the work of such painters as Rubens, and in the architecture of 17th-century German palaces.

The style is to be seen on Meissen and Vienna porcelain made during the early years of the existence of those factories both in form and decoration, and in such formal motifs as the *Laub- und Bandelwerk*. Metal-work, wood-carving, and all the decorative arts were affected by it.

About 1720 it began to give place to rococo, with which it is sometimes confused. One important point of difference, however, is that baroque is balanced and symmetrical, whereas rococo art is asymmetrical. For instance, the acanthus leaf is often used in baroque decoration, but it is always quite symmetrical, whereas the same leaf used during the rococo period has the tip twisted to one side. Likewise some of the baroque scroll-work used to frame porcelain painting bears some resemblance to rococo, except that the elements of decoration are the same on either side, whereas those in rococo scroll-work are different.

A typical Baroque porcelain vase with applied masks and pine-cone knop. Meissen, *c.* 1715

BÉRAIN, JEAN [1637–1711] and his son, also Jean [1674–1728], designers, whose work influenced the decoration of faience, porcelain, and many other kinds of decorative art.

The motifs associated with them have a grotesque and fantastic quality which is unmistakable. There is, commonly, a central subject, either slightly or elaborately framed with ornament, surrounded by symmetrical designs of grotesques, figures and half-figures, vases, drapes, *baldacchini*, and so forth. Reclining figures with the head and breasts of a woman and the haunches of a lion are to be seen. This curious concept caught the fancy of some of the beauties of the Court, and porcelain figures were thus modelled, notably at Sèvres in biscuit, and at Fulda. The fashion crossed the Channel, and the English actresses, Peg Woffington and Kitty Clive, were thus modelled at Bow and Chelsea.

BOW (EAST LONDON), PORCELAIN FACTORY

Bow was established about 1744 by Thomas Frye, an engraver, and Edward Heylyn, a merchant. Bone-ash was deliberately introduced into the body in 1749, although if any specimen prior to this date exists it is likely that it, too, will be approximately similar chemically. The presence of the phosphoric acid in bone-ash can be detected by the PHOSPHATE TEST (*q.v.*).

The earliest Bow porcelain is decorated in relief with sprigs of such Chinese flowers as the prunus. Early painting was in blue under the glaze, and the first enamelled examples copied the work of the Japanese decorator, Sakaida Kakiemon. Later Bow colouring includes a characteristic enamel blue, and a strong puce.

A few specimens were transfer-printed, and the first use of this method of decoration can be attributed to Bow, and perhaps to the enamel works at Battersea (also in London).

Table-wares of medium quality were the principal production, but many figures were also made. These are unsophisticated in comparison with those of Chelsea, but have always been sought by collectors.

Bow porcelain is usually heavy, and translucency is not often well marked. The early Bow porcelain is the most valuable, figures made after 1760 tending to be lower in price. The factory ceased working about 1776.

BRISTOL (GLOUCESTERSHIRE), EARLY PORCE-LAIN FACTORY

This factory was started in 1748 by

Benjamin Lund, a Quaker, together with others later connected with the factory at Worcester. A porcelain containing
a large proportion of soap-rock was made here until 1752,
when the manufacture was transferred to Worcester.

Most surviving examples are service-ware, and similar
small items, decorated with Oriental motifs. A figure copied
from a Chinese original and marked "Bristoll" is known.

Some of the porcelain made here is hardly distinguishable
from the early products of the Worcester factory, and such
things are often referred to as "Bristol/Worcester".

BRISTOL (GLOUCESTERSHIRE), HARD-PASTE
PORCELAIN FACTORY This factory was brought to
Bristol by William Cookworthy of Plymouth in 1770, and
transferred to Richard Champion about 1772.

The body was extremely hard, and the glaze thin and
glittering. There are often defects to be noted, such as fire-
cracks and black specks in the glaze. Wheel-thrown pieces
usually exhibit a fairly well-marked spiral wreathing in the
body, and handles are nearly always slightly askew.

Decoration frequently copied that of Sèvres and Meissen.
Coloured grounds are rare, and the Louis Seize and neo-
classical styles were generally used, as well as a few Oriental
subjects.

Most of the production was table-ware, but some figures
of good quality were made. Biscuit (unglazed porcelain)
plaques wreathed with modelled flowers also came from this
factory. It closed about 1782.

BRITISH ANTIQUE DEALERS' ASSOCIATION,
THE This Association, founded in 1918, now includes
almost all dealers of repute. The Association exists to promote
the interests of those engaged in buying or selling antiques in
any capacity, and it insists on a high standard of integrity from
its members.

It organizes exhibitions, acts as arbiter in cases of dispute,
and performs various other functions, such as that of examiners
of works of art and antiques intended for export to some
Commonwealth countries, the Association's certificate being
accepted as evidence of antiquity to enable the object to enter
free of duty.

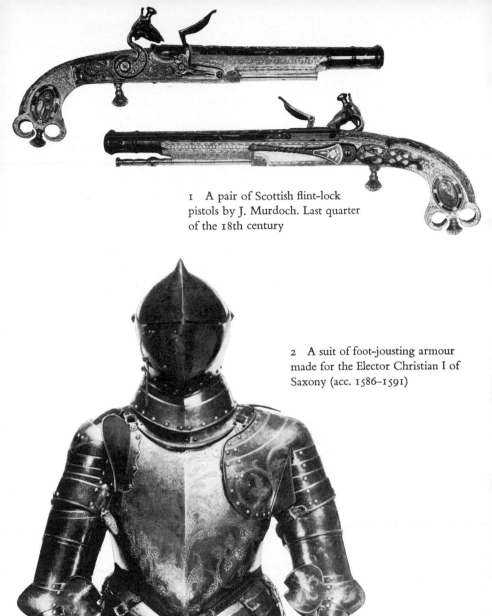

1 A pair of Scottish flint-lock pistols by J. Murdoch. Last quarter of the 18th century

2 A suit of foot-jousting armour made for the Elector Christian I of Saxony (acc. 1586–1591)

3 A large blue and white Chinese wine jar. Second half of the 14th century with 17th-century silver mounts

4 A pot-pourri vase of olive-green celadon stoneware from China, mounted in France about 1750 in gilt-bronze, the mounts in the manner of the goldsmith, Duplessis

A list of members (price 10s.) can be obtained on application to the Secretary at 20 Rutland Gate, London, S.W.7.

BRONZES, ANCIENT AND EUROPEAN Bronze has always been a favourite metal for works of art, either for statuary or ornament, and important specimens of bronze work are very highly valued. The metal itself is primarily an alloy of copper and tin, but zinc is a common addition, and lead not infrequent.

The proportions are, basically, ten parts of copper to one part of tin, but these are apt to vary considerably, especially if zinc or lead be added. There is nothing new in this addition, both lead and zinc being found in Roman bronze coinage.

The surface colour of the metal naturally varies somewhat with the composition. Casting is the usual method of fashioning articles from bronze, and the commonest method is called the *cire perdu* (lost wax). The artist first models the proposed work in a mixture of brick-dust and plaster of Paris, or casts it in this material from a clay original. The model is given a surface finish of wax of the same thickness as the metal cast intended. Over this is cast a mould, which is also of plaster and brick-dust, and pins are arranged through the mould, passing into the core. These are to support the two parts in position. Finally, the wax is melted out, and the molten bronze run in. The mould and core are broken away from the cast, and the bronze cleaned up with metal-working tools. This, of course, is a simplified description of a highly technical process. Duplicating is done in various ways, the modern method usually being to take a gelatine mould from which a number of cores can be cast. Casting in founder's sand is sometimes used for plaques and similar articles.

The finished cast is cleaned up with files, chisels, punches, and so forth, and polished. Large figures are cast in parts and joined up afterwards.

Thin sheets of metal were sometimes ornamented by methods appropriate to the silversmith (*see* p. 212), more particularly embossing, chasing, and engraving. Inlaying has also been practised from early times.

Exposure to the air causes chemical changes to take place in the surface of the metal, which eventually results in the

B

formation of a patina. Fine patination is regarded as exceptionally desirable, and can come only from exposure to the elements, or from substances present in the soil as a result of burial.

Attempts are sometimes made to reproduce natural patination, either by pickling in chemical solutions or by painting with lacquer or varnishes (*see* FORGERIES), but these are rarely deceptive to the experienced eye. Volcanic soils often lead to serious corrosion, and after centuries of burial parts may even be missing. The soil of Egypt also affects bronze badly, leaving the surface rough and pitted. Some soils have comparatively little effect.

Unlike gold and silver, the intrinsic value of bronze is small, and there has not been the same temptation to melt it down for purposes of coinage, although many things have undoubtedly been destroyed to provide metal for new work. For this reason, objects of bronze are not quite so scarce as those in the more precious metals.

The Egyptians were skilful bronze workers, and many important works exist from the Saïte period (664–525 B.C.). The extremely large statue is rare, most ranging from six inches to eighteen inches in height, although a few of larger size exist. Most Egyptian bronzes represent one of the gods, and small kneeling figures of worshippers making offerings are not uncommon. The bull is frequently represented, and the superb figures of seated cats are too well known to need more than passing mention. Less often seen are amusingly modelled representations of the cat with kittens. Less frequent than either of the two animals mentioned are figures such as the ichneumon, the ibis, and the jackal. The earliest regular use of bronze dates back to at least 1600 B.C., some excellent bronze vessels of one kind or another being made by hammering. Fluted ornament was used, as in later silver-work, to strengthen the body. Many early Egyptian figures are hollow cast by the lost wax method, most solid castings usually belonging to the Ptolemaic and Roman periods.

Sumerian objects of bronze or copper date from the beginning of the third millennium B.C., but, unlike Egyptian bronzes, specimens are extremely scarce and almost unknown outside museums. Much the same applies to Hittite bronzes, the few remaining specimens being mostly horse-furniture.

Assyrian bronzes, too, are scarce, although such things as the weight in the form of a lion with a ring in its back can be seen occasionally.

Of exceptional interest are the bronze standard heads and horse-bits from Luristan made during the first millennium B.C. Belt-plates with figures of animals can also be noticed, but less often. Phoenician bronzes are scarce, some specimens dating from the middle of the second millennium being in existence, but chiefly in museums. They are crude, but spirited.

Early Greek bronzes are to be found on the art market occasionally, although the price for good specimens is high. The first examples were merely hammered into shape, and figures in relief were made by embossing. Solid casting was used for the earliest cast work, but the introduction of hollow casting followed, although solid casting was retained for small figures.

The small formalized horses of the geometric period were made by hammering, but by the beginning of the 6th century we find that the art of casting had been mastered. Large statues have not survived in any quantity, probably because most of them were melted down in casting subsequent works, but small statuettes are not uncommon, and such things as mirrors, with decorative handles in human form and engraved decoration, are interesting and of fine quality.

Most of the larger statues are of athletes, and the style is extremely naturalistic. Bronze lends itself very well to work of this kind, and the essential difference between this and marble perhaps needs some comment.

The bronze statue is a reproduction of something in another medium. This medium is usually clay, or something equally plastic, and there need be no limitation, since free-floating pieces can always be given an internal support. A marble statue, on the other hand, has to be kept within certain well-defined boundaries. For instance, it is impossible to carve a standing figure so that it is supported only by its legs. The ankles and feet are much too slight to bear the weight of the head and torso with safety. For this reason marbles were made either with drapery, at least from the waist downwards, or with some such support as a tree-trunk. Likewise an arm thrown out from the body needs some support unless it is to run a grave risk of damage.

So far as the surface is concerned, there must obviously be some considerable differences in the subtlety of modelling between something which has been carved with a chisel and hammer and that which has been modelled in plastic clay. Although the Greeks finished their stonework with abrasives, they could not achieve in this medium the same kind of effect as may be seen in the bronzes.

Possibly the example of the difference which is nearest to hand, and best known, can be found in the work of Sir Jacob Epstein. His bronze portraits, which are first modelled in clay, are quite obviously completely different in technique and effect from his stone carvings, although his individual style is instantly recognizable in both instances.

Apart from modelling for bronze, the Greeks also used the art of engraving very effectively as decoration on boxes and mirrors, the subjects usually being superbly drawn.

The Etruscans were notable bronze-workers. The earliest statuettes of about the 6th century are curiously elongated, and the tendency reaches its limit about the 3rd century B.C., when votive or magical figures were made with a flat body which is fantastically long. Some extremely fine engraved work appears on mirrors and cylindrical covered boxes. The earliest Italian bronzes are usually of Etruscan workmanship, Greek artists being responsible for the later examples.

Some very fine portrait heads in bronze belong to the Roman period, but are rarely to be seen outside museums. Some can be identified by inscriptions, or in other ways. The small statuette was very common, and according to Pliny, one, Scaurus, had no less than 3,000 of them. These, and other small works in bronze of various kinds, have not uncommonly survived, the ruins of Herculaneum and Pompeii having yielded many such things.

The eyes of the portrait busts were originally filled with paste, enamel, or coloured stones, although these are now missing. Inlaying with silver was fairly often done, and the gilding of bronze frequently practised.

The ancient world used bronze almost exclusively for armour and weapons. The weapons were tempered by hammering – a process which hardens the metal and gives it a good cutting edge. A few examples of bronze used architecturally still survive. Even after the introduction of iron, bronze continued to be extensively used, and although weapon blades were eventually made of iron, hilts were often of bronze. When such weapons are excavated the iron blades are usually no more than flakes of rust, whereas the bronze hilts are still well preserved.

Early Christian work has been found in the catacombs and elsewhere, and can be recognized by the Christian symbols appearing on it. Byzantium supported a flourishing school of bronze-workers. The rigid formalism of the style can be well seen in bronzes either from Byzantium itself or from places influenced by it.

From the 14th century onwards bronze-work took on new life in Italy. The work of Lorenzo Ghiberti [1378–1455] and Donatello [c. 1383–1486] is especially notable, Ghiberti being a goldsmith, painter, and sculptor, who was responsible for the bronze gates of the Baptistery of St. John at Florence, which he decorated with scenes from the Old Testament, whilst Donatello did such magnificent things as the figure of *David with the head of Goliath* and the equestrian Gattemalata at Padua.

Andrea del Verrocchio, a pupil of Donatello, was born in 1435. He was distinctly a man of parts, being goldsmith, master of perspective, sculptor, carver, painter, and musician. His best-known work is the magnificent equestrian statue of the Venetian General, Bartolommeo Colleoni, in Venice, which was unveiled in 1496. A certain amount of work was done on this after his death by Alessandro Leopardi.

Antonio Pollaiuolo was a bronze worker of considerable skill and reputation, and Piero Torregiano, who was forced to flee from Italy after he had assaulted Michelangelo, came to England, where he completed a bronze shrine for Westminster Abbey and other works. Michelangelo undoubtedly worked in bronze, but nothing by his hand can now be identified. Much more is known of Benvenuto Cellini from his *Memoirs*, in which he describes the trials and tribulations of the bronze-founder. He is probably best known for his *Perseus with the head of the Medusa*, unveiled in 1554. Excellent work was also done by Giovanni da Bologna, who came, originally, from the Low Countries. His best-known work is a figure of

Mercury poised on one foot, later frequently imitated in bronze and other materials, including porcelain.

So far, I have mentioned only larger works, but many smaller bronzes were made, and those of the 16th century onwards have survived in appreciable numbers. They are either of religious subjects or of mythological figures, the latter being the more frequent. Apart from figures, such small pieces as plaquettes, as well as larger reliefs, medallions, door-handles, door-knockers, candlesticks, censers, and other things of the kind can be seen occasionally.

Early German bronze-work is important, as witness the bronze door for the cathedral at Hildesheim erected in 1015. Ecclesiastical work – fonts, censers, crucifixes, and the like – in the Romanesque style are characteristic of the period. Peter Vischer of Nuremberg was a notable bronze-worker of the 16th century, and Pankraz Labenwolf did excellent work, including a fountain in the Nuremberg market-place in the form of a peasant holding two geese. Not much important work was done in the 17th and the early part of the 18th centuries. Probably the bronze-founders and metal-workers were busy making arms and armour for the almost continual series of wars in which the German States were engaged. About the middle of the 18th century such works became a little more frequent. Ludwig Wiedmann did a large equestrian statue of Augustus the Strong of Saxony, which was erected in the market-place of Dresden Neustadt. Wiedmann was a cannon-maker of Augsburg. Johann Gottfried Schadow, who helped to model the "Wellington" service for the Berlin porcelain factory, also worked in bronze.

French bronze-work is at its best after 1600. In particular, much attention was devoted to such things as furniture mounts, clock-cases, candelabra, and a whole series of decorative bronzes of this kind. Much of this work was mercurically gilded, although mounts were sometimes only lacquered, and occasionally patinated in imitation of old bronze (verde antique). Among the finest work of the kind must be placed the elaborate mounts for Vincennes porcelain groups, in which the arts of the porcelain modeller and the bronze-worker were combined with great skill.

Of English bronzes, mention must be made of the monumental brasses to be seen in many churches. These were decorated with engraved ornament. They are not uncommon, and are usually very skilfully executed. Henry VIII imported Florentine artists, including bronze-workers, and mention has already been made of Torregiano. Grinling Gibbons, the 17th-century wood-carver, worked in bronze, as did the sculptor, John Bacon. There are a number of works by English sculptors in the public squares of London executed in the latter part of the 18th and the early 19th centuries, few of which do much credit to their originators.

Large works in bronze are obviously not suitable for the private collector. Apart from their intrinsic interest, however, they are used to attribute small works, since the larger works can obviously be dated, for various reasons, with some accuracy, and small bronzes are often reductions of large ones.

Prices for bronze-work vary greatly. Small Greek bronzes, particularly of the early period, often fetch high prices. There have been no recent sales of consequence, but Renaissance Italian bronzes have been appreciating very steadily in price during the past few years.

19th century French bronzes by a group of animal sculptors called the *Animalistes* are now much sought, and the work of such well-known sculptors as Rodin brings very high prices.

BRONZES, CHINESE Bronzes made in China before the present era are particularly important examples of the art of the metal-worker. Those principally sought belong to the Shang-Yin Dynasty [1766–1122 B.C.], the Chou Dynasty [1122–249 B.C.], and the Han Dynasty [206 B.C.–A.D. 220]. The bronze-work of the T'ang period, particularly its bronze mirrors, is sometimes important, but rarely does it approach the earlier. Little is known of bronzes made later than this, although they are now beginning to attract the attention of collectors, especially those of the Sung and Ming dynasties.

The earliest reference to bronze casting in China can be dated to about 2200 B.C., during the legendary Hsia Dynasty, but nothing exists which could be reliably attributed to a period earlier than Shang.

Although the first method of formation to be used was casting into stone moulds, the so-called "lost wax" method (*see* p. 33) may have been introduced into China at a comparatively early date; whether it was employed to cast the magnificent series of ritual vases, however, is uncertain.

Many of these vases have been buried for millennia, and the effect of burial has caused a certain amount of corrosion of the metal, known as patination, which incidentally improves the appearance to modern taste, and large sums are paid for a specimen with exceptionally good patination.

The principal types still existing are briefly described. The *ting* is a bowl of hemispherical shape with three legs and two upstanding handles. Like most of the other shapes mentioned, this was frequently copied in pottery and porcelain. The *li* is a curious vessel with hollow legs which seems to have been based originally on the udder of a cow. The *hu* is a vessel of baluster form which is also common in Han pottery. The *yu* is a covered jar with a swing handle, and the *ku* a slender, trumpet-shaped vase which is particularly graceful. A vessel shaped like an inverted helmet, with three legs and two upstanding bars, which were probably used to lift it from the fire, was used for warming wine on the altar, and is known as a *chüeh*. The *i* is a ewer, shaped rather like a sauceboat, whilst the *p'an* is a shallow circular bowl on a low foot, with two handles. There are a number of other shapes, all of which have different names, but those named are the most usually seen. The *ting*, in particular, sometimes reached a very large size during the Han period.

In addition to these, we find such things as bells, chariot furniture, numerous weapons (including an early form of cross-bow lock which is very rare), as well as mirrors ranging in date from the Han to the T'ang period.

Decoration is extremely fine, being at its best in the early period. It is principally formal in type, and cast in relief, although the later *hu*, and the mirrors, sometimes show much more naturally delineated motifs. Inlaid work of various kinds is to be seen. Inscriptions in archaic characters are not uncommon, and are of some assistance in dating, although dated examples are very rare.

This would, perhaps, be an appropriate place to mention the animal bronzes found in the Ordos Desert, since this is on the Northern frontiers of China. Actually, the makers were nomad hunters who ranged from northern Russia and the Caucasus to the Ordos Desert, and their delineation of animals is well observed. The most usual form is a simple model of the animal itself, or a plaque with the animal in relief. Most are quite small, and were ornaments of one kind or another. They range in date from about the 8th century B.C. to the 2nd or 3rd century A.D.

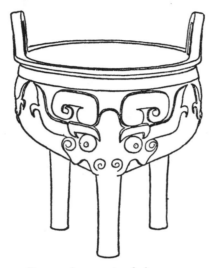

Bronze ting or tripod altar vase with characteristic formal ornament of the Chou period

CARPETS, CHINESE These are nearly always of fine quality. The material used for the pile is camel-hair, sheep's wool, or silk and wool. Occasionally some of the pile is cut to raise part of the decoration above the level of the rest.

Colours are comparatively few and good. Dark blue is extensively used, a golden yellow is excellent in shade, and the red is brownish. Motifs of decoration are those commonly employed in Chinese art.

Chinese carpets are better used where they will not be subjected to continuous traffic, but they are hard-wearing, and very decorative.

Pillar carpets are intended to decorate pillars, and are not now seen from elsewhere. They are often handsomely decorated, and their purpose can be deduced from the disposition of the motifs.

Chinese silk rugs are of extremely fine quality, and the use of metal thread is to be seen occasionally.

CARPETS, EUROPEAN   Eastern carpets were known in Europe from comparatively early times, and were first used as bed-covers, table-covers, and in such private rooms as the boudoir. Early European tapestries were sometimes used for similar purposes, as well as for wall-hangings.

As an industry, the making of tapestry carpets in France dates back to the beginning of the 17th century, when Henri IV established a factory in the Louvre. In 1665 Colbert, the minister of Louis XIV, assisted the foundation of a factory at Beauvais which made both carpets and tapestries. Carpets were certainly made at the Gobelins Factory after 1826, and they were quite commonly made at Aubusson. Very few specimens earlier than the 19th century now survive, and most Aubusson carpets one sees are little more than 100 years old, if as much. They are particularly in demand for decorative schemes which include French furniture, and French styles do not blend so happily with Oriental rugs and carpets as do English.

Both Brussels and Savonnerie-type carpets are in demand for period furnishing schemes. These are pile carpets inspired by Turkish techniques. The Savonnerie* carpet dates from the 17th century, and was made with a close-cut pile, the number of knots per square inch varying between 16 and 60. The early specimens in particular are very sumptuous, with rich patterns, and these follow the various changes in fashion in the decorative arts generally. They are at their best during the 17th and 18th centuries, but specimens can rarely be found for sale. Manufacture continued during the 19th century, and the factory is still in operation. Upholstery for furniture was made occasionally, but examples are rare. The difference in technique between these and the tapestry weaves is immediately apparent.

The manufacture of the pile carpet was introduced into England at Kidderminster about 1750, but the most notable of all English carpets were made by a Mr. Moore of Chiswell Street, Moorfields, in London, shortly after the middle of the century. The "Moorfields" carpet was knotted in the Turkish manner, using about twenty knots to the square inch. Moore

* So-called because they were made in a disused soap factory.

worked for the Adam brothers, and specimens of his work are to be found in some of the great houses of England, notably at Syon House. Axminster carpets were first made in England by Thomas Whitley in 1755, and were usually made to order for a particular room. These, too, were based on the knotted Turkey carpet.

All European carpets woven before about 1840 are extremely expensive, and the price rises steeply in ratio to age. Very high prices indeed are asked and obtained for 18th-century carpets in good condition. This must necessarily be so. They were expensive in the first place, a contemporary recorded price for a Moorfields carpet being 250 guineas – no small sum at the time. Specimens are now very few, and they need to be used with appropriate care for their fragility.

Further information on the carpet and tapestry weaving factories of Gobelins, Beauvais, and Aubusson is given under the heading of TAPESTRIES.

CARPETS – HOOKED RUGS A type of rug very popular in the U.S.A. The foundation is of coarse canvas, and a substitute for the pile is contrived from pieces of cloth which are *hooked* through the canvas. The older specimens are essentially a kind of folk art, and the patterns are unsophisticated and amusing.

CARPETS, INDIAN Those usually to be seen have a cotton foundation and a long, coarse pile. Patterns are not detailed because of the length of the pile, and they show distinct differences from most Persian decorative motifs. Colouring is usually poor, and garish. The inferior qualities wear very badly.

Old Indian rugs and carpets are of better quality, and the patterns are usually much closer copies of those more familiar from Persia.

CARPETS, PERSIAN Oriental rugs and carpets are especially valuable in any scheme of decoration which uses antique furniture. The colouring is usually harmonious, and the patterns interesting without being obtrusive. Rugs can be used on the polished boards of old floors very effectively, and often obviate the need for close carpeting. They can be found in all sizes and shapes, from the saddle-bag and prayer rug to the runner. Silk rugs, and those of silk and cotton, are very decorative when used as wall-hangings.

Most rugs and carpets from the Orient have a pile. The foundation is made of a large number of vertical parallel threads (the warp), with a similar series of horizontal parallel threads crossing at right angles (the weft). The weft is passed alternately over and under the warp threads. The pile itself consists of short lengths of wool, camel-hair, silk, or something of the same kind, and these are looped or tied through two adjacent warp threads, the ends being free and left as tufts. The weft threads locate the knots horizontally. The quality of the carpet is estimated partly by the approximate number of knots to the square inch, 250 being fine and 20 very coarse. The knots can be counted on the back. The closest weaves

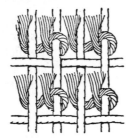

Warp and weft of a Persian rug, showing the method of knotting the pile

The experienced eye can form some idea of the closeness of the weave from the definition of detail in the pattern – the more detailed the pattern, the finer the weave.

come from Persia, Kashān silk rugs approximating about 250 knots to the square inch, and much finer rugs are known.

To some extent, the closeness of the weave affects the price, the finest being the more expensive, but allowance must also be made for other factors, such as condition, and quality of the patterns. A good Persian rug should have the following points: the dyes must be fast colours; it must show few signs of wear; the patterns should be good, and the design well balanced.

The price will be increased by exceptionally good design or a rare pattern, and very old rugs are naturally worth considerably more than comparatively new ones. One authority suggests, as a rough guide doubling the value of a rug for each century of its age. The estimation of antiquity in a rug is very much a job for the expert, and few genuinely antique rugs are to be seen. Wear is not evidence of age. Whilst an old rug will almost certainly be worn, so are many relatively modern ones. To have an antique value a rug should have been made before the introduction of aniline dyes – that is to say, before about 1870. These have now largely replaced the older vegetable dyes.

Some aniline dyes are quite as good as the earlier varieties, but others are apt to fade, especially in sunlight, or to run when wetted. A clean pad wetted and rubbed on the pile should show no sign of colour if the dyes are fast. Some fading, even with vegetable dyes, has to be accepted, but excessive fading is a serious detraction. Aniline colours are inclined to make the pile brittle, and to reduce the wearing qualities of the rug.

When buying furnishing rugs there are a number of important points to consider. The rug should first be inspected for condition. The foundation must be sound. If it has been exposed to damp it may be rotten. A good test is to pull a suspected part with the fingers. If it is rotten it will tear.

The pile should be inspected for wear. There is no remedy for a worn pile, and the price should be commensurate with condition. Small parts can be repiled, but this is expensive, and, for large areas, prohibitive. Much the same applies to holes. Cuts and tears are less serious if the foundation is in good condition. They can usually be sewn up inconspicuously at comparatively small cost. Most repairs are visible if they are looked for carefully, and if the price is high inspection by ultra-violet light is an excellent plan.

The pattern should be inspected to make certain that nothing has been cut away. Frayed ends, for instance, are sometimes dealt with in this way, and subsequently overcast.

Threads from the pile in a used rug should not come away when it is brushed. This is common with some Indian rugs, and the fault often persists throughout their life, which is correspondingly short.

The colours should be clear, and there should be no running. This fault is due to bad dyes in the first place, continued use in a damp place, or careless cleaning and washing. Slight running of one colour can, perhaps, be disregarded.

Stains are usually irremovable without removing the colour from the stained area of the pile. For example, what will remove ink is virtually certain to remove the dye from the wool, although if it is done immediately washing with water will often remove most of an ink stain without further damage. The remedy in such cases is to have the stained area repiled. Although stains are sometimes disguised with paint, this is always obvious on really careful inspection. When the pile of a rug is very short it has probably been cut. Dirty rugs are sometimes treated in this way, but their life is correspondingly short.

Two points sometimes regarded as faults by the uninitiated can safely be disregarded. These are more than one shade in a field colour and an irregular shape, which are seen only in rugs woven by nomads. The first is due to the use of more than one separately dyed batch of wool, each with a slightly different shade, which is almost inseparable from work done in such conditions, and the second is due to primitive methods of manufacture. Nomadic rugs have, in fact, the defects of their qualities, and such things do not affect value.

It must be emphasized that these remarks are intended to apply to rugs made within the last fifty years or so to be used for furnishing. The purchase of an antique rug by a collector is something quite different. Many old rugs are so tender that it would be impossible to put them to practical use, and if the pattern is of especial beauty and rarity a degree of wear is accepted which would cause the instant rejection of a furnishing rug.

Really old rugs are nearly always infinitely better in the quality of decoration than those made more recently, since a kind of factory system grew up with the increasing popularity of these products in Western countries. Among the Persian rugs and carpets thus prized by collectors may be numbered those which have the figures of huntsmen and animals portrayed amid floral motifs (hunting carpets), those with floral motifs simply, and those which have vases amidst the flowers (vase carpets). A pattern based on the plan of a garden, with flower-beds and footpaths, is extremely effective, and various kinds of central medallion form an early design which has continued in use to the present day.

The transmission of these patterns has gone on from one century to the next, and the various rug-making districts have characteristic patterns and colours which enable the expert to identify the place of origin with some degree of certainty. It is impossible to go into this question in detail in the space available, but as a very rough guide Turkish, Caucasian, and Turkoman designs are usually geometric. Most Persian designs, on the other hand, are more naturalistic and less angular. The so-called Polish carpets are, in fact, Persian silk carpets, often with the addition of gold and silver thread, and made during the reign of Shah Abbas I for export to Europe. Some have the arms of Polish families.

A type of carpet much less frequent in the West is the Kilim. This is a tapestry, or pileless, carpet, made in much the same way as the European Aubusson. The weft is used to form the pattern. Such rugs have the advantage of being reversible. The Soumac is also a tapestry weave, but it, too, is rarely seen in the West.

Rugs are of various kinds. Perhaps the most important is the prayer rug, which is usually of good quality. This has a prayer niche or *mihrab* in the pattern on which the worshipper kneels, the point being turned towards Mecca. The *mihrab* represents the door of the mosque. Three small medallions, one for each knee and one for the head, may replace the *mihrab*.

Patterns resembling a double-ended *mihrab* are hearth or tent rugs. Grave rugs, used to cover the dead before burial, often have a formalized cypress, a sign of mourning, in the pattern. "Mecca" rugs were commonly used as offerings to a mosque. The most usual are those made at Shirāz, and these are often called "Mecca Shirāz" by dealers.

Saddle-bags are of various sizes, those for camels being the largest; saddle-covers are approximately the same size, but have a hole for the pommel. Carpets are mostly comparatively modern, and, because of the difficulty of handling them on the looms, the large ones are much more expensive in relation to prices asked for rugs and small carpets. Runners are used in Persia to lay along the sides of a room. Fine silk rugs are used as hangings and for coverlets.

It is difficult to give much guidance in the realm of values. The number of knots per square inch must obviously have a considerable bearing on price, since it takes at least five times as long to make 250 knots as 50. Of the commoner varieties, Turkeys have about 20 knots per square inch, Chinese about 45, Baluchistan about 55, Caucasian about 70, Kirman about 80, Tabriz about the same, Bokhara about 200, and Kashān, 250, but these figures cannot be regarded as invariable.

As a very rough guide, a Kashān rug is worth about four times as much as a Chinese rug of comparable quality. If we take, as an example, £2 per square foot for the latter, a rug of 25 square feet will be worth about £50, and for the former (at £8 per square foot) about £200. This estimate compares favourably with actual market prices. Turkey carpets are always the cheapest on this basis, being about one-tenth of the cost of a Kashān rug per square foot, but if the prices are reduced to knots per square inch the Turkey carpet is actually the more expensive at about £1 per 50 knots, against 16s. per 50 knots for the Kashān specimen.

Many other factors are, of course, involved – condition, design, age, and so forth – and this can only be a very rough guide, but it helps to put a background of intelligence into the guess-work. The price per square foot may vary, but the method is a reasonably sound one.

CARPETS, TURKEY The name is applied to carpets made in Anatolia and Kurdistan.

The weave is always fairly coarse, and the foundation heavy. Most of the dyes are now aniline. The patterns are angular, and well marked, and red and blue predominate in the colouring. The Turkey carpet is strong, and wears well. The colouring is usually unsubtle, and the patterns uninspired.

CAUGHLEY (SHROPSHIRE) PORCELAIN FACTORY Founded in 1772 by Thomas Turner, a Worcester engraver, who was later joined by Robert Hancock. Thomas Minton was also apprenticed here. The *Willow Pattern* was introduced for the first time in 1780, and the still-used *Broseley Blue Dragon* also started at Caughley.

The body closely resembles that of Worcester, the glaze being bluish-white in colour. The early wares were printed in underglaze blue, the subjects usually being Oriental. Hancock-engraved plates which had been previously used at Worcester were also used by Caughley. Some decoration in enamel colours can be attributed to Humphrey Chamberlain working as an outside decorator.

Production was of table-services and decorative ware. No figures have been attributed.

The factory was sold in 1799 to John Rose of Coalport.

CERAMICS – AMERICAN POTTERY AND POR-
CELAIN Perhaps the most important name in the history
of early American ceramics is that of Andrew Duché of
Savannah, Georgia. He owned a pottery here, and some
time during the 1730s discovered both china clay and the
feldspathic rock necessary to make true porcelain. From
records still existing it appears that by 1738 he had actually
succeeded in making porcelain, and that production was
started in 1741. Due to lack of financial support he found it
necessary to try to sell his discovery to English manufacturers,
and he was in London during 1744, and in Plymouth in 1745.
A Bristol paper in 1764 refers to the importation of some
pieces of porcelain manufactured in Georgia. From this it
seems undoubted that American production of porcelain
antedated that of England by about five years.

Despite this early start porcelain manufacture was not
followed up, and most of 18th-century requirements were
imported from England and from China. Both the English
manufacturers and those of the Continent made various kinds
of pottery and porcelain especially for the American market,
decoration being of American subjects. Much ware was
printed in blue in Staffordshire at the turn of the century and
later with American views and portraits of notabilities.

A number of factories operated in the U.S.A. during
the 19th century whose products are now regarded as antique.
These include the products of a factory at Bennington,
Vermont, and the porcelain of Tucker in Philadelphia.

American ceramics, apart from those of native races and
tribes, are not generally sought outside the United States.

CERAMICS – BELGIAN POTTERY AND POR-
CELAIN The principal Belgian factory was at Tournai.
Faience was made as early as the 17th century, and later a
brown glazed earthenware (the *brun de Rouen*), and faience-
fine in imitation of Wedgwood's cream-ware. The faience of
both Rouen and Strasbourg was copied.

The manufacture of porcelain was started here in 1751 under
the patronage of the Empress Maria Theresa. Tournai had
a number of indeterminate connections with the English
Chelsea factory, and there was some interchange of artists.
Many copies of Sèvres porcelain were made during the

18th century and after, and some 19th-century copies of Chelsea and Worcester probably emanated from here. A good deal of the painting was *en camaieu*, and the 18th-century bird painting was excellent in quality. Some Tournai porcelain was decorated at The Hague, and when the mark of the latter factory is overglaze the inference that the porcelain came from Tournai may safely be drawn.

St. Amand-les-Eaux, not far from Tournai, was connected with it, and made similar wares.

An early faience factory at Brussels was much influenced by Holland, and a later 18th-century factory made many large tureens in the form of poultry, vegetables, fruits, and so forth.

CERAMICS – CHINESE POTTERY AND POR-CELAIN   The earliest Chinese pottery has been recovered from the Pan Shan Cemetery in Kansu Province. The approximate date of specimens is between 2000 and 2500 B.C. and they are offered occasionally by specialists in Chinese art. They have geometric decoration in black and red pigment and sometimes reach a very large size. Somewhat similar types have been recovered from other sites of about the same date.

Not much pottery is known from the Shang and Chou periods, which were more remarkable for their bronze vessels, but it becomes more plentiful from the Han Dynasty [206 B.C.–A.D. 220] onwards. Much Han pottery is covered with a green lead glaze, and it often copies the shapes of contemporary bronze vessels. Less frequent are unglazed examples decorated with unfired painting. The custom of burying pottery representations of household objects, animals, retainers, and so forth, with the deceased is responsible for the preservation of many things of this period.

Little is referable to the troubled period between the end of the Han Dynasty and the beginning of the T'ang [618–906]. The T'ang Dynasty was one of great progress in the arts, and its products are particularly sought. It is, perhaps, best known for its pottery tomb figures, some of which are remarkably fine, especially the large figures of camels and horses. The distinctive method of decoration at the time was by coloured glazes, either as monochromes or in conjunction with each other. Dishes, bowls, and vases from the same period are decorated in this manner, and some are of considerable interest. The occasional Greek influence can be traced to the conquests of Alexander the Great in the Middle East. Unglazed figures are very numerous, and these were sometimes painted with unfired pigments. Most forgeries belong to this class.

At this time translucent porcelain was first produced. The line of demarcation between earthenware and stoneware is sometimes very vague from the Han Dynasty onwards, hard-fired specimens frequently being better regarded as stoneware.

The following Sung period [960–1279] is noted for its fine stonewares, and these are sometimes mistakenly called porcelain. The difference is mainly one of definition, the Chinese regarding any ceramic material which will give a ringing tone when struck as porcelain, whilst the Western definition insists on the presence of the property of translucency in addition.

The most important wares made during the Sung Dynasty are the so-called classic wares. These are Ju-*yao* (*yao* means *ware*), Kuan-*yao*, Ko-*yao*, Lung Ch'üan-*yao*, Ting-*yao*, and Chün-*yao*. Of these, Ju, Kuan, and Ko are extremely rare, and the reader is referred to the specialist works mentioned in the Bibliography. The kilns at Lung Ch'üan made stoneware covered with a celadon glaze which is usually green in colour, although it can range from grey to brown. This glaze was much prized at the time, and celadon dishes were extensively exported. The foot-ring is dark reddish brown, and the glaze inclines to brown wherever it is thin. An unglazed circular band within the foot-ring proper usually denotes manufacture during the Ming period at Chu Chou, whence the Lung Ch'üan kilns were removed. The celadon glaze was also used in north China and Korea.

Ting-*yao* approaches much more nearly to the conventional definition of porcelain and has an orange translucency. It ranges in colour from a chalky-white to an ivory-white. Decoration is moulded or incised, the latter being the more valuable. Good specimens of incised Ting-*yao* are among the most valuable kinds of Sung porcelain.

Chün-*yao* is probably thought more desirable in the West than in China. It is a trifle more showy than most other things of the period. The glaze colour is usually lavender grey splashed with a colour varying between crimson and purple. "Soft" Chün and Fatshan Chün are imitations of the classic ware, generally made in the Ming period.

Copies of some of these classic wares were made in the 18th century in porcelain, the unglazed foot-ring being washed over with a brown pigment to imitate the appearance of the earlier pieces. If it is remembered that the originals were hard-fired stoneware whereas the copies are in porcelain, it should not be difficult to distinguish one from the other. The type of porcelain with which we are most familiar was not, in fact, made until the 14th century.

Ying chi'ing ware is a Sung porcelain with a pale blue glaze. Forgeries are numerous. The pottery of Tz'ŭ Chou is an interesting Sung type. It is noted for painted decoration in sepia, and for incised and carved decoration of various kinds. The first use of enamel colours on pottery in China can be seen here during the 13th century. The black glazed wares of Honan are of great interest, and tea-bowls with a variegated dark brown glaze, known as "hare's fur", came from Chien-an in Fukien Province.

Wares of the Yüan Dynasty [1280–1368], during which China was governed by the Mongols, usually look backwards to the Sung period, with perhaps more florid shapes and decoration. The earliest painting in underglaze blue pigment is probably referable to this period.

The porcelain of the first part of the Ming Dynasty [1368–1644] began to approach the type which later became more or less standard in China. It is white and translucent, and painted decoration of one kind or another replaces the earlier coloured glazes. Most early Ming glazes are thick and uneven, potting is not always very precise, and there are similar minor defects. Generally, however, the technical differences between Ming porcelain and that of the 18th and 19th centuries is one of degree, the later usually being more precisely finished. This lack of precision, however, cannot be used as the sole criterion of judgement. Later provincial wares also show the same tendencies, and form and decoration are obviously the more important guides. For the most part later painting is "tighter" than earlier, and the brush is used with much less freedom.

Early blue-and-white Ming porcelain is much prized, particularly that of the reigns of the Emperors Hsüan Tê

Chêng Tê, and Chia Ching. On the other hand, the blue-and-white of the later Emperor, Wan Li, exists in fairly large quantities and is not, except in special cases, regarded as particularly important. A most important and rare colour introduced during the Yüan dynasty was the underglaze copper red.

Enamel colours increased in importance and excellence of quality throughout the Ming period, and coloured grounds were introduced. The practice of using enamels directly on to biscuit porcelain, without an intervening glaze, dates from the reign of Ch'êng Hua [1465–1487], and such items are always sought after.

San tsai (three-colour ware) is actually porcelain decorated with coloured lead glazes kept apart by threads of clay. The technique was probably suggested by *cloisonné* enamelling, which it much resembles. Imitations of *cloisonné* enamelling on a pottery body, using wire to keep the enamels apart, was actually done by the Japanese during the 19th century.

Throughout the Ming period the manufacture of porcelain was increasingly concentrated at the Imperial Kilns of Ching-tê Chên.

The wares of the following Ch'ing Dynasty [1644–1912] are by far the best known to most people. During the reign of K'ang Hsi [1662–1722] technical excellence was allied to good taste in decoration. The blue and white was of fine quality, the porcelain body being exceedingly white, without the blue tinge in the glaze noticeable at other periods, and the blue was exceptionally pure in colour. Enamelled wares are usually divided into families, the two most commonly seen being the *famille verte* and the *famille rose*. The former has a palette in which a brilliant green enamel predominates, whereas the latter has an opaque rose-coloured enamel which was introduced soon after 1700 from Europe.

New ground colours were devised. Powder-blue (the pigment in powder form being *blown* on to the porcelain through a bamboo tube) is an example of a Ch'ing ground, but many other colours and shades were employed. The painting of floral and figure subjects was usually of excellent quality, and much more ambitious in scope than can be seen in the work of the preceding period.

Generally, the work of the Ch'ing Dynasty is sophisticated,

that of the Ming Dynasty being notable for a simplicity preferable to the later flamboyance. Nevertheless, the best Ch'ing wares are magnificent decoration.

19th-century Chinese porcelain is not particularly important. Some quite pleasing derivations from earlier wares were made during the reign of Tao Kuang, but most things of the kind are tawdry.

Figures were not commonly made in China after the T'ang Dynasty, except at Tê Hua, Fukien Province, where a white porcelain known as *blanc-de-chine* was used for the purpose. The magnificent coloured figures of birds of the K'ang Hsi period have always been highly valued, and some rare figures of dogs are also much sought.

A fine brown stoneware from Yi-Hsing dates from the 16th century. Most surviving specimens are such things as teapots, and they were highly valued for brewing tea when it was first introduced here. They were copied in such European stonewares as those of Böttger at Meissen, the Elers of Staffordshire, and Arij de Milde of Holland.

Values in Chinese porcelain can be learned only by long experience. High values are put on most of the classic Sung wares, on early Ming blue-and-white, and on some Ming enamelled porcelain. Good examples of *san tsai* ware always fetch high prices, and fine specimens of *famille verte* and *famille rose* can never be bought cheaply. Value in Chinese porcelain depends far more on an informed appraisal of quality and artistry than in some other fields. Rarity plays some part, but the tendency to pay for mere scarcity (common with some Europeans wares, for instance) does not exist to the same degree. As an example, a really fine *famille verte* dish will fetch much more than a Pan Shan funerary urn, although the latter is infinitely rarer. This, however, is not true of the market in Chinese export porcelain – wares made for export to Europe and the United States in the 18th century. Specimens are rarely important artistically, but because of their European affiliations the price has always been much higher than their status as works of art warrants. This is principally due to the demand for such wares in the United States and France.

CERAMICS – DUTCH DELFT Dutch delft (or tin-enamelled ware), particularly the blue-painted variety, is quite often mistaken for English, and the art of tin-enamelling was introduced into England from Holland in the 16th century. The first specimens from Holland were in the Italian style, but Far Eastern motifs of decoration soon superseded it.

About mid-century manufacture began to be concentrated in the town of Delft, from which the ware derives its name, and many of the factories were located in disused breweries. For this reason they sometimes have such fanciful names as *The Four Roman Heroes, The Three Golden Ash Barrels,* etc.

The trade was almost entirely in the hands of the members of the Guild of St. Luke, a craft organization which included art workers of all kinds.

The industry commenced to flourish about the middle of the 17th century, and from then until towards the end of the 18th century much tin-enamelled ware of all kinds was manufactured. The competition of Wedgwood's cream-ware had caused all but two of these factories to close down by 1800.

A great deal of the work was blue-painted, and included such themes of decoration as copies of Oriental porcelain, landscapes, biblical scenes, mythological scenes, shipping and seascapes, and other things of the kind. A distinctive feature is the large landscape or seascape made up of a number of flat tiles. Tiles used in this way, often in sets, were very commonly made, and painted, usually, in blue or manganese purple.

Later wares are also in polychrome, in typical faience colours, and the normal tin-glaze was often covered with a powdered lead glaze (known as *kwaart*) which gave it a brilliant appearance. The coloured decorations, particularly those imitating the more sumptuous Oriental styles, are often extremely elaborate, and gilding is occasionally lavish.

Enamel colours were introduced about 1720, and some copies of styles current at Meissen are to be noticed. The use of the *famille rose* palette from China is also to be seen.

There are many small and unusual objects in Dutch delft. Ladies' shoes, sledges, and cow milk jugs are examples. Figures are usually naïvely modelled.

A class of crudely painted ware, sometimes with portraits of members of the House of Orange, is sometimes mistaken for English delft. Specimens can be found in blue or in faience colours. There is a considerable difference in value between the two, English delft being the more expensive.

Forgeries are fairly numerous, the worst on earthenware with a clear lead glaze. Marks are also numerous, but often not particularly reliable. They are given at length in the books of marks recommended in the Bibliography.

Probably due to a lack of information in English, Dutch delft has not been in great demand here for some years past, and does not fetch particularly high prices in relation to English. An exception, of course, must be made in the case of really sumptuously decorated specimens (of a kind never made in England), for which the market is international in character and prices much higher.

CERAMICS – DUTCH PORCELAIN   There were a number of porcelain factories in Holland during the 18th century. Some excellent work was done at Weesp after 1764. The factory was transferred to Oude Loosdrecht in 1771, and again to Oude Amstel in 1784. The work of France and Germany was freely copied. The Hague both manufactured porcelain and decorated that made elsewhere, particularly from Tournai (*q.v.*).

CERAMICS – ENGLISH PORCELAIN   The principal factories will be found under appropriate headings. Generally, English porcelain is largely derivative, and its principal sources of inspiration are fourfold – Arita porcelain from Japan, Chinese porcelain, the work of Meissen in the early period, and of Sèvres after about 1760.

Much of the early work is naïve, and the bodies and glazes obviously experimental. Perhaps the most finished work comes from Chelsea, and it also shows much the highest standard of artistry. Some original work was done here, particularly in the case of such early figures as those wrongly attributed to the sculptor, L. F. Roubiliac, and Continental influence is always strong. The other factories cannot even approach Chelsea in quality, although their work is often pleasant enough.

Possibly second in importance is Worcester. Here Japanese

patterns were not used to the same extent in the early period, and, when they do appear, they have a much closer relationship to the Imari styles than to the work of Kakiemon. Chinese styles in the early years are much more frequent than elsewhere, and are copied with some fidelity. After about 1765 the mid-century styles of Meissen, Sèvres, and Berlin (the *Mosaik* and scale-patterns, for instance) were freely copied, the earlier simple patterns tending to disappear.

The best things at this time can be found in the paintings of the miniaturists, O'Neale and Donaldson, and a great deal in addition was done outside the factory by an outside decorator (an English *Hausmaler*), James Giles.

The figures of Derby are not particularly original, but they are usually well modelled. The later painted decorations of Boreman and others are not at present in especial favour, although they are excellent in quality and peculiarly English in style. The work of Bow and Longton Hall particularly appeals to those who like *incunabulae* and unsophisticated wares. Artistically, the other factories are not very important, although their work is always in demand.

Prices for English porcelain have usually been good, and for many years the only important movements have been upward. Most Chelsea fetches extremely high prices. Those for the early periods are much the highest, prices tending to ease for items made after 1756, except for unusually fine things. Small scent bottles, patch boxes, and similar items have always been expensive whatever the period.

The decorative scale patterns of Worcester have regularly realized good prices, the lowest being paid for scale-blue and the highest for the other, very rare, scale-colours. The work of Donaldson and O'Neale is also extremely highly valued.

Derby and most Bow figures hold their prices extremely well. Many examples are less than £150, only rarities and exceptionally fine examples exceeding this by any considerable amount. Longton Hall figures, never cheap, have recently taken a pronounced upward turn. Much the same applies to the service-ware of these factories, although prices for plates and such things are not nearly as high as those for figures.

These remarks on the prices of English porcelain are intended to be considered relatively between factories. The level of prices over the whole field is liable to a certain amount of fluctuation from time to time.

The best general rule for the neophyte collector, to my mind, is not to pay high prices for rarity which is unaccompanied by artistic merit, although even this can be disregarded to some extent when an unusual documentary piece – one bearing a signature or something of the kind – is offered. For instance, no one would reject a Bow inkwell of 1750 inscribed "Made at New Canton" on the grounds of lack of artistic qualities.

CERAMICS – ENGLISH POTTERY   English medieval pottery is comparatively rare, and reasonably perfect specimens are seldom to be seen.

The slip wares – that is, pottery decorated with trailed and dotted slip – date from the early years of the 17th century, specimens from Wrotham, in Kent, being valued highly. Large dishes from Staffordshire by Thomas Toft and others made during the second half of the 17th century are also in demand. This kind of work did not long survive the turn of the century, except in a few of the smaller centres.

The tin-enamelled glaze was introduced into England about the middle of the 16th century, and was probably brought here by Dutch potters. Of considerable importance are the rare examples, known as "Malling" jugs because the first example was excavated in a churchyard in West Malling, Kent. Probably made in London, they often have a mottled tin glaze intended to represent the Rhenish stoneware jugs known as "tiger-ware". Tin-enamelled wares made in England are known as delft, after the town of Delft in Holland, which was a considerable centre of Netherlands production. Dated pieces are found after about 1625, and these are often decorated in blue in the style of Chinese porcelain of the late Ming period. About mid-century wine-bottles inscribed with the name of the wine and the date are fairly common. The dishes distinguished by blue dashes on the rim – the "blue dash" chargers – are an interesting series which were made apparently in London and Bristol and which were not discontinued until almost the middle of the 18th century. The manufacture of delft was continued almost to the end of the 18th century, when it was finally discontinued owing to pressure of competition from Wedgwood's cream-ware. The high-temperature faience colours were used, as well as enamel colours (late) and transfer printing (after mid-century). Blue and manganese purple were commonly used from the beginning. Plates and dishes are the commonest survival, bowls are somewhat rarer, and tea wares exceptionally so. Such things as fine examples of the posset pot often fetch very high prices.

Salt-glazed stoneware, introduced into England for the first time by John Dwight of Fulham towards the end of the 17th century, was undoubtedly inspired by the stoneware of the Rhineland. Jugs with the mottled glaze known as "tiger-ware", and with a mask on the spout, called "Bellarmines", were imported into England in large quantities at the beginning of the 17th century and earlier. The "Bellarmine" is the German *Bartmannkrug*. The brown glazed stoneware from Fulham is fairly well known, particularly from later reproductions. The drab and the white stoneware is much less common.

The manufacture of stoneware found its way to the Midlands soon after its introduction in London, a distinctive brown variety being made in Nottingham. Manufacture of a fine cream-coloured stoneware in Staffordshire was on a large scale, one variety (the "scratch blue") being decorated with incised designs touched with blue. High prices are paid for good early salt-glazed figures, particularly such naïvely modelled examples as the well-known "Pew" groups. With the introduction of plaster moulds about 1745 more highly finished ware became possible, and such things as teapots in the form of a house or a camel are to be seen. Plates and dishes were often moulded in imitation of contemporary silver. Enamelled decoration was first introduced from Holland during the 1750s, and enamelled service-ware and figures are much sought after.

In the early part of the 18th century tea and other ware was made in a red pottery body imitated from the wares of Yi-Hsing, and from the red stoneware of Böttger at Meissen. This was first made by the Elers brothers, and later by Astbury and others. Astbury also made brown ware decorated with relief stamping in white, and probably made the first experiments towards the elaboration of the cream-ware body.

Pottery covered with coloured glazes, often sponged on in a mottled fashion and called "tortoiseshell" or "clouded" glazes, appears to have been introduced by Thomas Whieldon, who started work in 1740. He later entered into partnership with Josiah Wedgwood, when wares in the form of cauli-flowers and such things were made and covered with good green and yellow glazes.

Black-glazed ware was made at Jackfield, and in Stafford-shire generally. It was decorated with designs in unfired gilding of which traces still remain.

The work of Wedgwood is separately treated (*see* WEDGWOOD), but he introduced a cream-ware body which was later imitated in France (*faience-fine*) and Germany (*Steingut*). So great was its success that the manufacture of faience was largely discontinued.

Wedgwood's jasper and basaltes wares were much copied in Staffordshire and elsewhere by various manufacturers, and a modeller, Jean Voyez, who at one time worked for Wedg-wood, did some excellent work in cream-ware in conjunction with Ralph Wood.

Ralph Wood and his son, Ralph Wood, Junior, were responsible for some of the best figure work in pottery to come from Staffordshire during the 18th century. Some, possibly many, were modelled by Voyez, who based much of his work on the models of Paul Louis Cyfflé of Niderviller and Lunéville. The Wood figures were either in plain cream-ware or decorated with coloured glazes. They are hollow cast and light in weight.

A relative, Enoch Wood, was a prolific maker of figures until well into the 19th century. These were decorated with overglaze colours, and although competent are far more numerous and less expensive. Most of the other figure-makers, Walton, Salt, Sheratt, and so forth, worked in the early part of the 19th century. Their work is seen fairly often, and only isolated examples are important. Of the work of Pratt and others it is impossible in the space available to do more than mention its existence, but the books recommended in the Bibliography will give more details.

The use of lustre is peculiarly English and owed little or nothing to the use of metallic pigments elsewhere. The metals most commonly used for this purpose are copper, which more or less retains its natural colour, platinum, which yields a silver colour, and gold, which gives an iridescent purple of varying shades and intensities. Silver, under these conditions, gives a pale straw colour, and was rarely used in England. Lustre pigments were in vogue from about 1775 to 1830, although copper lustre continued to be used at small factories for many years afterwards.

The main varieties are painted lustres, pottery covered entirely with lustre, and the so-called "resist" lustre pottery. Complete covering with lustre was usually carried out in copper or platinum, the latter being known as "poor man's silver". In the "resist" variety the glaze was covered with glycerine in the places where the pigment was not required, the whole then being dipped into a solution of platinum dissolved in *aqua regia*, a compound of nitric and hydrochloric acids which will dissolve both platinum and gold. The rarest and most valuable examples are those in which the "resist" design is used in conjunction with a coloured ground. Most of the important English manufacturers made lustre ware.

There were few potteries of importance outside Staffordshire by the end of the 18th century, but Leeds is an important exception. The commonest types are a cream-ware elaborately pierced in the manner of contemporary silver, sometimes decorated with printing, or painting in black and red overglaze in a free style. Particularly important are large centrepieces and cruets.

Latterly much interest has been shown in Victorian figures manufactured in Staffordshire, many of which represent personages of the day. These range from Queen Victoria, through such notabilities as Garibaldi and Dr. W. G. Grace, to the infamous in the form of notorious criminals.

CERAMICS – FRENCH PORCELAIN The first record of attempts to make porcelain in France date back to 1664, and Louis XIV was himself a collector of Oriental porcelain.

The first undoubted success in manufacture was at St. Cloud (Seine-et-Oise), where soft porcelain was made shortly before 1700. The factory had existed for the manufacture of faïence since the middle of the 17th century, and it closed about 1773.

The porcelain was excellent in quality, slightly yellow in colour, and, commonly, the early things were in white with a relief or moulded pattern of such things as overlapping scales, or sprays of prunus blossom in the Chinese manner. Painted decoration included polychrome patterns in the Kakiemon style, and underglaze blue painting was often in the contemporary style of Rouen faïence.

The factory of Chantilly (Oise) was founded about 1725 under the protection of the Prince de Condé. The early ware can be distinguished with a certain amount of facility, since the porcelain body is covered with a white tin-enamel glaze. Polychrome decoration included many Kakiemon patterns. Much more rarely German flowers (*deutsche Blumen*) and the moulded ozier borders of Meissen, as well as landscapes and Watteau scenes in black and green enamels, are to be seen, together with the occasional use of coloured grounds. Figures are rare and highly valued.

The later porcelain was covered with the normal clear glaze, and a frequent pattern is one of small cornflower sprigs – the so-called "Chantilly sprig". This has comparatively small value in comparison with the early wares. The factory closed about 1800.

A factory at Mennecy was started by a faïence manufacturer, François Barbin, in 1735. The body ranges in colour from an ivory white to a milky white, and the glaze is always good. Kakiemon patterns were among the earliest themes of decoration. Probably the commonest survival is the small fluted custard cup and cover. Some excellent figures were made, and this porcelain has always maintained its value. The faïence is practically unknown, only one or two specimens having been recognized.

The factory which was later to become the Royal factory was established in the Château de Vincennes about 1738, but little porcelain was made until after 1745. By 1750, however, production was on a fairly large scale, and the biscuit figures, for which the Sèvres factory later became noted, were first made here in 1751 at the instance of J. J. Bachelier, the Art Director. The white-glazed figures are also of superb quality, and very rare. On the few occasions on which specimens appear in the saleroom, they are the subject of keenly competitive bidding.

The Vincennes factory made porcelain flowers which were mounted on metal stems, and a certain amount of service-ware. Decoration is always of the finest quality.

The mark of the crossed L's (for Louis Quinze) was confirmed to the factory in 1753, and the system of date marking by letters (*see* Appendix) was adopted at the same time. The L's alone had occasionally been used before this.

The Royal factory was removed to Sèvres in 1756. It was under the patronage of Madame de Pompadour, and made the finest soft-paste of any factory of its period. Its porcelain is noted for magnificently coloured grounds, and for the quality of the painting.

A rich blue enamel ground, the *bleu de Roi*, was introduced in 1749, and was later the subject of many attempts to steal the secret. *Gros bleu* was a dark blue used underglaze. Turquoise was a brilliant ground colour of the highest quality, and particularly well known and much copied from the 18th century onward was the *rose Pompadour* (sometimes called, erroneously, the *rose du Barry*), introduced in 1757.

Such patterns as the *œil de perdix* (partridge eye), which consists of dotted circles, and the *caillouté* (pebble) pattern – a gilded network over a coloured ground – were also extensively copied elsewhere.

Flowers, landscapes, figure subjects, mythological and pastoral scenes, birds, elaborate battle scenes, and musical instruments were all used as painted decoration, and were executed with great skill.

In 1770 a hard-paste body was introduced, and the earlier soft-paste was progressively discontinued, although it was still made almost to the end of the century. A kind of soft-paste, inferior to the 18th-century body, was used for a time towards the end of the 19th century for reproductions and imitations of the old wares.

Glazed and painted figures are extreme rarities, and very high prices are willingly paid for them. Biscuit figures were made in much greater quantity, the original models being done by contemporary sculptors of distinction. The soft-paste examples are, generally, more valuable than the hard-paste variety.

The Empire style was introduced about 1800, and the Sèvres factory played a part in popularizing it in Europe. Sèvres is still in existence, and is one of the great European factories.

18th-century soft-paste Sèvres porcelain is greatly in demand, and specimens are few. Consequently prices are always high, the highest amounts being paid for rich ground colours and fine painting. Prices for hard-paste are somewhat lower. The porcelain of Sèvres has been much copied and forged, and a great deal of white soft-paste was sold just after the Revolution and subsequently painted in decorators' studios in the old styles. For this reason it is inadvisable for anyone but the expert to buy from sources about which little is known.

The Sceaux factory (Seine) was founded in 1748 and closed in 1784. A little porcelain was made in the early period, but this greatly increased in quantity after 1775.

The manufacture of porcelain was well established at Strasbourg by 1752, but pressure from the King on behalf of the Vincennes factory compelled removal to Frankenthal (*see* CERAMICS – GERMAN PORCELAIN). It was started again in 1766, and continued until about 1781. The early porcelain, and in particular figures by J. W. Lanz, is the most valuable.

Porcelain was first made at Niderviller about 1765. Its best work was undoubtedly figures by the sculptor, Lemire, and by Paul Louis Cyfflé. Biscuit porcelain was commonly used for this kind of work. Painted decoration often resembles that of Strasbourg.

The factory at Limoges (Haute-Vienne) was founded in 1771 and acquired by the King in 1784. It made a good deal of porcelain for decoration at Sèvres. Other factories were started in or near the town during the 19th century, since there are large beds of suitable clay in the neighbourhood. Limoges porcelain is of good quality, but almost all of the production has been purely commercial.

A factory at Fontainebleau was founded by Jacob Petit in 1795 and closed about 1830. It made a good commercial porcelain, including the VEILLEUSE (*q.v.*), which is in demand for decoration. The factory in the Rue Popincourt, Paris, of Johann Nepomuc Hermann Nast, founded in 1782, also made decorative porcelain of much the same kind, as well as

5 An Italian Comedy figure by
Franz Anton Bustelli.
Nymphenburg, *c.* 1760

6 Two German ivory
tankards with silver-gilt
mounts. Mid-17th
century

7 A Wedgwood
teapot decorated in
jasper of three colours.
c. 1790

8 A covered cup with a
green ground and painting in
reserves by Dodin. Sèvres,
1759

copies of Wedgwood's jasper ware. A factory in the Rue Thiroux [1775–c. 1800] was under the protection of Marie Antoinette and copied the productions of Sèvres.

Soft-paste French porcelain of all kinds is sought after, and high prices are often paid for it. Prices for the later hard-paste are a little uneven, much depending on its value as decoration.

CERAMICS – FRENCH POTTERY The most important group of French pottery is the tin-enamelled ware.

Specimens of the work of Bernard Palissy and his contemporary imitators are occasionally to be seen. It has moulded decoration, and is covered with lead glazes in various colours. Perhaps the least rare in this class is the "rustic" ware, which has such things as moulded lizards, snakes, and insects against a natural background. These have been extensively copied in Portugal, and the imitations are quite common. Genuine examples are not. At one time prices were very high; they have, however, dropped during the past century, probably because of a general diminution of interest in the period. Unusual and exceptionally fine specimens still fetch comparatively large sums, however.

The earliest French faience (tin-enamelled ware) was in imitation of that of Italy, and dates from the 16th century. During the 17th century the most notable factories were at Lyons, Nevers, and Rouen.

The Nevers factory introduced painting in white on a brilliant blue ground (*bleu Persan*). A Rouen innovation was the use of *lambrequins* in decoration. These motifs are a kind of formal ornament derived from such sources as book-binding, lace-work, and ironwork. Similar decoration was used on some early French porcelain. At a slightly later date the grotesques of JEAN BÉRAIN (*q.v.*) were also employed, particularly at Moustiers.

Much faience was made in and around Marseilles, and although the name of the Veuve Perrin is the best known, it is not necessarily the most important.

An extremely influential factory was situated at Strasbourg in Alsace, with a branch factory at Haguenau. Enamel colours were introduced about 1740. It was noted for flower painting in a style which was widely copied elsewhere.

Niderviller made much faience of excellent quality,

including some very good figures. It introduced the *décor bois* – the representation of a piece of grained wood with an engraving pinned to it. Lunéville, in addition to faience, made figures in a type of biscuit porcelain known as *terre de Lorraine*, as well as in a softer material called *terre de pipe*. Faience from Sceaux is of fine quality, the painting being particularly good.

Faience-fine (a similar material to the English cream-ware and the German *Steingut*) was manufactured towards the end of the 18th century, and eventually replaced faience. Imitations of salt-glazed stoneware in the English manner were made at Pont-aux-Choux.

Prices for good French faience have always been firm. The work of Nevers, Moustiers, and Rouen is particularly sought after, and the finer wares of Strasbourg and Sceaux are also very desirable. Figures from Lunéville and Niderviller are often of fine quality, and, in particular, those of the modeller, Cyfflé, are usually expensive but worth the money.

CERAMICS – GERMAN PORCELAIN   The discovery of the secret of manufacturing hard-paste porcelain was due to the researches of a member of the Saxon Court, Ehrenfried Walther von Tschirnhausen, who had the assistance of an alchemist, J. F. Böttger.

The first factory to be established was at Meissen, some twelve miles up the River Elbe from Dresden which was under the patronage of the Elector, Augustus the Strong.

Von Tschirnhaus died in 1708, and the first commercial production took place in 1710. For several years the porcelain was experimental and decorated with somewhat primitive enamel colours. Specimens are very rare.

In 1720 an enameller, Johann Gregor Höroldt, came to Meissen from Vienna, and made many changes, including improvements in the body and glaze. His most important innovation, however, was the introduction of a new range of brilliant enamel colours. From 1720 until about 1745 most Meissen painted decoration is of extremely fine quality, and much sought after by collectors. After this date painting becomes less important.

Meissen is particularly noted for its figure work, the figures of Johann Gottlob Kirchner and Johann Joachim

Kändler in particular being highly valued. Kändler introduced the art of *Kleinplastik* – the small figures often used for table decorations – and is regarded as the greatest of all porcelain modellers. His early work, in particular, is exceptionally fine.

There were many other modellers and artists of distinction, and until the beginning of the Seven Years' War in 1756 Meissen set the fashion for porcelain in Europe, almost every other factory copying its products to a greater or lesser extent.

The Vienna factory was started in 1719 with the aid of workmen from Meissen. The most sought-after period is that during which it was under the control of the founder, Du Paquier, when the painting of service-ware was remarkably good, much original work being done. In 1745 it passed to the control of the State, when some excellent figures by Johann Josef Niedermayer and others are to be seen. A later modeller of distinction, Anton Grassi, worked in the Louis Seize style. Vienna is also important for the workmen who left to help in establishing factories elsewhere.

Höchst-am-Main started to produce porcelain shortly after 1750 with the aid of Benckgraff and Ringler, two Vienna workmen. An artist of note was Simon Feilner, who later worked elsewhere. Best known, however, was Johann Peter Melchior, a modeller whose figures of children in particular have always been extremely popular.

The Berlin factory was started in 1752, probably with information furnished by Benckgraff. The first owner was a merchant named Wegely. The factory was revived in 1761 by another merchant, Gotzkowsky, with the aid of Frederick the Great, who later took it over as a State enterprise. Berlin was particularly noted for finely painted service-ware. Much of the later figure modelling was done by Friedrich Elias Meyer, formerly a Meissen artist, and his brother.

The extremely important factory of Nymphenburg started production about 1753 at Neudeck, not far from Munich, with the aid of Vienna workmen. This factory is particularly noted for the figures of Franz Anton Bustelli, a superb modeller in the rococo style. Within recent years prices given for figures by his hand have often broken saleroom records.

Fürstenberg was founded in 1747, but manufacture did

not commence until 1753, when the aid of Benckgraff was obtained. Simon Feilner was very active here after he had left Höchst, particularly in the administration of the factory. Figure work was excellent in quality.

Frankenthal was started by Paul Anton Hannong in 1755 after he had been compelled to close his porcelain undertaking at Strasbourg (*see* CERAMICS – FRENCH PORCELAIN). It is noted for fine figures and groups by Johann Wilhelm Lanz, Karl Gottlieb Lück, Konrad Linck, and others, and figures were an important side of the production.

The Württemberg factory of Ludwigsburg was started in 1756, and was under the directorship of J. J. Ringler, formerly of Vienna. The figures are excellent in quality and much sought after, particularly a series of folk types depicting workmen and artisans of the period.

There were a number of other smaller factories in Thuringia, Bavaria, the Rhineland, Hesse-Darmstadt, and elsewhere, all of which are of interest to the collector. The work of outside decorators (or *Hausmaler*), who bought white porcelain and decorated it in their homes, is also important (*see* HAUSMALEREI).

Good German porcelain is always in steady demand, and high prices are paid for fine work. It is, generally, the most original of 18th-century productions in this field, and although the smaller factories did a good deal of copying from Meissen, they were also responsible for much work of importance.

All German porcelain, apart from a handful of experimental specimens preserved in museums, is hard-paste, and this remains the standard Continental body to this day.

CERAMICS – GERMAN POTTERY   The first German productions of interest to the collector date back to medieval times, and were the product of stove-makers. These were lead-glazed tiles from which the stoves were made, and are called *Hafner*-ware – *Hafner* meaning a stove-maker. Vessels made by these people are also called, by extension, *Hafner*-ware. Complete stoves are very unusual.

An important group of German pottery is the salt-glazed stoneware (*Steinzeug*) made in the Rhineland, the principal centres being Westerwald, Cologne, Siegburg, and Raeren. These vessels were very popular at the time, and were extensively exported. Most of them were tankards and beer-jugs. The so-called "Bellarmine", and the "tiger ware" which has a mottled glaze, are frequently found in England. The "Bellarmine", thus named because the grotesque bearded mask was assumed to be a satire on Cardinal Bellarmino, was, in German, a *Bartmannkrug*.

This ware is best known from later reproductions, which are comparatively common, but it has not been in great demand in recent years. It can, at present, still be bought relatively cheaply, although really important specimens fetch good prices.

Red stoneware was made at Meissen during the lifetime of J. F. Böttger, who died in 1720, and for a decade or so afterwards. It is very important, and much sought after. This stoneware is probably the hardest ceramic substance, apart from hard porcelain, to be made, and some of it was decorated with incised patterns by lapidaries and glass-engravers.

The manufacture of faience first began on a large scale towards the end of the 17th century. The early wares are rare. A notable factory was that of Bayreuth, under the patronage of the Margrave, which did a great deal of painting using the popular *Laub- und Bandelwerk* motifs (*see* MOTIFS OF DECORATION – ABSTRACTIONS). A number of porcelain factories made faience of good quality, among them being Ansbach, Höchst, and Ludwigsburg. The early work of Hanau, Frankfurt, and Nuremberg is also of great importance.

Factories were exceptionally numerous, and it is impossible in the space available to list them, but the work of many of them was excellent in quality. The faience of Höchst and Bayreuth is among the best. For much of it, prices are not excessive, but well-painted examples from the two factories mentioned are sought after, and the decorative value of such things as tureens in the form of animals, birds, vegetables, and fruit has caused them to be very highly valued.

The lack of interest in the less showy examples of German faience is probably due to the fact that almost no information exists in English, and collectors like to know something of the background against which their specimens were produced. Apart from Honey's *Dictionary of European Ceramic Art*, which gives much information in a compressed form, the work of Riesebieter (*Die deutschen Fayencen des 17. und 18. Jahrhunderts*), published in Leipzig in 1921, is probably the most comprehensive for those reading German. This has many excellent illustrations.

Many copies of Wedgwood's cream-ware (*Steingut*), as well as the basaltes and jasper wares, were made in Germany during the 18th century, and since.

The work of HAUSMALER (*q.v.*) on German faience is particularly important, and that of such artists as J. L. Faber, Johann Schaper, and Abraham Helmback is sought after and expensive.

CERAMICS – ITALIAN MAIOLICA AND PORCELAIN

The term *maiolica* is applied to tin-enamelled pottery made in Italy from the 15th century onwards.

There were many centres of manufacture, the most important being Faenza (whence the term faience), Orvieto, Florence, Siena, Deruta, Gubbio, Caffagiolo, Castel Durante, Urbino, and Venice.

The lustre pigments of Spain were introduced about 1500, and had a limited popularity at Deruta, Caffagiolo, and Gubbio. Maestro Giorgio Andreoli of Gubbio was, perhaps, the most notable practitioner of the art, but it was not particularly effective on *maiolica* in the later stages of its development and was soon given up.

The earliest *maiolica* was a series of wares painted in green and manganese purple at Orvieto and elsewhere, and most are loosely called "Orvieto ware". Slightly later there is a series of wares decorated in a heavily applied dark blue (*impasto* blue) from Florence. This was followed by a decoration of grotesques (derived in the first place from Roman frescoes), *arabesques*, and foliage, which gave place in popularity early in the 16th century to the *istoriato* style. The latter was a new departure in ceramic decoration, and was undoubtedly inspired by the changes which were then taking place in pictorial art generally. The surface was used to paint what was, virtually, the equivalent of an easel picture, and the work of such artists as Mantegna, Raphael, and Dürer was extensively employed, principally by way of engraving. At Urbino, and a few other places, this kind of decoration often covered the whole of the surface of a dish, although a few centres used it as a central motif, with other designs on the ledge of the plate.

This type of ware was made primarily for decoration, and it was fashionable to display it on side-tables and buffets. It was also fashionable for pharmacies to be gaily decorated with painted drug-jars, the most popular being the tall, waisted jar known as the *albarello*, which was originally derived from Persia by way of Moorish Spain.

Definite attributions to a centre of production are not always possible, although some wares – particularly those of Urbino – are comparatively easy to place. At one time prices for Italian *maiolica* were high, and justifiably so. From about 1930 prices tended to be low, but prices for all *maiolica* made before 1600 have recently been rising rapidly.

All Italian *maiolica* is decorated in high-temperature colours on a raw tin glaze, the glaze and colours being fired in one operation. This needed great skill, since erasures were impossible. Most things had a layer of lead glaze, which was known as *coperta*, added over the tin glaze, thus giving it a smooth and glassy appearance.

The names of a few artists are known. Nicola Pellipario did some extremely fine work at Castel Durante. Another artist who worked at the same place, and in his style, is known as Pseudo-Pellipario.

Italian *maiolica* offers a fruitful field for the collector interested in the Italian Renaissance. It is the first example of the use of the tin-glaze on a considerable scale in Europe, and the art of tin-enamelling spread from Italy to France, Germany, Holland, England, and Scandinavia. It remained popular until the decline of the technique, which was due to the rise to popularity of Wedgwood's cream-ware towards the end of the 18th century. Small tourist souvenirs in *maiolica* are still made today at Deruta and elsewhere.

An experimental soft porcelain was made in Italy at the end of the 16th century at Florence. This was done with the assistance of the Medici family, and it is, therefore, called Medici porcelain. Examples are very rare, plates, for instance, fetching something over £1,000.

There were several factories in Venice, the earliest being founded by the Vezzis in 1720 with the aid of C. K. Hunger. Specimens are rare, but those from another factory started by Geminiano Cozzi in 1765 are somewhat less scarce. Best known is a factory at Capo-di-Monte, near Naples, which was founded in 1743 by the King of Naples, and which made very fine soft-paste figures and service-ware. These are scarce and very expensive. A relief decoration, subsequently coloured, which has always been associated with Capo-di-Monte was, in fact, made at the Doccia factory, near Florence, which was founded by the Marquis Carlo Ginori in 1735. This ware has been much copied and forged. The Capo-di-Monte factory was removed to Buen Retiro, near Madrid, in 1760.

A factory at Nove, near Venice, started about 1720, made both faience and porcelain. The latter has a greyish paste, easily recognized, which was manufactured from about 1752. A soft-paste porcelain was made at Vinovo, Turin, from 1776 to 1820, but specimens are scarce.

The most valued porcelain from Italy is that made at Capo-di-Monte. Care is necessary, however, since forgeries are common, and many earlier suppositions have now been superseded by the researches of Arthur Lane, whose recent work, *Italian Porcelain*, should be consulted.

CERAMICS – JAPANESE POTTERY AND POR-CELAIN

Japanese pottery is not well known in Europe, the so-called "Satsuma" ware apart. This clumsily over-decorated pottery was especially manufactured for export during the 19th century, and was probably made at Kyoto. It is not representative of Japanese art, and now has small value. True Satsuma ware is quite unlike the export rubbish, and is rarely seen in Europe.

Within the last few decades interest has been shown in the type of wares used for the Tea Ceremony. These have a primitive appearance, and are often hand-modelled. They depend for understanding on the ability to appreciate subtleties of Japanese aesthetics. To this group belongs the low-fired *raku* pottery.

Most other varieties of Japanese pottery, such as Bizen stoneware, the work of Kenzan and Dohachi, and things of the same kind, are rare in Europe, and are very much for the specialist.

Japanese porcelain was first imported into Europe during the early part of the 17th century, the Dutch being the nation principally engaged in the trade. For many years it rivalled, and even exceeded, the porcelain of China in popularity.

Most porcelain of this kind was made at Arita (Hizen Province), although a few specimens made at Kutani and elsewhere can be seen occasionally, most of which have probably been imported later.

Arita porcelain is decorated with a very distinctive palette consisting of iron-red, bluish-green, light blue, yellow, and sometimes a little gilding. The forms were often octagonal, hexagonal, and even rectangular. Rims were frequently defined by a chocolate brown line.

The decorative motifs have the typical Japanese quality of asymmetry, with much of the glaze left white and undecorated.

A typical asymmetrical decoration of the type associated with the painter, Sakaida Kakiemon, and much copied on early European porcelain. *c.* 1700

European copies are sometimes extremely close, the nearest being made at the English Chelsea factory. The style was also extensively employed at Meissen.

The finer examples are attributed to a member of a family of artists, Sakaida Kakiemon, who worked towards the end of the 17th century, and the word "Kakiemon" has now become a generic term for work in this style.

At a slightly later date Dutch merchants persuaded the potters of Arita to use native brocades as themes for porcelain decoration. These designs, called "Imari" from the port of shipment, are overcrowded, and are usually inferior to the earlier styles. They became popular among English manufacturers under the name of "Japan" patterns, but did not attract much favour elsewhere in Europe. Copies of this kind of work were done in China, and are called "Chinese Imari".

CERAMICS – PERSIAN POTTERY Persian pottery of good quality is important, but the supply is extremely limited.

Specimens range from the 9th to the 17th centuries. The early examples have usually been excavated, and most are damaged in one way or another. This must be accepted, and perfect specimens are usually unobtainable. Care has to be taken to avoid excessively restored examples. In some cases a complete object has been built up round one or two fragments, and then carefully overpainted to make it appear perfect or nearly so. A small and obvious area of restoration should not be accepted as the only damage. Eastern restorers often assume that if one such place can be easily detected the unwary purchaser will not look for others which are more important, and much more cunningly concealed. Usually they are right. The ultra-violet lamp is a great enemy of this kind of chicanery.

With Persian pottery, and with most other early wares of the kind, the best type of restoration is one in which missing parts are replaced by plain or tinted plaster, without overpainting.

The glaze of early specimens is quite frequently iridescent, and this often reaches a point where the decoration is completely obscured. If desired, this iridescence can be subdued with a little vaseline.

The Persians rediscovered the tin-enamel glaze first used by the Assyrians, and it later spread to Europe by way of Moorish Spain. They also discovered the use of lustre pigments, made from finely divided particles of copper, silver, and gold, and this kind of decoration was used from the 9th century onwards. The art of lustre painting spread to Europe by the same route.

Much use was made of both the *neskhi* (or running) script, and the Kufic script, which is angular and formal, as decoration, and good calligraphy was regarded (as in China) as an art.

Painting of one kind or another was commonly used as decoration under clear and coloured glazes. *Sgraffito* ware, in which the decoration is incised through a white slip to a reddish-buff body and covered with a yellowish lead glaze, is called "Gabri". "Lakabi" ware is decorated with incised lines which serve to limit the flow of coloured glazes. Coloured enamels were used in the manner of Persian miniature painting, and referred to as *minai* decoration. Coloured glazes, including an excellent turquoise, were used frequently. Underglaze blue preceded the use of this pigment in China.

Up to the 14th century the best-known centres of production were at Rakka, Rhages, Sultanabad, Samarkand, and Kashān. Related wares were made in Syria, and at Fostat (Old Cairo) in Egypt. Most attributions are to some extent conjectural.

Later Persian wares, from the 14th century onwards, frequently copy the porcelain of China. Until the 17th century the source of inspiration was often Ming blue-and-white porcelain. During the 18th century the *famille rose* palette was copied, as well as the Chinese monochrome glazes. Copies of Chinese celadons are comparatively early, and another early technique copied later is to be found in "Gombroon" ware, in which designs are pierced through the body and subsequently filled with clear glaze. The wares of Isnik were also copied.

Prices for Persian wares are uneven. Nondescript specimens are not very expensive. Good examples of Lakabi ware, lustre decoration, and *minai* painting can be extremely high in price.

CERAMICS – RUSSIAN PORCELAIN A good deal of interesting porcelain was made in Russia, and the Imperial factory at St. Petersburg (Leningrad) was founded in 1744 with the assistance of C. K. Hunger of Meissen and Vienna. The independent discovery of the formula for hard-paste porcelain has been claimed for Dmitri Winogradoff. Production was on a fairly large scale, and much good work was done, some of which was obviously influenced by Sèvres. Probably the later figures of peasants and folk types are the most interesting.

There were also several factories in and near Moscow, one being founded by an Englishman named Gardner in 1758. Here, too, the figures of peasants and folk-types are extremely good. The Popoff factory was founded in 1806. There were a number of factories elsewhere in Russia, including one at Baranovka (now in Poland). Some of these factories appear to be still in existence, although little information is available.

Russian porcelain is very scarce in Western Europe. Prices are good for original figures, and somewhat less for those derived from Meissen and other factories farther west. Prices for service-ware are a little uneven.

CERAMICS – SCANDINAVIAN POTTERY AND PORCELAIN The tin-enamelled wares of Scandinavia are often of extremely good quality, and some (particularly those from Kiel, Germany, and Marieberg, Sweden) are much sought after.

A faience factory was established at Copenhagen in 1724. Much of the decoration was in blue, although some work in polychrome was done. Here, and at other places, a bowl shaped like a mitre was made for brewing a kind of punch known as "bishop".

Both Schleswig and Kiel made a good deal of faience of excellent quality. The former was established by a Meissen modeller, J. C. L. Lück, in 1755, and the latter by the *faïencier*, J. S. F. Tännich, who had the assistance of the Dukes of Holstein.

The factory at Rörstrand, in Sweden, was founded by Johann Wolff of Copenhagen in 1725, and C. K. Hunger of Meissen was at one time manager. It used the *Laub- und Bandelwerk* motifs, and the *lambrequins* of Rouen. Work was done in *bianco sopra bianco* (white on white) which was copied from Italian *maiolica*. Enamel colours were introduced in 1758, and good quality painting in the rococo style, and of *famille rose* subjects, appears. A workman, Anders Stenman, is reputed to have discovered transfer-printing independently.

Marieberg was founded by a Court dentist in 1758. The factory was sold to Rörstrand in 1788. Very good enamel colours were used, and many styles were adopted from Rörstrand. Much sought are the rare "terrace" vases, in the form of a vase decorated with applied flowers at the top of a winding flight of steps, sometimes with an animal at the foot. Pierre Berthevin of Mennecy, and later of Frankenthal, was at the factory, which accounts for the influence of Mennecy to be seen in some of its work.

A number of small factories elsewhere in Scandinavia made wares of good quality, as well as copies of Wedgwood's basaltes, *rosso antico*, and cream-ware.

The principal porcelain factory was at Copenhagen, founded about 1759. This still exists, and is one of the principal European factories. The porcelain made after 1780 is in the neo-classical style. The famous *Flora Danica* service – decorated with exact representations of native botanical specimens – is in Rosenborg Castle.

The manufacture of porcelain was started at Marieberg about 1786, and the influence of Mennecy is particularly to be noted. Its work is excellent in quality, and it made very effective use of the rococo style.

CERAMICS – SPANISH POTTERY AND POR-CELAIN Most Spanish pottery can be conveniently divided into two kinds – the Hispano-Moresque ware and faience.

Hispano-Moresque pottery is decorated with lustre pigment (introduced by the Moors, who got it from Egypt and Persia), as well as in blue and, to a much lesser extent, manganese purple. The designs are usually extremely good, and specimens which belong to the 15th and 16th centuries are the most important, earlier examples being virtually unobtainable. The lustre on the best specimens is normally a straw colour. The decoration is commonly based on such plant forms as the bryony and the vine, together with Moorish Kufic script. Frequently there is a central armorial bearing which indicates the family for whom the piece was made. Many dishes have remarkably fine designs on the reverse. A later coarse ware with lustre of a deep coppery colour is often interesting. It was made for peasant use, and is not valued highly. Some of it was exported to England during the 17th and 18th centuries, and is not uncommon in this country.

Much faience of good quality was made at Talavera and elsewhere during the 17th and 18th centuries. Prices are similar to those for other good European faience.

The principal Spanish porcelain factory was situated at Buen Retiro, near Madrid, and was started in 1760. It was a continuation of the Capo-di-Monte factory from Naples. A soft porcelain of excellent quality was manufactured, mostly in the neo-classical style. Specimens are comparatively rare in England.

CERAMICS – SWISS POTTERY AND PORCE-LAIN   The earliest work was in the style of the German *Hafner*-ware, mostly stove-tiles. Tin-enamelled glazes were introduced in the 16th century, and used at Winterthur and elsewhere. Faience and cream-ware was made at Zürich, where a certain amount of transfer-printing was done.

The manufacture of porcelain at Zürich was started about 1763 by Adam Spängler. During the first few years a soft-paste was used, but hard-paste porcelain was introduced about 1765. Some excellent figures were made about this time which are much in demand.

The factory at Nyon, near Geneva, was founded about 1780 and closed in 1813. Most of its work was in imitation of styles current in Paris.

CERAMICS – TURKISH POTTERY   A type of pot-tery characterized principally by good floral decoration, and the use of a thick pigment known as Armenian red, was made at Isnik (Southern Anatolia) from the 16th century onwards. The earliest examples are painted in blue only, but this soon gave place to a brilliant palette of high-temperature faience colours. A border pattern of scrolls (called "Ammonite" scrolls, from a resemblance to the fossil ammonite) is derived from an early Chinese pattern of the Ming Dynasty.

Turkish pottery of this kind is not uncommon in England, and makes very colourful decoration. Plates and dishes are the most often seen, other things being somewhat rare. Examples with Elizabethan and other early silver mounts are very highly valued.

This pottery was at one time called "Rhodian" ware, since it was assumed that it had been made in the Island of Rhodes on the evidence of some fragments discovered near Lindos. The name still lingers in some quarters.

CHELSEA (WEST LONDON) PORCELAIN FAC-TORY   This factory was started about 1743 by Huguenots. It was later in the proprietorship of Nicholas Sprimont, a silversmith of French descent. It enjoyed the patronage of the

Duke of Cumberland. Chelsea was the premier English factory of the 18th century.

Several bodies were used. The first, up to about 1750, was extremely glassy. From 1750 to 1753 a body noted for its "moons", or patches of greater translucency, was employed, and by 1755 a bone-ash body similar to that of Bow, but better in quality, had been adopted. The glaze is usually soft and glassy, and three small, more or less equidistant marks ("stilt" or "spur" marks) can be seen on the base of most service-ware.

The earliest decoration is Oriental, mainly of the Kakiemon type, but soon after 1750 copies of Meissen wares were being made. Decorations based on Aesop's fables are particularly important. After 1757 the work of Sèvres was extensively used as a source of inspiration.

Chelsea is especially noted for the quality of its figures, the finest fetching extremely high prices, and some are equal to any made in Europe at the time.

Especially during the early period, the forms of contemporary silver were much used.

The factory was sold to William Duesbury of Derby in 1770.

CHELSEA-DERBY PORCELAIN The term refers to porcelain made and/or decorated at Chelsea after its purchase by William Duesbury in 1770. The factory was closed finally in 1784, and for some years was little more than a decorating studio. It is difficult to be certain whether any given example of this period was made or only decorated at Chelsea.

CH'ING DYNASTY, THE [1644–1912] The Ming Dynasty, which ruled China from 1368, collapsed towards the middle of the 17th century, one of the principal reasons being the imposition of excessive taxation. It was replaced by the Ch'ing Emperors. The latter were Manchus who invaded the country from the north. The first Ch'ing Emperor was Shun Chih, but the dynasty is particularly noted for three important rulers – K'ang Hsi [1662–1722], Yung Chêng [1723–1735], and Ch'ien Lung [1736–1795].

The Emperor K'ang Hsi did much to encourage the arts, and, in particular, that of porcelain. The principal manufacture was located at Ching-tê Chên, and many technical innovations and improvements were introduced. A picture of the industry at this period which had much influence on porcelain manufacture in Europe is contained in the letters of Père d'Entrecolles, a Jesuit missionary.

The art of painting in enamel colours on porcelain was brought to a high degree of technical excellence, and porcelain with the *famille verte* palette, introduced in the early part of the reign as a development of a pre-existing Ming style, is much sought by collectors of the later wares. It is characterized by the presence of a brilliant green pigment, as well as by an enamel blue which affected the surrounding glaze, giving it a slight halo. At the end of the 17th century a rose colour was introduced from Europe and helped to establish the no less noteworthy *famille rose* palette which was at its best during the reign of Yung Chêng. Some variations on the *verte* palette, such as the *famille noir* and the *famille jaune*, are much prized as decoration, but are inclined to be overcrowded and overelaborate for modern taste.

The blue-and-white porcelain of the period is very white in body, and shows an exceptionally brilliant and pure blue, but it deteriorated during the 18th century and later, the glaze developing a bluish tinge. Some exceptionally good monochromes were devised during the early part of the dynasty, and the reign of Ch'ien Lung saw the manufacture of *flambé* glazes in great variety.

Services of all kinds were made especially for export to Europe and America, and, in both form and decoration, were frequently done to special order. Armorial porcelain, and the so-called "Oriental Lowestoft", belong to the latter part of the 17th and the 18th centuries.

Apart from porcelain, such things as embroideries, tapestries, lacquer, enamels, jades, ivory carvings, and carpets were exported to meet the great and growing demand for Chinese art and crafts of all kinds.

The 18th century saw an increasing decadence, together with much over-detailed work for its own sake. The emphasis on sophistication and mere prettiness was due to the export trade, since Europeans demanded intricate workmanship and decorations which appealed to Western taste. During the past half-century collectors and students have achieved a much better understanding of the basic principles of Chinese art, with the result that emphasis has shifted to the works of the T'ang, Sung, and Ming periods.

During the 19th century little work of merit was done, although much Chinese craftwork was shipped to Europe. Most of it is very little above the level of tourist souvenirs, although some good porcelain was still being made at Ch'ing-tê Chên.

CHINOISERIES   Chinese works of art and craft of all kinds were extremely popular in Europe during the 17th and 18th centuries, and many important personages of the period had collections of one kind or another. The fashion was not limited to porcelain, but included embroideries, lacquer, and other things of the kind.

European artists took Chinese subjects as inspiration for their own work, but, apart from examples of Chinese art, information about the country was extremely scanty, and few people had actually visited it. Work in this style, therefore, took on a fantasy element quite unrelated to the real Chinese forms, and these motifs are referred to as *chinoiseries*.

Although the popularity of Chinese art was, at first, mainly due to Dutch traders, it soon became fashionable in France. The Jesuit father, Bouvet, presented forty-nine volumes of drawings to Louis XIV which were used by designers, and Cardinal Mazarin had a collection of porcelain and textiles as early as 1658. One of the Prince de Condé's retainers, a painter named Fraisse, made a collection of Chinese and Japanese drawings, and he published the *Livre de dessins Chinois* in 1735. Huet combined Chinese designs with the current vogue for monkeys as decoration, dressing them in Chinese costume. Books of Chinese engravings were published by Le Comte and others, and Boucher and Watteau adapted Chinese motifs. Watteau was responsible for decoration of the kind for the Pavillon de la Muette, and Boucher's *Suite de Figures Chinoises* became the inspiration for porcelain figures at several European factories. The fashion came to an end with the work of Jean Pillement (1727–1808), which was also exceedingly popular. In Germany the porcelain of Meissen was decorated with *chinoiseries* after engravings by its *Obermaler*, J. G. Höroldt, and others, and porcelain figures of the kind were also manufactured, mainly in the rococo style, although a few early *baroque* figures were made at Meissen. In England the furniture of Chippendale was decorated with pseudo-Chinese motifs, and the same motifs also appear on rococo silver.

The fashion had run its course soon after the middle of the 18th century. From then onwards, most of the Chinese patterns are copies of the overcrowded "Mandarin" style which was first used at Canton for export porcelain towards the end of the 18th century.

The English "Willow" pattern is a true *chinoiserie*, having no Chinese origin, either in design or in the story attached to it. Fairly exact copies of Chinese decoration were done at Worcester and some other places. These, of course, cannot be classed as *chinoiseries*, since the fantasy element is lacking.

Chinoiseries of all kinds have always been extremely popular with collectors. In porcelain those of Meissen are particularly sought after.

CLOCKS Old clocks are not only extremely decorative accessories to a period furnishing scheme but they are also the subject of much interest to collectors. For both purposes desirable specimens include those made in the 17th, 18th, and early 19th centuries.

So far as English clocks are concerned, the examples of the greatest interest to collectors are those made in London by members of the Clockmakers' Company, provincial clocks being somewhat less in demand. The latter are excellent for furnishing purposes, and less costly than the London-made clock.

The most valuable are those made by clockmakers who are recognized masters of their craft, such as Thomas Tompion, Daniel Quare, Edward East, and George Graham. Britten's *Old Clocks and Watches and Their Makers* gives a comprehensive list of clockmakers, and inclusion in this list is regarded as providing evidence of the good standing of the maker.

Clock movements are rarely in original condition. They are pieces of moving mechanism which are subject to wear and tear with the passing of time. The part most frequently renewed is the escapement, on which most of the wear falls, and a clock with its original escapement would almost certainly be a very bad timekeeper for this reason.

Clock movements are driven either by weight or springs, and these provide the motive power which drives the chain of wheels. The power, however, needs to be released in a controlled and orderly sequence. This is done by the escapement and the pendulum. The escapement is an arrangement of a wheel which engages with two pallets (verge escapement) or with an anchor (anchor escapement), which allows the weight to fall, or the spring to unwind, tooth by tooth. The *speed* of the escapement is governed by the pendulum, which regulates the rate at which the pallets are allowed to escape from the wheel. If the pendulum be removed the escapement will work at a tremendous rate, and the hands will cover an hour in a

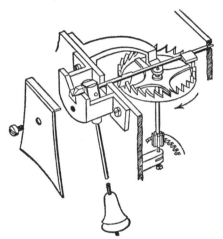

Details of the verge escapement, showing the crown wheel and pallets and the connection to the pendulum. The latter raises each of the pallets in turn as it swings and allows one tooth of the crown wheel to "escape". Hence the name

matter of minutes. If the escapement be removed as well the weights will fall in an uncontrolled manner, and the hands will circle the dial at a prodigious speed. It can be seen, therefore, that the actual time-keeping of the clock depends on the escapement and the pendulum. Variations in time-keeping can be adjusted by raising or lowering the weight of the pendulum on its rod, and an adjustment is provided for this purpose. In practice, a very slight movement up or down is all that is required.

Clocks fitted with anchor escapements need to be exactly true and level to work properly. Experience will enable the owner to judge when his clock is functioning correctly from the sound of the tick – that is, the noise made by the escapement. If the clock is level, and the escapement is in good condition, this should be smooth and even. An uneven tick suggests either that the clock is not level or the escapement itself is in need of attention.

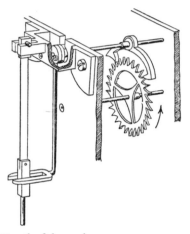

Detail of the anchor escapement,
showing the top of the pendulum and
the anchor-shaped release mechanism

Some early clocks have had the escapement altered from the original verge to the later anchor. The anchor escapement was invented by Robert Hooke towards the end of the 17th century, and was devised to allow the use of a long pendulum of 39·1 inches. This swung once for each second, and replaced the much shorter pendulum which had been in use until that date. The long pendulum, of course, had to be used in conjunction with a case long enough to accommodate it; hence the rise to popularity of the long-case clock. The table-clock, driven by a spring, retained the verge escapement for about a century after Hooke's invention, probably because it was moved from room to room, and the verge escapement was a little more tolerant of uneven surfaces. Many such clocks were fitted with anchor escapements in the 19th century, and it is better, in cases of this kind, to have the original verge escapement restored. When examining an old clock it is advisable, if there is suspicion of tampering, to look at the back-plate and see whether there are holes which were originally the bearings for shafts carrying wheels, and which are no longer used. When these are present it argues that the clock has been altered, and parts of the original train omitted.

Table-clocks driven by a spring are usually of the fusee type. The spring is contained in a cylindrical barrel, and the fusee is a cone-shaped drum connected to it by a small chain or a length of gut. A spring will obviously exert more force when it is completely wound than when it has run down, and the cone-shaped drum provides a method of compensating for variation in the pull of the spring. It is still used sometimes in clocks of fine quality, and it appears impossible to improve upon it in cases where great accuracy is demanded from spring-driven mechanism.

In assessing the value of old clocks, it should be remembered that, where a high price is asked, case, dial, and cast ornament should be in original condition. In assessing the quality of the spandrels decorating the dial, the remarks on the quality of ORMOLU MOUNTS (*q.v.*) can be used. Apart from renewal of a worn escapement, the movement should be otherwise untouched, although if replacements have been made by a skilled workman detection will be very difficult.

The earliest clocks likely to be found date from Elizabethan times. These are rare, and are not good timekeepers. They are, in fact, of much more interest to the collector than as furnishings. These early clocks were known as "lantern" clocks and hung on the wall. Most have a large hemispherical bell on which the hours were struck. They have an engraved dial, and were provided with a single hand. The escapement should be of the verge type, and the short rapidly-swinging pendulum was sometimes placed in front of the dial. If the clock has been altered to an anchor escapement it will have a long pendulum which will swing behind the clock.

This type persisted until the invention of the anchor escapement, after which the long-case clock became popular. 17th-century long-case clocks are usually in oak cases veneered with ebony or walnut. Towards the end of the century these cases were decorated with MARQUETRY (*q.v.*). This was floral at first, but later of a seaweed pattern. The hood was flanked by columns in the form of a spiral twist, and the hood either lifted up as a whole or slid forward. A door to the hood came later.

The dials were small, and cast spandrels in the form of a cherub's head can be seen in the corners. Most long-case clocks were designed to run for eight days, but thirty-day clocks, and even those made to run for three months or a year at one winding, are not unknown.

During this period the bracket (or table) clock had a basket-top – that is, an elaborately pierced top of brass which contained the bells. Slightly more elaborate, and rarer, is the double basket-top. These clocks had a square dial, and the use of two hands became common after 1680. Cases were of oak veneered with ebony, walnut, or, very occasionally in the finest examples, tortoiseshell. The use of lacquered cases can also be seen in these and in long-case clocks of the period.

By the reign of Queen Anne the square dial was sometimes replaced by the arched dial, which eventually became the rule. The earliest cases had seaweed marquetry, the later are in plain walnut. The walnut case persisted into early Georgian times, and was then replaced by mahogany. Applied ormolu mounts, and rococo motifs replacing the cherub spandrels, can be seen about 1755. By 1760 clocks began to show the phases of the moon in the arch of the dial, and the whole of the dial began to be silvered or, in the cheaper clocks, painted. During the latter part of the century many concessions were made to the neo-classical style in the design of clock cases, and the enamel dial became the rule.

A feature of most clocks during the period under discussion is fine-quality engraving, to be seen at its best on the back-plates of bracket clocks. (See Appendix V.)

COALPORT (SHROPSHIRE) PORCELAIN FACTORY This factory was started by John Rose, who purchased the Caughley works in 1799. In 1822 he bought the NANTGARW FACTORY (*q.v.*) and took the moulds to Coalport. He also obtained the recipes of William Billingsley for the Nantgarw bodies.

The body of Coalport porcelains is white, and excellent in quality. The glaze is equally good. At one time the factory was especially noted for its copies of Sèvres porcelain, and for certain reproductions of early Chelsea, although some of the latter seem to be a little doubtfully attributed.

Many good ground colours were introduced, and in general technical excellence Coalport was fully the equal of any 19th-century factory. Its decoration was in much better taste than most. Its decorative styles were mainly imitated from Sèvres and other Continental factories. No figures were made.

Its closure has recently been announced (1958).

COLLECTIONS Collecting objects of one kind or another is a basic human activity. Even the humblest home has its quota of ornaments, although they have usually been acquired haphazardly and have no obvious relationship apart from sentiment. When objects are brought together according to a definite plan, then the assemblage assumes the status of a collection.

Usually the serious collector tries to illustrate a particular theme, and the themes he can select are many in number. To take porcelain as an example, he can illustrate the work of a particular factory throughout its life, or he can take a cross-section through the work of several factories at a particular period. He may decide to collect *incunabulae*, or examples of the rococo style. He can limit his acquisitions to porcelain from one country, or he can take in several. He can collect blue-and-white or enamelled porcelain. In the latter case he can limit it to flower painting, bird painting, figure painting, or the work of a particular artist, such as O'Neale, Billingsley, or Boreman. Transfer-printing offers a fruitful field, as at least one important collection has demonstrated. He can collect figures or service-ware. The service-ware can be general, or limited to a particular type – teapots or cups and saucers. Whatever he does, there is much to be learned from the result if he carries his project to its ultimate conclusion.

Much the same applies to other fields. If the collector be attracted to clocks he can acquire lantern clocks, bracket clocks, or long-case clocks of a particular period, or the work of one or several makers. In furniture he must be guided by household necessities to some extent, since it is for use as well as ornament, but the same principles apply.

A collection may take in a wide variety of objects of a

particular period. For instance, a room devoted to Queen Anne furniture with appropriate accessories, such as clocks, silver, and some Oriental porcelain or delft-ware, is an excellent example of this. Such reconstructions as those of Colonial Williamsburg in the United States or the period rooms at the Victoria and Albert Museum are models of how this should be done.

Collections generally can be roughly divided into vertical and horizontal. Vertical collections are those which are limited in scope, but cover a considerable period of time – for instance, bracket clocks of the 18th century. Horizontal collections are wider in scope, but cover a limited period of time. An excellent example would be lantern, bracket, and long-case clocks of the last quarter of the 17th century. Both methods are equally important from the viewpoint of the student.

A necessary ancillary to a collection is its records. It is important to keep adequate records of the purchase of various items – the price paid, information on previous collections of which they may have formed a part, and so forth. It is also an excellent plan to add information about similar examples culled from reference books and art journals, and, if the object is important enough to have been illustrated, a record of where such illustrations are to be found. Apart from the interest of such records, if objects are subsequently sold information of this kind often adds considerably to their value.

Loose-leaf books are useful for recording information of this kind, and an additional photographic record has much to commend it. Particular care should be taken of documentary specimens. This term includes signed objects, those of which there is contemporary mention, those known to have come from an important source (a particular country house or excavation, for instance), those with armorial bearings, and those which bear a date.

An important collection is a matter of interest to students and specialists as well as to the owner, and the collector does valuable work for posterity in assembling and caring for art objects of all kinds. The value of this work is much greater if adequate records are kept.

Collections need to be preserved from numerous destructive agencies, which are more dangerous with some things than with others. Porcelain merely needs to be kept from damage, whereas furniture has to be watched for woodworm, ironwork kept from rusting, and pictures need an atmosphere free from damp and deleterious substances. Apart from other considerations, lack of care can considerably affect value. Professional restorers can deal with existing defects, and museums are usually prepared to give advice on care and preservation. Nothing ought to be left to deteriorate or perish for want of attention.

COROMANDEL LACQUER *See* LACQUER, CHINESE.

CREAM-WARE *See* FAIENCE-FINE.

DEALERS I have elsewhere commented on the high standard of honesty to be found among reputable and established antique dealers. This, of course, does not mean that they will refuse to drive a hard bargain occasionally, or that they will necessarily pass on something important for which they paid very little at much less than a fair market price. They could hardly be expected to do so. The occasional "plums" must help to pay for the many disappointments.

The dealer has to pay rent and rates for his showrooms, as well as lighting, heating, wages to staff, and similar expenses, and he has to lock up a good deal of capital in his stock. The largest item in his annual budget is likely to be for travelling, since antiques are hard to find, and for every ten journeys he makes to auction sales, or to see things which have been offered to him, he is lucky to be able to buy something worthwhile on one of them. Many of these journeys, too, involve travelling long distances. This applies rather more to the specialist than to the general dealer in minor antiques, who can often keep his stock at a reasonable level by attending auctions within the comparatively small radius of fifty miles or so.

The more important dealers spend a good deal of time and money in acquiring the necessary knowledge to carry on business efficiently, and to keep in touch with markets, and inevitably much of what is bought takes time to sell. Very few dealers have the connections and the knowledge to buy only those things which can be sold easily and quickly, and many good things may remain in stock for years, not because they are too highly priced, but because no one comes along who likes them sufficiently well to buy them. For this reason, a large proportion of any dealer's business is done with other dealers. The things which one cannot sell may be readily saleable in the hands of another.

The risks of the antique trade are probably lower than in many trades, because stock properly bought rarely deteriorates very much in value, but a considerable supply of ready cash is important to the dealer so that he can take advantage of buying opportunities as they arise. Since few people are fortunate enough to have unlimited supplies of this kind, it is sometimes advisable to sacrifice old stock at less than cost in order to buy new things.

A friendly dealer is the collector's greatest asset. By constant practice he learns to value saleroom lots with a high degree of accuracy in very unfavourable conditions. Inspection at sales is often difficult, with a large number of people trying to examine the various lots offered, and catalogue descriptions often leave a good deal to be desired.

At the actual sale the dealer is usually sufficiently knowledgeable and well connected to know when the bidding is genuine and when it is being forced up artificially. Above all, he knows when to stop, because his judgement is not clouded by a desire to possess an item at all costs. Many collectors have paid too much because an inordinate desire for possession has clashed with determined bidding on the part of the seller.

The dealer also renders the collector an inestimable service by keeping prices at a safe level, and thus protecting the value of his investment. If a class of antiques becomes temporarily unfashionable the price eases. The dealer, seeing this and knowing the phase to be temporary, buys for stock, thus preventing a fall to catastrophic levels, and ensuring that market prices remain reasonably stable. To do this he must necessarily tie up capital, and, if his subsequent rewards make it worth it he has earned them.

Lastly, the dealer, by distributing antiques to the people who want them both makes the market and keeps it in existence, so that the collector is reasonably assured of being able to sell what he has bought if he needs the money, or if his estate has to be sold after his death.

The collector, therefore, has to pay more than he would if no dealers existed. In return he is relieved of the necessity to spend money in searching for what he wants, he gets an assurance of authenticity from an expert, and the value of his purchase is protected. On balance, he is certainly not the loser by the arrangement.

It sometimes happens that the collector eventually makes a profit beyond the wildest dreams of the dealer, because the dealer cannot afford to hold the things he buys in order to make a long-term profit. An example from my own experience proves the point. In 1941 a dealer (now deceased) bought a very rare and interesting item from a London porcelain sale for £7. Subsequently, in 1948, I acquired it from him on behalf of a friend in the United States for £70 who, about eight years later refused £500 for it. This was not a matter of something being sold at less than its true value at any time, or of its true nature not being known to any of the parties. It simply recorded the rise in value due to inflation and a greater demand, and this is the kind of profit that only the collector can make. The dealer is precluded, by the nature of his business, from keeping objects for so long. I do not want my reader to think that such instances are common, but they do happen.

There are other ways in which the dealer can help the collector. Questions of valuation and disposal often need expert handling. The dealer is in touch with markets which are closed to the collector and can often dispose of items reasonably quickly which would otherwise wait a long time for a buyer at a fair price. If an object has to be disposed of too quickly a loss is certain to result, and the quicker the disposal, the greater the loss as a general rule.

The twin problems of where to sell an object and at what price frequently bedevil the collector, and, still more frequently, his executors, who do not have the benefit of his knowledge and connections.

I have found in the past, in the course of my own work, that estates can be involved in quite heavy losses if the executors have to realize on a large number of antiques quickly, and without expert guidance. Even if it is decided to put the objects into a saleroom, the question of which auction room remains. Specialized objects put into a general sale usually realize far less than they are worth. The same position exists with dealers. A general dealer in antiques will not be able to give the price which would willingly be paid by the specialist.

A word of caution is advisable. The collector is safest in keeping to one dealer whom he trusts, and whose knowledge is sound. It is not smart to tell several dealers of an interest in a particular kind of antique, because they will then bid against each other to get what is wanted, and the price will be forced up in consequence. If only one dealer is involved the collector knows that he is not competing against himself. Moreover, a dealer will look after a good customer, and will make concessions in price to someone whose business he values and who is a regular buyer.

Most important dealers are members of the British Antique Dealers' Association. In buying from any of them the collector knows that he is in safe hands, and if he does have reason to complain, the Association will see that he is fairly treated. I do not, of course, mean that he is necessarily in unsafe hands if this advice is disregarded, since one or two large dealers are still outside the Association, but as a general guide, and particularly in a strange town, the advice is sound.

Dealers, as a class, are unregenerate individualists. They range from the little man in the back street who earns his bread and butter selling junk for shillings, and who occasionally adds a little jam to it by picking up an unsuspected antique from a working-class household, to the glittering showrooms of London, Paris, and New York, presided over by men who know the best when they see it, and who are willing to spend in tens of thousands of pounds to get it. They range from the "knocker" (*q.v.*) and the "runner" (*q.v.*) to the specialist who has spent his lifetime finding out most of what there is to be known about one or two aspects of the subject, and who is the trusted agent and *confident* of millionaire collectors.

The buyer can take his pick according to the depth of his purse, but he will not be able to complain of lack of variety in the people he meets in the course of his career as a collector. He will, in fact, meet a much more colourful selection, both among dealers and his fellow-collectors, than can be found in most walks of life, and he will have a common ground on which to meet them.

DELFT   *See* TIN-ENAMELLED POTTERY.

DERBY (DERBYSHIRE) PORCELAIN FACTORY

This factory was established about 1750, but little is known of its early work. A class of figures characterized by a lack of glaze round the sides of the base – the so-called "dry-edged" type – are attributed to this period. In 1756 the manufacture of porcelain was started by a partnership headed by William Duesbury, who had earlier owned a decorating studio in London.

From 1811 until 1848 it was in the hands of Robert Bloor and his family, and it closed, finally, a few years afterwards. Some of the moulds passed to Copelands of Stoke, who still have them. The present Crown Derby Porcelain Company is a new concern started in 1877.

The first porcelain to be used at Derby resembles an inferior Chelsea body of the period, and is sometimes mistaken for it. Bone-ash was introduced about 1770, and variations of one kind or another are to be noticed throughout the factory's life. The glaze also varied. In the 1760s it is noticeably thick, and inclined to run and to pool in hollows. During the Bloor period the glaze used frequently developed a fine network of cracks.

Derby was noted for its figures, which were well made but never rose much beyond the mediocre. Many were copied from Meissen. Derby introduced the biscuit figure into England in imitation of Sèvres. Figures nearly always have three marks – known as "patch" marks – on the unglazed base, but until 1770 specimens never have a factory mark.

Derby was also noted towards the end of the 18th century for its painting, and a number of artists have been recorded about which a good deal is known. "Japan" patterns, copied from export Imari ware, were a factory speciality which has since been continued by the new Crown Derby Porcelain factory.

EMBROIDERY

Unlike tapestry, embroidery is done on a foundation, such as canvas or linen, which has a normal warp and weft. The pattern in tapestry-weaving is made by the weft itself. *Petit point* is a kind of needlework consisting of a canvas ground on which a tapestry effect is obtained by fine stitching in silk or wool over the whole ground. It is sometimes used for upholstery and cushions.

Embroidery generally is executed in a wide variety of techniques and styles, of which there is only space to mention a few of the more outstanding. The art has a long history, and the Egyptians achieved a considerable reputation for it in the ancient world. Penelope, of course, was engaged in work of this kind during the years in which she waited for the return of Ulysses, and the early Christian Church made much use of embroidered vestments, altar-cloths, and so forth.

Embroidery was an occupation for women of all ages and ranks. Probably the most important surviving example is the so-called Bayeux "tapestry", which is not a tapestry, but needlework. This depicts scenes from the conquest of England by William of Normandy, and is reputed to have been worked by Queen Matilda and her ladies-in-waiting, although the tradition has little to confirm it.

Pictorial embroideries became fashionable in medieval times, and remained so for many years. An unusual development of the pictorial style started in the reign of James I and continued until that of Charles II. This was "stump" or "stamp" work, which used stuffing and padding to raise parts of the design in high relief. Figures, especially, were raised in this way, but other elements, such as trees, rockeries, animals, and so on, were also given the same treatment. The technique was used to decorate caskets and boxes of various kinds, and such things as mirror frames.

The subjects frequently refer in one way or another to the House of Stuart, and the fashion obviously was popular in Royalist circles. Biblical, classical, and allegorical subjects, as well as flowers, fruit, landscapes, and many similar things, are to be found. The work was executed with silk and metal threads, with the occasional addition of pearls, beads, and bits of glass. Dated examples range from about 1640 to 1660, but the method was undoubtedly in use both before and after these dates.

Related to "stump" work is *appliqué* work, in which various materials are attached to the foundation and finished off with ornamental stitching of one kind or another. This kind of work dates from medieval times.

Beadwork is closely allied to embroidery, the two often being used together, but small objects composed entirely of beadwork were done until towards the end of the 19th century.

A comparatively common survival from the 17th and 18th centuries is the sampler, which was originally a series of motifs to be used as patterns or exercises, or as displays of skill.

Samplers of the 17th century exhibit considerable ingenuity, a great variety of stitches being employed, as well as cut-work and lace-work. At a later date the sampler became a pious exercise for children and young ladies, and most have the name of the executant and the date of execution, as well as a text or two, and sickly exhortations. The sampler has always been popular among collectors, and the most important were done before about 1830. They are becoming much rarer.

Embroidery of one kind or another was frequently used in England for upholstery, much in the same way as the French used tapestry for the same purpose. Tapestry was rarely used in England, and most such panels are *petit point* needle-work. Today, genuine 18th-century embroidered covers of this kind are extremely rare, and those in good condition still rarer. Such work was usually done at home in wool or silk, and can be very elaborate. If it is of good quality it adds considerably to the value of seat-furniture.

This apart, much upholstery was carried out in silk damask, often elaborately patterned. Silk velvets were used for finer things, and woollen velvets for the less important. The ravages of moth, however, have made surviving specimens of woollen velvet upholstery exceedingly scarce. Printed materials came into use during the latter part of the 18th century, and leather was used for hard wear and economy.

Most such fabrics have now faded, due to exposure to light, and artificially faded reproductions are sometimes used. This can be detected if it is possible to examine the reverse, since artificial fading has the same effect on *both* sides, whereas fading from exposure to light will occur only on one side.

ENAMEL AND ENAMELLING   Enamel is a kind of glass coloured with various metallic oxides, and it is used for a variety of decorative purposes.

Enamel colours on pottery and porcelain are painted over

the glaze and subjected to a second firing, which must be below the melting-point of the original glaze. To ensure this substances known as fluxes are added to the pigments to lower the melting-point below that of the glaze. Enamels were in use in China late in the Sung Dynasty, and in Persia (*minai* painting) from about the 12th century. Although the first pigment to be used on porcelain was blue underglaze, which is a high-temperature colour, enamels were introduced in Europe early in the 18th century at Meissen and elsewhere. Enamel colours were first used on faience during the 18th century, and the tin glaze is, in itself, an enamel on a pottery base (*see* TIN-ENAMELLED POTTERY).

The art of enamelling was first developed to decorate metal-work of all kinds. It was applied in the form of powder to the metal base and vitrified by heating. There are two kinds of enamel paste – opaque, to which a proportion of tin oxide has been added, and translucent, which is clear glass with a colouring oxide.

There are several methods of application, as follows:

Champlevé   Small cells are scraped in the metal and filled with the glass paste. This is subsequently vitrified by heat.

Cloisonné   Wires are fixed to the metal base to form compartments to contain the glass paste.

Basse Taille   The design in metal is covered with a transparent enamel through which it can be seen.

Plique à Jour   This is similar to the *cloisonné* technique, except that there is no metal background, the enamel being held in position by the wires. These enamels are translucent or transparent.

Painted enamels   These are similar in principle to enamelled faience and porcelain, inasmuch as the painting is done on a foundation of opaque enamel, with no confining wires. The base, however, is metal, and not a ceramic substance.

The art of enamelling is of considerable antiquity, and it probably followed fairly speedily on the discovery of glass. It has always been much used in the manufacture of jewellery, especially during Renaissance times. The Celts were skilled craftsmen in enamel, and much work of the kind was

9 A fine jade buffalo of the
Ming dynasty (1368–1644)

10 A creamware
model of a
pillion horseman
on a mare,
decorated with
coloured glazes.
English, mid-18th
century

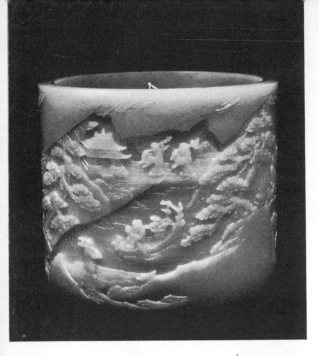

11   A fine brush-holder
in apple-green translucent
jade. Chinese, 17th
century

12   A fine quality Japanese
lacquer box. 18th century

13   A Worcester vase painted
with a Teniers subject by
Donaldson. *c.* 1765

done at Byzantium. The painted enamels of Limoges are famous.

From the collector's viewpoint, the types most usually collected are the Chinese *cloisonné* and painted enamels (much work of the latter kind being done at Canton for export to the West), and the painted and printed enamels of Battersea, in London, and of various provincial centres in England.

Chinese *cloisonné* enamels appear to belong, at the earliest, to the Yüan Dynasty, and were probably introduced from the West during the 13th century. The reign of Ch'ing Tai [1450–1457] is celebrated for enamel work of fine quality. Ming *cloisonné* enamels are very rare, and the surface of probable examples is pitted, with a dull polish. Most such work seen in Europe belongs to the reign of Ch'ien Lung [1736–1795] and later. These are usually well finished, but the ornament is more fussy and over-detailed than the broader treatment of those awarded a Ming dating.

Much of the Cantonese painted enamel work is on forms inspired by contemporary porcelain. Themes of decoration are very similar. Perhaps the most sought after are specimens based on Western forms decorated to order, which are analogous to the so-called ORIENTAL LOWESTOFT (*q.v.*). 18th-century examples are the more highly valued, but dating is often difficult, and depends on the style of decoration for the most part.

Among the painted and printed enamels, those of Battersea have always held a high place. Many Bilston and South Staffordshire enamels are wrongly attributed to Battersea, however, which was a small factory founded by Alderman Stephen Theodore Janssen in 1750, and closed in 1756. Anything in a style other than rococo, therefore, can at once be dismissed as having no connection with Battersea.

The factory was situated at York House, and made such things (to quote from a contemporary advertisement) as "snuff-boxes, pictures of the Royal family, bottle tickets, wine labels with chains, watch cases, tooth-pick cases, coat and sleeve buttons, crosses, and other curiosities, mostly mounted in metal, double gilt".

Much of the work was decorated with transfer prints from engraved plates by Robert Hancock, who worked later at the Worcester porcelain factory and a few examples exist painted by a hand familiar on early Chelsea porcelain which I believe to be William Duvivier. Battersea employed the Irish engraver, John Brooks, who invented the process of transfer-printing.

Enamels were made at Bilston, Birmingham, and Liverpool, and doubtless most of the larger pieces, such as candlesticks, inkstands, jugs, cups, salts, tea caddies, plates, and so forth, came from one or other of these. The same factories also made many small items, such as patch-boxes, snuff-boxes, and so forth, most of which are indubitably in the Adam style. Boxes with such coloured grounds as pink and green are especially sought.

ENGRAVING Decoration incised or cut into a metal surface with a tool known as a graver. Flat plates thus worked upon were inked and used for printing, and the prints are called, by extension, engravings.

Printed engravings of the 17th and 18th centuries not uncommonly survive, but the subject is too large for discussion here. Many of them were copied from original paintings by important artists, whose work was, in this way, widely disseminated.

Much use was made of engravings of all kinds by the painters of pottery and porcelain, and it is, in many cases, possible to trace such work to its source. Many porcelain figures were inspired by contemporary engravings, and some of these have likewise been traced.

Books of engravings of formal ornament, such as the German *Laub- und Bandelwerk*, were published on the Continent, and used by craft-workers of all kinds as a basis for designs.

Engravings are of several kinds. The line engraving is probably the commonest, and the term is self-explanatory. The mezzotint is a later process in which burrs were first raised over the entire surface of the plate with a chisel known as a rocker, the design then being formed by a scraper, which flattened the ink-retaining burrs where required. Stipple engraving, best seen in the work of Bartolozzi, is made up of many small dots, much in the same way as a modern half-tone block.

Etchings are made from printing plates which are first prepared by covering them with an acid-resisting material.

The design is then scratched through this in such a way as to uncover the metal beneath. The plate is finally immersed in a bath of acid which "bites" the design into the metal through the incisions thus made.

Engraved plates were extensively used during the 18th century for the process of transfer-printing on pottery and porcelain.

FAIENCE   *See* Tin-enamelled Pottery.

FAIENCE-FINE   Cream-coloured earthenware covered with a clear lead glaze. This material was popularized during the 18th century by Josiah Wedgwood, who exported it to the Continent in large quantities. From a utilitarian viewpoint it was superior in many ways to the earlier faience (tin-enamelled earthenware) which was then in use, and the faience factories were forced to meet the competition of Wedgwood by manufacturing a similar ware which was termed "faience-fine". As a result, the manufacture of faience proper was progressively discontinued until, by the end of the 18th century, it had almost entirely disappeared.

FASHION IN WORKS OF ART   This is a subject which any writer would approach with caution. It depends on many factors, almost all of which are unknown and unknowable.

Fashion can be divided into two kinds: that which arises naturally and spontaneously from the circumstances of the period, and that which is deliberately manufactured.

To make the point clearer, the fashion for neo-classicism in the 18th century was started primarily by the discoveries at Pompeii and Herculaneum. Nevertheless, to make a revived classical style fashionable, these discoveries needed to come at the right time. People were tiring of rococo, and such contemporary figures as Winckelmann, Sir William Hamilton, the Brothers Adam, Diderot, and Goethe all aided its development, each for their own reasons. In the absence of this assistance neo-classicism as a vogue would probably have been stillborn.

The kind of fashion which is manufactured can be seen most easily in the modern picture trade, where all the resources of publicity are brought to the task of creating a vogue for a particular artist. Fashions of this kind are precisely the same as those of Dior.

Fashion affects some things more than others. Antiques are rarely affected seriously. Although Queen Anne furniture may be temporarily eclipsed to some extent by Chippendale or Sheraton, or English porcelain by German, market values do not drop catastrophically. Objects out of fashion once tended to ease considerably in price, but at present a consistent increase is to be observed over the whole field, and this for a number of reasons is likely to persist indefinitely.

The purchase of modern art is a gamble which occasionally pays fantastically high dividends. If the collector acquires specimens that please him at a price he can afford, then no harm is done. If the artist subsequently becomes fashionable the owner can, if he wishes, take his profit, happy in the knowledge that it is capital appreciation and probably non-taxable. In the meantime, he has enabled the artist to continue working by helping to provide him with an income.

To borrow from Shaw, the golden rule is that there are no golden rules. The ability to anticipate fashion is partly luck and partly good judgement. It is the result of a careful watch on saleroom prices, of mingling with people who are in touch with the art market and evaluating small talk and gossip, of studying contemporary trends in other spheres, and then putting all these pieces of the jig-saw together in the right order.

Even this may not give the answer. The market for an important class of antiques was distinctly affected for several years by the purchases of a close friend of mine. He started collecting by buying a gift for his wife in a New York art dealer's store, and wondering why he had to pay so much money for it. His curiosity eventually led him into the possession of one of the world's finest collections of its kind, which was made with scholarly care and skill. This is the kind of intervention which no one could predict, but because of it many collectors paid higher prices, and many estates were richer when their antiques reached the saleroom than they might have been.

It is, perhaps, advisable to consider the special position of the 19th century in relation to fashion. From time to time a minor vogue for Victorian things occurs, but it is difficult to think that anything made during this period will ever attain the status of the products of the 18th century and earlier.

The reason for this was so well set forth by the late W. B. Honey that I feel I cannot do better than quote his words, "It may be remarked that the charge of artistic insignificance in the nineteenth-century wares is by no means due to the familiar contempt for the insufficiently antique. The period of the Napoleonic wars marks a definite break with the old traditions of craftsmanship. The financial and cultural impoverishment they caused left the industrializing process ... irrevocably complete."

FONDPORZELLAN Porcelain decorated with coloured grounds. A "mother-of-pearl" lustre introduced in the Böttger period at Meissen was sometimes used in this way, but the first ground colour clearly to fall into this category was the *Kapuzinerbraun* (or *Kaffeebraun*) devised by Samuel Stölzel some time between 1720 and 1722. *Kapuzinerbraun* (lit. Capuchin brown) was probably derived from the colour of a habit worn by Capuchin monks.

Underglaze blue was used at Meissen in imitation of the Chinese powder blue, and a yellow ground was first used in 1727, a vase formerly in the Dresden Collections signed by Höroldt bearing this date. Yellow grounds of several shades were subsequently devised. Following these came several shades of green, including a sea-green which is markedly turquoise in colour. Pale grey, lilac, lavender, and a pale greyish ground in imitation of the 18th-century Chinese copies of *Ko* ware are infrequent, and a celadon glaze is extremely rare. A rich crimson-purple which is fairly close to a raspberry in colour is among the best of the coloured grounds. Much porcelain of this kind was also made at Sèvres, where the *gros bleu* and the *rose Pompadour* are worthy of special note. The use of ground colours at the English factories was, for the most part, inspired by these sources.

Coloured grounds were mostly employed in conjunction with panels reserved in white which were painted in enamel colours.

Fondporzellan gradually fell into disuse with the introduction of MOSAIK PATTERNS (*q.v.*).

FORGERIES, FAKES, AND REPRODUCTIONS

To begin with some definitions, forgeries are objects made to simulate something of value for the express purpose of deception; fakes are objects which have been altered or added to for the same purpose; reproductions are honest copies of antique objects and works of art made for decorative purposes, and not primarily intended to deceive, although, in unscrupulous hands, they are sometimes used for this purpose.

In general, the materials from which almost all works of art were made in the past were naturally-occurring substances containing a number of accidental impurities which could not be removed. It must be remembered that, before these days of the scientific preparation of pure materials, most were taken from natural sources, and were selected for certain desirable properties. Unrecognized by the craftsmen of the time, these properties were, quite often, the result of the occurrence of impurities which affected the final result. These cannot now be added in the form, or the proportions, in which they then occurred. For instance, in some kinds of old pottery impurities in the clay, glaze, or pigments joined together to produce a result which cannot be repeated except by the use of materials from precisely the same source in the same way. Therefore a forgery must be as near a replica as can be obtained with other materials, and this can never be close enough to withstand proper examination.

Next to materials, we have the methods used in making the article. Tools are very different today from what they were. The old tools are unobtainable, and, even if they are reproduced, workmen are not trained in their use. Craftsmen have to serve a long apprenticeship to the use of hand tools for fine work, and they cannot handle unfamiliar tools effectively without a great deal of practice. The circular saw was unknown to the maker of antique furniture, and it leaves traces of its use which are, in most cases, unmistakable. Therefore, the forger of antique furniture, even when he uses old wood, is often accused by his tools.

Then there is the effect of age, and of the vicissitudes which time necessarily brings with it. The colour of old silver is unmistakable to the expert. The colour of old wood can rarely be simulated convincingly. This question of the PATINA (*q.v.*) conferred by the passing of time is an important one to the expert.

The forger not only has to use modern purified materials, but frequently synthesized substances prepared by modern chemical methods. The paintings of van Meegeren, which passed several unscientifically minded experts, were unhesitatingly pronounced to be forgeries the instant they were subjected to chemical analysis, because he used synthesized materials which do not occur naturally.

The forger, therefore, no matter how expert, is in a very difficult position. He cannot expect his work to stand up to anything more than superficial examination. He fears the chemist, ultra-violet light, and scientific approaches generally, and most of all he likes people who think they have a "flair" which absolves them from using the ordinary processes of close examination and reasoning. A "flair" may, if it is good enough, suggest that an object is a forgery, but more often than not only scientific examination can prove it.

The notes which follow are by no means exhaustive, and the collector should develop the habit of mind which questions any apparent departure from the normal, no matter how slight. Perhaps this is the best place to say that what follows may be a little frightening to the beginner, but it should be regarded as a challenge. Little would be accomplished if we considered the merely difficult to be impossible, and the forger rarely deceives the expert and the sceptic. His target is the gullible and the over-enthusiastic, and it is not often that anything wiser has been said on this subject than the remark of Giovanni Morelli, "Enthusiasm is not a method of judgement."

The best safeguard, at first, is to buy from the expert who is prepared to back his judgement with a guarantee, and acquaintance with genuine examples will ultimately make the collector proof against almost anything. No one is proof against the occasional error of judgement. It is enough to ask that one is not deceived by the obvious at any time, and by the really skilful forgery very rarely.

Examination of porcelain should first be addressed to the body. Old soft-paste examples are copied in a hard-paste body. This should be the first point of agreement. The finer points, such as the absence of glaze inside the foot-ring of most old Worcester, must also be learned. The decoration should be examined, particularly with the possibility in mind that a piece of white porcelain might have been decorated later.

When decoration of white porcelain outside the factory is contemporary the price may not be affected. Indeed, in some cases it may be higher. But when it is a fake, then the value is negligible. Slight enamelled decoration is sometimes removed with hydrofluoric acid, and the piece re-enamelled with a more expensive decoration. Fortunately, this cannot be done without affecting the glaze more or less seriously. It causes "bubbles" and black specks, the presence of either of which is usually a cause for suspicion, although both appear on some primitive soft porcelains as a manufacturing defect.

Because of its high value, old porcelain has always been a target of the forger, but faience of the more desirable kinds has also been forged, particularly polychrome delft. The tin-enamelled ware most to be treated in this way, however, is Italian *maiolica*. German stoneware has been copied in the Rhineland and elsewhere. These are principally detected by clumsiness of form. In some cases old moulds have been used. Forgeries of German faience are more or less limited to the enamelled wares of Ansbach, and to such popular things as tureens in the form of vegetables and birds made at Höchst and elsewhere. French faience of the more colourful kinds has been copied extensively, including some of the early work of Nevers, and anything in faience which seems to be in brilliant condition should be suspected and made to prove its innocence. The material was too soft and fragile to survive at least without minor damage, except in rare cases.

Forgeries of Sèvres porcelain reached a point where one 19th-century writer on the subject stated that the greater proportion in private collections, and in some museums, was not genuine. The increase in expertise, and the adoption of more rigid standards since then, have improved the position, but many of these things are still in circulation. The soft-paste of Chelsea has been copied extensively, both in hard-paste and in a later variety of soft-paste which never approaches the original in quality. Gold anchor marks are added to figures and groups of a kind known not to have been made at Chelsea in the first place. Raised and red anchor models are rarely copied, but the triangle mark is to be seen on forgeries of such things as the early Goat and Bee jugs.

The moulded decorations of Doccia have been commonly forged, and are usually called Capo-di-Monte by the small dealer, who is often an innocent party to the deception. Even English creamware has been copied, particularly that with decoration sought after for the U.S.A. market, and contemporary copies from Germany and elsewhere are far from unknown.

Forgeries of German porcelain are numerous, and in the same hard-paste as the originals. In a few cases the old moulds were used for reproductions at a later date. These are, however, always accused by the enamel colouring, and by the style of the decoration.

Chinese pottery and porcelain, apart from being the subject of innumerable copies in Europe, has been extensively copied in China. T'ang tomb figures, particularly the unglazed variety, can be very deceptive, and it would be a bold man who would give many such figures an unqualified certificate of genuineness. Knowing that European buyers view undamaged specimens with suspicion, the Chinese break and repair forgeries. Glazed figures are much safer, and although attempts are made to imitate the effect of burial on the glaze, it is rarely done convincingly. T'ang styles were repeated in the Ming Dynasty with some differences.

Of the Sung wares, the showy varieties, such as Chün ware, have been copied from the Ming Dynasty onwards, and many types were reproduced in the 18th century in porcelain instead of stoneware, and given a wash of brown pigment over the foot-ring to imitate the appearance of an antique specimen. Some of the painted wares have been extensively copied, and were frequently given false marks, often more as a token of veneration than as a serious attempt to deceive. Close copies have been made in modern times for export to the West, particularly of the Ch'ing wares, and recently factories in China have made use of European catalogues of Chinese porcelain.

The Chinese are also skilful forgers of other materials. Jade, for instance, is treated with acid to reproduce the effect of burial. Ivories are faked to give them the patina of age. Girls are given small ivories to wear between their breasts, the sweat eventually producing a passable imitation of an antique patination which can usually be detected by ultra-violet radiation, and old pieces are altered and recarved to make them more desirable. Ultra-violet light is particularly useful in revealing fakes in ivory.

The corrosion (or patina) of old bronze is imitated in various ways. Archaizing bronzes of the Sung Dynasty are damaged and given a heavy artificial patina of copper carbonate mixed with lacquer. Although this is often very convincing superficially, it will scrape off with a penknife, and this cannot be done with genuine corrosion. Patination is also imitated both in China and the West by immersion in chemical solutions. In such cases it will be seen that the surface has been attacked with suspicious evenness. This never occurs when the corrosion is the result of burial.

Despite the stringency of the laws relating to articles of gold and silver, forgeries still exist, although the vigilance of the Goldsmiths' Company has greatly reduced their number.

There are relatively few examples of modern imitations stamped with false marks, although marks are sometimes cut from old pieces of little value and inserted into modern copies. Faking in silver is still common. Complete objects are made from damaged ones, the bowl of one spoon, for instance, being attached to the handle of another. Heavy ornament has been added to plain examples. If an old specimen is worth (say) £10 an ounce, and 6 ounces of modern ornament is added, the faker is doing well, since he is getting £10 an ounce for modern work worth perhaps £1 an ounce. In these days this fraud is not so common, since the principal demand is for plain silver. It should be remembered that any new additions greater than 25 per cent. of the original weight must be hall-marked, which, of course, would reveal the fact that it was modern work.

Adapting comparatively minor articles to make something more valuable is often fairly easy to the skilled silversmith. Thus, a plain mug sometimes receives a cover, or the addition of a spout to turn it into a jug; spoons are turned into the rarer and much more valued forks; saucepans become porringers or caudle-cups; plates are refashioned into baskets and bowls, and pap-boats into sauceboats. Teapots have even had spout and handle removed to make them into tea-caddies.

Another trick is to insert a piece of silver shaped like the bottom, and bearing old silver marks, into a modern coffee-pot, giving it a double bottom.

All these have perfectly genuine marks, but false punches have been made and used, although possession of them means a heavy term of imprisonment.

Furniture is an exceptionally fruitful field for the forger. If an article of furniture is not genuine it may be one of several things. At best it may be a copy made during the 19th century, when the copying of old styles was commonplace. These are sometimes difficult to detect, since they are made with good materials by a craftsman, and they will have some of the signs of age. At best they are accused by clumsiness of form. Such things are sometimes replacements – in a set of chairs, for instance – and sets of this kind often contain genuine examples mixed with later copies. The presence of French polish is not a good guide, since some 18th-century furniture was later maltreated in this way, with consequent loss of value. French polish was not introduced until the 19th century. It is sometimes used on forgeries and rubbed down to simulate the old beeswax and turpentine finish, which it never does convincingly.

An object may be completely new, but made of old wood. Indeed, there is always a good demand for old wood for this purpose. Careful examination, however, usually succeeds in discovering the fraud. Old panels, for instance, have to be sawn to size, and the signs of this can nearly always be found somewhere. Such things as the transverse slicing of worm-tunnels (*see* WOODWORM) is a valuable indication. Reveneering in a more ornate style is not so easily detected, since the carcase is genuine. Elaborate marquetry designs can be machine-cut and used on what was a plain veneered example. The addition of painting in the style of Angelica Kauffmann and others has increased the price of many nondescript cabinets.

"Marrying" is not uncommon. Chests can be "married" to stands, for example. The process is taken a little further when tripod stands are joined to old mahogany trays to form occasional tables.

Carved work has been extensively faked. Much work of this kind has been done to plain specimens, but quite obviously insufficient wood is present in such cases for the carving to be anything but flat and shallow. On genuine pieces the craftsman allowed himself plenty of wood to cut away, and the resulting work is much more vigorous. Carving which appears too shallow, therefore, is obviously suspect. In some cases, where the potential profits have been great enough, blocks of wood have been let in for subsequent carving, and the skill with which joints of this kind can be disguised is known only to someone who has had the opportunity to watch a really skilful cabinet-maker at work.

Furniture was made for use, and after two or three hundred years of wear it would be remarkable if it were intact. A few minor repairs, therefore, are passable, although a damaged set of a dozen chairs from which half a dozen seemingly perfect specimens have been made up hardly comes under this heading.

Mounts for fakes of French furniture are often cast from moulds taken from old mounts. Some have a spongy and granulated appearance at the back, and they are rarely finished with much attention to detail.

FURNITURE, AMERICAN During the 17th century the early American colonists made their own furniture, although a few of the finer examples were imported from Europe. Most of this early colonial furniture is plain and simple, and somewhat roughly made. American furniture generally shows an assortment of styles in which those of England and Holland predominate.

Furniture made by the colonists during the early period is often in such woods as pine, maple, cedar, hickory, and ash, as well as the more familiar walnut and oak. Fruit-woods were also used with comparative frequency. At a later date such woods as mahogany and satinwood were employed for better-quality pieces, usually in English styles. Until the 19th century a certain amount of furniture was made in the black walnut (*Juglans nigra*) of Virginia, a wood which resembles mahogany, but native sources became exhausted.

The Jacobean and William and Mary styles (*see* FURNITURE, ENGLISH) are to be seen with minor modifications during the 17th and early 18th centuries. The black walnut was used for furniture in the Queen Anne style which was made principally in Philadelphia. The wood was also exported to England during the same period. The designs of Chippendale were used soon after mid-century, particularly in Boston and New York. Probably the best-known maker working in this style is William Savery of Philadelphia.

After the middle of the century furniture became more

noticeably American in style, although the Hepplewhite and Sheraton designs were used, principally at Baltimore. The neo-classical style was adopted both in architecture and furnishings, and French influence became stronger.

The most widely known name in the history of American furniture is that of Duncan Phyfe, a Scottish settler who arrived in 1780. His early work was extremely good, and he used the styles of Sheraton and Hepplewhite. Later he was influenced by the Directoire and Empire designs of France. His later work in the Regency style is less happy and not so important.

Primarily he was a designer, and he employed craftsmen of various kinds to do the actual work of manufacture. He used most of the contemporary decorative motifs, such as lion masks, paw feet, lyres, and the acanthus leaf, which is usually simpler than the English version.

American innovations include the block front, probably introduced by John Goddard of Newport, Rhode Island, during the 1760s. This was applied to such things as chests, tallboys, secretaires, and so forth, and has raised panels in the form of blocks running from the base to the top, usually decorated at the top with a carved shell. This is never seen on furniture made outside America. The rocking-chair, too, is reputed to have been an invention of Benjamin Franklin. The Hitchcock chair is a light, painted chair first made by Lambert Hitchcock, a Connecticut furniture-maker of the 1820s, who introduced mass-production techniques into manufacture.

Turning was much used for chair legs and similar parts of some American furniture, and the surface was painted on some things, usually pieces made of pine or, less often, maple, from about 1700 onwards.

Most of the Victorian derivations from earlier periods were copied by the American furniture-maker. Such styles as Victorian Gothic and rococo, as well as various revived French styles, were popular. Some particularly intricately worked and unpleasant examples of pseudo-rococo were produced by John Belter of New York.

FURNITURE, BELGIAN Much furniture was exported to England from Belgium during the 19th century, and examples are common in the provincial salerooms. Most of it was stained with a very dark colour, and extensively decorated with extremely bad carving. Specimens are worthless to the collector. Most of it appears to find its way to seaside boarding-houses.

FURNITURE, DUTCH   Dutch furniture is common in England. Some of it was imported from Holland, but much was made here by Dutch cabinet-makers who came to this country when William, Prince of Orange, ascended the throne. It is therefore a little difficult to tell exactly where furniture of this class was made.

Large bureau-bookcases and similar objects decorated with marquetry belong to the end of the 17th century and the beginning of the 18th. The so-called "seaweed" pattern remained in vogue until the death of Queen Anne. Many of the lacquer cabinets on stands of the period are of Dutch workmanship, and the *bombé* front, with heavy outcurving feet, is another Dutch characteristic borrowed from France. Scroll pediments to bureaux and wardrobes are Dutch in origin. The occasional addition of ivory and mother-of-pearl to marquetry is to be seen.

Later in the century copies of the Chippendale and Hepplewhite styles were made in Holland, but were somewhat heavier than their English prototypes. Ebonized furniture painted with seascapes and figure subjects belongs to about the middle of the 18th century, but is not in great demand.

A certain amount of furniture decorated with marquetry was also made in the 19th century in Holland and exported to England. The designs are usually floral, and they can be detected by the poor quality of the workmanship.

FURNITURE, ENGLISH   The following notes on English furniture are intended to survey its history very briefly, and to provide some guide to the succession of styles.

Gothic

The earliest English furniture, of which specimens can be seen occasionally, is in the Gothic style. These are usually in museums, or, less often, in churches. Most of the things thus preserved look vaguely ecclesiastical because, in England, the commonest architectural survival from this era is the church, most secular houses having long since yielded to time. Churches, and buildings of stone, are the only things sufficiently durable to have remained. Most Gothic furniture was uncomfortable, and was undoubtedly destroyed when less austere things became common with the increase of material prosperity under the Tudors. Most examples remaining are chests and cupboards in oak, usually carved with easily recognized motifs, especially the pointed arch.

Henry VIII

When Henry VIII came to the throne foreign influences in decoration were becoming fashionable, and these modified the plainer Gothic ornament of the earlier period with arabesques, and floral and foliate carving. By 1520 the influences of Italy, France, and the Netherlands can all be traced, with that of Italy predominant at first. Italian carvers and decorators were brought to England to work on Hampton Court, and they influenced the design and decoration of furniture as well as plaster and stone-work. Classical columns, heads in relief in medallions, and little figures of *putti* (small naked boys) are all to be seen. Later, Flemish influence replaced the Italian, and can be seen in such things as the bulbous legs fashionable to the end of the century and beyond. Chests and cupboards are the commonest survivals, but chairs and tables were now being made in larger quantities, although the stool was still more common than the chair. Tables made to be permanent replaced the earlier Gothic trestle tables.

Elizabeth I

The reign of Elizabeth saw the development of earlier 16th-century styles. Inlaid ornament in a variety of coloured woods became fashionable. The use of carving continued, becoming more florid with the passing of time. Turning, which dates – in England – from mid-16th century, was used to fashion the bulbous legs already mentioned.

Turning was done on a lathe, the block of wood being held at either end and rotated. Various stationary wood-cutting chisels were brought into contact with the rotating wood, first shaping the block into a cylinder, and then cutting away the unwanted wood to give the final shape. By using cutting tools of different kinds and lengths, a variety of shapes could be obtained, and the surface of the plain turning was usually ornamented with carving in addition.

James I

The reign of James I shows for the most part a gradual refinement of the somewhat coarse and exuberant styles current during the Elizabethan period. Upholstery, hitherto little used, became fashionable for chairs, and the arms (which had been an invariable part of the chair since Gothic times) fell into disuse to some extent, the armless chair taking the place of the stool. The use of drawers in chests and cupboards became more common.

Mirrors were introduced from Venice during the reign of Charles I, but it was not until the Duke of Buckingham started the manufacture of glass mirrors at Vauxhall in 1670 that they became in the least usual.

Commonwealth

The period of Cromwell and the Puritans hardly deserves mention. It was mainly a continuation of the earlier Jacobean styles in a ponderous form, almost unrelieved by ornament of any kind. Chairs sometimes had slung leather seats and backs. Turned legs were common.

Restoration

The Restoration was a period of reaction from the excesses of Puritanism, and Continental influences of various kinds were fairly well marked.

Lacquer cabinets were imported from China some of which were magnificently decorated, and elaborately carved stands, gilded or silvered, were made to carry them. Black lacquer was the most usual, red being much rarer and valued accordingly. Imitations of Chinese lacquer were made in the West, mostly by amateurs, but the quality of the workmanship was much inferior to the Far Eastern varieties. Lacquered cases for clocks are examples of Western lacquering.

About 1675 oak, which had been the preferred furniture wood in the earlier periods, gave place to walnut – a wood of much finer grain and more suitable for detailed carving. Veneering was also introduced at the same time. Veneers are thin sheets of wood selected for an interesting grain or "figure" which are used to cover a carcase of commoner and cheaper wood. Unlike oak, walnut takes a high surface polish, and for this reason cabinets of polished wood, without carving became fashionable, the grain (or figuring) of the wood being employed as decoration.

The marquetry of this period is usually Dutch in origin, and the method of cutting was similar to that used by André Charles Boule for his brass and tortoise-shell inlays (*see* FURNITURE, FRENCH).

William and Mary

Chairs of the period often have woven cane seats and backs first to be seen in the reign of Charles II, which lasted until the end of the reign of William and Mary. The day-bed, made in this manner, was popular during the same period, but is not seen thereafter. Turned legs were still common, spiral turning was introduced, and carving was often elaborate. Cherub heads were a frequent motif, but the use of the crown commemorates the Restoration of the House of Stuart. Chairs often had a deep front rail decorated with carving, and an extremely high back.

The work of the great English carver, Grinling Gibbons, belongs to the period of 1670 and after. Most of his carving was done in pear-wood, and his favourite subject was fruit and flowers in high relief. The amount of work attributed to him suggests a life-span comparable with that of the Biblical patriarchs. Mirrors were often elaborately framed with marquetry or carved decoration.

The first import of Indian furniture of ebony (or "blackwood") belongs to this period, but specimens are very rare. At this time, too, imports of exotic woods for decorative purposes from the West Indies began. Mahogany was first imported into England in Elizabethan times, but did not come into use for the making of furniture before about 1720.

Writing bureaux made their appearance during the Restoration. The earliest had a sloping fall-front, and were placed on stands. Later examples had drawers under, and a bookcase top was added. This quite often had glazed doors, although mirrors were sometimes used for the same purpose. China cabinets came into use about the same time, and the fashion for collecting ceramics was probably started in this country by Queen Mary, who assembled a collection of Japanese porcelain at Hampton Court. Glass was still difficult to produce in large sheets, and most glazed doors were divided into sections by glazing bars, each section having a comparatively small pane. The glass of the period did not have a flat surface, and, looked at from an angle, these surface irregularities are nearly always quite obvious.

During the reign of William and Mary most of the styles current in the following reign of Queen Anne were developed, and Dutch influence is particularly strong, many Dutch craftsmen having been brought from Holland.

Queen Anne

The Queen Anne period marks the beginning of the extensive changes to be seen in the design and making of furniture during the 18th century.

Veneering of all kinds was extensively practised at this time. Walnut was the preferred wood for veneers and some interesting effects were obtained. Good figuring is particularly valued in plain walnut veneers. Thin sheets with knot-like markings called "burrs" were used for burr-walnut veneers. Similarly, four thin sheets were sometimes sliced successively, two of them being reversed to form panels which were mirror images. This was called "quartering", and was often used on such comparatively large surfaces as the fall-fronts of writing-cabinets. Dutch seaweed marquetry was also much used. As a general rule, plain walnut veneers of good figure are more expensive than marquetry, and particularly is this so with long-case clocks.

Another innovation was the cabriole leg, mucl used for chairs of all kinds. The better-quality chairs had carvings on the knee, usually the Dutch shell ornament, and the feet were either the rounded club type, the ball and claw (without webs between the claws), or the hoof. The same leg was used for cabinet stands, lacquer cabinets especially being given stands of this kind. Small lacquer cabinet stands were still sometimes provided with the earlier turned leg, or with stands which were based on Chinese furniture designs. At first, lacquer boxes were imported into Europe and utilized as panels in the making of furniture. When demand outran the supply the deficiency was supplied by craftsmen of Holland, England, and France, with varying degrees of success, English lacquer being, for the most part, the least successful.

Backs of chairs of this period were somewhat lower than previously, although they were still a little high in comparison with succeeding styles. The top rail was rounded, and solid splats (urn-, fiddle-, or vase-shaped) occupied the centre of the back. Seats were stuffed, and, for the first time, removable.

Bureaux became much larger, with drawers below. These,

A Queen Anne period walnut chair with a solid splat and cabriole legs

and the larger bureaux-bookcases, were fitted with bracket feet. Interiors were much more elaborate, with drawers, pigeon-holes, and small cupboards. Concealed drawers became common, and can be reached in various ways. The commonest is probably by sliding forward the whole of the centre section, for which purpose it may be necessary to release a secret catch. The best way of tracing the existence of such drawers is by measuring, and then by trying to gain access to any space unaccounted for. The finest bureaux-bookcases were perhaps those handsomely decorated with red and gold lacquer.

Chests of drawers were often decorated with marquetry, and cabinets on stands, with two large outer doors giving access to a series of drawers, were often ornamented in this way. Corner cupboards now had glazed doors, and were in walnut instead of oak. These, and glazed bureaux-bookcases, were used for the display of china and pottery, the collecting of china having by now become a fashionable pursuit.

The tallboy, a tall chest of drawers which started as a chest on a stand and gradually became a double chest, one on the other, was introduced at this time. Mirrors were made in greater quantities, those with the original glass now being the most valuable. Pier glasses were sometimes made with the glass in two sheets. The dressing-glass, which had a swing mirror above a stand containing a series of small drawers, came into use.

The settee, which looks like two or three chairs joined together, became popular. The splats were similar to those to be found on chairs. Small footstools with cabriole legs are to be seen.

Tables had tops veneered in walnut, and small tables were especially designed to be put together to make a large table when a number of persons were to be accommodated.

Side-tables for serving and other purposes became fashionable, the sideboard not being introduced until much later in the 18th century, and the Jacobean gate-leg table, with hinged flaps supported by movable legs, gave place to a rectangular table with a flap opening upwards and out, supported by movable legs. These were often card-tables, although slightly sunken wells at the corners were used to accommodate candlesticks, and not money for gambling as is sometimes supposed. Money-wells, when they are provided, are much deeper and nearer the centre of the table. Console tables belong to this period and later.

George I

The reign of George I is principally a continuation of these styles, and little change is to be noticed until the period of George II, when a certain amount of French influence becomes evident. From about 1733, when the tax was removed, mahogany began to oust walnut as the preferred wood for cabinet-making. This was Spanish mahogany from San Domingo – a dark wood with slight figuring and unsuitable for veneering. For this reason solid wood became the rule, and veneering in mahogany did not become popular until Cuban and Jamaican wood was imported. This is lighter in colour and has a comparatively well-marked figure.

The work of this period has been well described as pompous. Carving became much more common, and furniture was heavier and more ostentatious. The wing easy chair was fashionable, and chairs without arms but with stuffed high backs came into use. These were often covered with designs in *petit point* needlework, usually floral.

Chests of drawers had serpentine fronts and chamfered corners. The plain bracket feet of the earlier period were now sometimes heavier and carved on the more expensive pieces.

Secretaires were sometimes combined with tallboys. Usually the writing section pulled out like a drawer and was fitted with a fall-flap.

The classical pediments of the PALLADIAN STYLE (*q.v.*), together with such carved motifs as the eagle and the lion mask, can now be seen. William Kent was a designer in the Palladian style, to which he added elements of Italian baroque. Primarily his work was done only for those people to whom money meant little. The remark of J. P. Morgan on the subject of yachts might well have been applied to interior decoration by Kent: "If you have to ask how much it costs, you can't afford it." His forms were massive, and intended only for large and spacious houses. He used marble freely, particularly for the tops of side-tables, which were usually elaborately carved and moulded and gilded lavishly. Often they had swags of fruit and flowers with a central carved shell motif as an apron.

Much use was made of carving at this time, and bureaux-bookcases and such things were topped with a broken pediment, usually with a central block for a bust. The effect at which contemporary designers aimed was an ostentatious display of wealth.

The later Kent designs contained some elements of rococo decoration without being in the true rococo style. This is seen at its best in the carved gilt mirror frames called "Chippendale" which frequently have the light and airy scrollwork which is similar to painted and moulded scrollwork on contemporary porcelain.

At mid-century we have the fashion for Chinese designs best termed *chinoiserie*, of which furniture in the style known as Chinese Chippendale is a good example. The plainest specimens were based on imported Chinese furniture, but canopied beds in particular were much more elaborate, with motifs only distantly recalling those of China. Painting and japanning decorated a good deal of furniture in this style. The style can be seen at its most elaborate in the mirror-frames of the period.

Mixed with Oriental motifs were elements of the rococo style, and sometimes of Gothic. Gothic enjoyed a brief revival in the 18th century, and it owed its popularity to Horace Walpole's imitation Gothic villa at Strawberry Hill. Such Gothic motifs as the pointed arch were more or less confined to the glazed doors of bookcases, and grouped pillars in an architectural style were used for table-legs. The revived style is far more often seen in the 19th century.

Many of the designs of this period came from Thomas Chippendale, already mentioned, who published his *Cabinet Makers' Director* in 1754.

The extravagance of rococo and Chinese ornament was a short-lived fashion, and a return was soon made to plainer styles. Veneering was once again employed, this time the veneers being of mahogany.

The knee-hole writing desk, with drawers on either side, came into use. The partners' desk, a much rarer type, is much longer and was made with four sets of drawers, or drawers and cupboards, enabling two persons to work facing each other.

Perhaps Chippendale's greatest contribution to the art of design can be seen in the chair. This was now much better proportioned and more comfortable. The pierced and carved splat took the place of the old solid splat, and although the shell carving is still to be seen on the knees of cabriole legs, its place was sometimes supplied by the acanthus leaf. The terminals to the arms of carvers and similar chairs were sometimes carved with such motifs as eagles' heads, or, more rarely, dogs' heads, while the claw and ball foot is fairly common. Settees were still fundamentally two or three chairs joined together, although the splats were now carved and pierced in the Chippendale manner. Tables with two tripod supports were made to take extra leaves, and side-tables were plain and well proportioned, with a little well-carved ornament, and sometimes with fret-cutting.

The small occasional table on a central pillar terminating in a tripod support was introduced, and the Pembroke table belongs to the same period. This has two wide flaps, hinged on either side of a narrow centre. It takes up little space when not in use. It was a smaller version of the later sofa-table, and is said to have been named after Lady Pembroke,

A mahogany chair in the style of Thomas Chippendale (*c.* 1760)

who was the first to order one. Silver-tables had a fretted gallery.

Generally, most Chippendale furniture depends for its effect on good proportions and the quality of the wood, which was selected for its figure. Carving is not excessive and frequently slight, but always in good taste.

By 1760 Robert Adam (*see* ADAM STYLE) had returned from his tour of Italy, and had started to popularize neo-classicism. He was associated with his brother, James, and as architects they built houses, but they also designed the interior fittings as well.

Cabriole legs now disappear, to be replaced by straight and tapered legs. These were made in either circular or square section, and were quite often fluted. Such motifs as medallions, classical urns, swags and pendants of husks, the ram's head, and the Greek fret were used as ornament, and shape was to some extent based on surviving records of Greek and Roman furniture. Greek vase painting and Pompeiian wall-painting were two of the sources used for this purpose. A number of catalogues of newly formed collections of antiquities, such as that of Sir William Hamilton, were published, and provided source books for designers.

Towards the end of the century furniture was painted, seat-furniture – usually of beech or birch – being coloured white or cream, and less often green or black. These ground colours were then painted with decoration, generally floral. This kind of ornament was comparatively slight on chairs or settees, but much more elaborate figure-subjects after Angelica Kauffmann, Cipriani, Francesco Piranesi, and others were painted on cabinets. These artists also worked for the Adam brothers, and painted wall panels which were fashionable as decoration. Occasionally ceilings were painted in the same way. Much of the more elaborate painting on furniture was done on such things as the half-circular commode, or pier-tables of similar form. Some painting was *en grisaille* – a revival from the early years of the 17th century. Most was done directly on to the wood, but some on to sheets of copper, which were subsequently let in to the wood. The plaques of Wedgwood were also frequently inset. Many of them were after models of John Flaxman, R.A. [1755–1826], the most important exponent of neo-classicism in English sculpture. As in France, friezes of classical ornament are not uncommon in the decoration of case-furniture.

Chairs underwent radical changes in design, the backs becoming oval, shield-shaped with a central lyre in place of the more usual kind of splat, heart-shaped, and in the form of a wheel. These backs were designed not only by the Adam brothers, but by such makers and designers as Sheraton, Hepplewhite, and Gillow. The half-circular commode, either painted or decorated with marquetry, is a new departure. It had a central door and shelves.

The decoration of looking-glasses became symmetrical – that is, the scrolls and volutes on either side of the frames were more or less mirror-images of each other, and not asymmetrical as with the rococo style. Usually the frames are surmounted by an urn, or by a similar neo-classical motif.

A great deal of the ornament was modelled in *gesso* and was given an internal strengthening of thick iron wire or thin rod.

To this period belongs the introduction of the sideboard. This was at first an ordinary side-table with two large cupboards at either end, often surmounted by urns. The urns contained knives and forks, and sometimes the water for washing them. The sideboard proper was introduced by Hepplewhite. Essentially it was a large serving- or side-table with the addition of drawers and cupboards.

The half-circular occasional table became common, and such woods as satinwood and harewood were even more popular than mahogany for fine work.

Approximately contemporary with the Brothers Adam is the work of Hepplewhite. The *Cabinet Maker and Upholsterer's Guide* was first published in 1788. The firm of A. Hepplewhite & Co. was founded by George Hepplewhite, first apprenticed to the noted cabinet-maker, Gillow, who later opened a shop in Cripplegate, London. Among the more frequent kinds of carved ornament used by them are the wheat-ear and the Prince of Wales's feathers, and there is an ambiguous reference in the *Guide* to the shield back, about which it says: ". . . it has been made with good effect for the Prince of Wales."

The designs in the *Guide* exhibit many departures from the severity of those of the Adam brothers. The variations to be seen in the backs of chairs are considerable, although the shield shape is the more frequently used. One or two outlandish designs, such as a back in the shape of a silhouetted urn, for the most part remained on paper. An outcurving leg reminiscent of the earlier cabriole leg was sometimes used for stools, and the frames of small settees with outcurving arms at either end in the Roman style were elaborately carved. These had no backs. The larger settees had backs of various forms from those appearing as a simple triple or quadruplicate chair, to the high, curved, stuffed back.

Pedestal cupboards surmounted by urns appear quite frequently in the *Guide*, but the sideboard proper was still comparatively simple in design. These and commodes were veneered with mahogany and satinwood, often inlaid with other contrasting woods, or painted. Added brass rails to the backs of sideboards were used for displaying silver plate, and for mounting candle-holders. Side-tables continued in use, some with SCAGLIOLA tops (*q.v.*) which imitated marble.

Hepplewhite designed many large bookcases, examples of which are not infrequent.

Thomas Sheraton published his *Cabinet Maker's and Upholsterer's Drawing Book* in 1793. He was principally a designer and a draughtsman, and made very little furniture.

A chair with a shield-shaped back and an urn splat. A design by George Hepplewhite (*c.* 1790)

His designs often resemble those of Hepplewhite closely, but are usually much lighter and less sturdy. They called for little carving, and most of his effects were achieved with veneers, inlays, and marquetry. Although he used such curves as may be found in serpentine-fronted commodes, his furniture is much more a matter of straight lines. The shell motif occurs very frequently. Pierced metal galleries to the tops of cabinets, and similar things, are not uncommon. In France his designs were called "*Louis Seize a l'Anglaise*".

The frames of wall-mirrors of the period were exuberantly ornamented. Swing-mirrors on stands were used for the dressing-table, and are not an uncommon survival. They were in keeping with the Sheraton designs as a whole.

After 1800 Sheraton was influenced by the Empire styles prevailing in France, but these were the least successful of his designs. The Empire style, in fact, never became so popular in England as in France. Napoleon liked replicas of the furniture of the Roman Empire, with the same florid forms and decoration, but the Romans were a dangerous source of inspiration for any but the most disciplined designer. To these motifs of the Roman Empire were added those of Egypt. Most

A chair in the style of Thomas Sheraton (*c.* 1800)

Greek motifs were either drawn from a late and degenerate period or were at second-hand from Roman and Italian sources.

Belonging to this period in English furniture are occasional examples of decoration with dolphins, tridents, anchors, capstans, rope, and other marine motifs which owe their existence to the victories of Nelson.

The lion and the sphinx are a common variety of ornament. The griffin is perhaps a little less frequent. Caryatids were used and animal legs, hoofs, and paws were commonly employed for the feet and legs of tables and other items of furniture. Gilt bronze and ormolu mounts decorated the best pieces as they did in France.

The Empire style was absorbed and Anglicized to become

the REGENCY STYLE (*q.v.*). Much Regency furniture was in rosewood, and inlaying with brass, first employed by Sheraton, became a common practice.

Although the rococo revival started before 1837, it was most popular during the early years of Victoria's reign. A Gothic revival was also fashionable, influenced by Pugin, and the Great Exhibition of 1851 did little to improve the situation.

A chair decorated with classical motifs in a manner based on the French Empire style (*c.* 1810)

Perhaps the best that can be said for Victorian furniture is that it was made from good materials with honest workmanship – something which almost disappeared between the two world-wars, and has been even harder to find since. For this reason some of the less offensive Victorian furniture is worth pre-serving. Much of it, even though it be a century old or more, has a great deal more life left in it than many modern produc-tions.

These notes refer principally to furniture made in the metropolis for the better-class trade. During the 18th century a good deal of country-made furniture was produced which followed metropolitan styles at a distance, or even ignored them altogether. Belonging to the latter category is the Windsor chair, first made in the Queen Anne period. The early specimens sometimes have cabriole legs, and the backs were made of turned supports stretching between the seat and the top rail. Later examples had a central splat as well as turned supports and legs. Towards the end of the century the back was altered, and the splat pierced with wheel-shaped ornament.

The ladder-back chair dates from about mid-18th century. The backs were made up of several flat cross-members

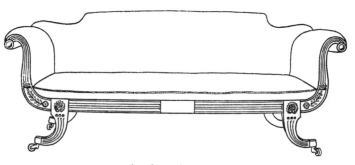

A typical sofa in the Regency style

between two upright rails. The seats were usually of rush-work, which had been used since the last decades of the 17th century.

The Lancashire spindle-back chair is similar in many ways to the ladder-back. These had three cross-members between the upright rails, a series of spindles in two rows joining them together.

Apart from these regional and country types, the mahogany chairs of Chippendale and others were copied in a clumsier version and in less valuable woods, usually beech. Such chairs are extremely useful for furnishing, and are rarely expensive.

The earliest constructional methods in the making of English furniture were distinctly crude. Much of it was joined by cutting tenons (or tongues of wood) which slotted into holes called mortises. The tenons were secured by oak pins (dowels) which were driven in through holes drilled at a right-angle. This joint was extremely strong, but was not adapted to fine work. Nails were always made by hand, the first machine to make nails only being introduced in 1790.

Wood-screws were introduced about 1675, but the threads were hand-cut with a file, and there was little or no taper. The pointed screw was invented in 1851. Slots of old screws are usually a little off-centre, enabling them to be recognized by the appearance of the head.

Veneers were sawn in a saw-press, and were usually about $\frac{1}{16}$ inch thick. The underside was roughened with a toothing plane, and the veneers laid, after gluing, with a veneering hammer. Glue began to be used for joints about the same time as veneers were introduced.

There are few more satisfying things than to furnish with good antique pieces. Apart from the superiority of design, workmanship, and materials over almost all modern productions, it is comforting to know that one's possessions are likely to appreciate in value rather than depreciate. Just as the first run of a few miles takes 10 per cent. off the value of a new car, so most modern furniture acquires a second-hand value, which is a good deal less than its showroom price, immediately it is delivered.

Generally, most antique furniture of different periods mixes fairly well. Of course, a rococo mirror will clash with Jacobean oak, and Sheraton styles do not look well in a thatched cottage, but Queen Anne will blend quite happily with Chippendale, and Chippendale with Hepplewhite. 18th-century furniture in particular fits much more easily into most modern houses than might be imagined, and even blends well with carefully chosen modern furniture.

Prices for antique furniture vary greatly, and it would be impossible to give any exact guidance. It does not need a fortune to furnish with antiques. The high prices paid in sale-rooms are usually for showpieces of superb craftsmanship. Much the same applies to clocks. High prices are paid for clocks by Tompion, Quare, and a few other London makers, but those by provincial makers are usually cheap enough, and good time-keepers. Some antique furniture is scarcer than it was because much has been exported to the United States. Veneered furniture and pieces decorated with marquetry are not, however, in great demand in the States, because central heating causes veneers to lift and warp, although a satisfactory but expensive process has been developed to obviate the trouble.

Walnut is always dearer than mahogany. Usually it looks better but needs more attention, and it must have care and protection from woodworm.

It is worth taking a little trouble to get accessories which are in keeping with the furniture. A few pounds spent on some old delft to go with Queen Anne walnut, for instance, and a little care spent in finding fabrics which are in keeping, will enhance the appearance of the furniture, and will improve the look of mediocre specimens immensely.

The dealer will usually be pleased to help and advise, and will tell potential buyers when he has something which fits their scheme of decoration. The beginner wishing to furnish with antique pieces, therefore, could hardly do better than enlist the help of a reputable dealer.

FURNITURE, FRENCH The first French furniture of which specimens can normally be acquired belongs to the period of Louis Quatorze [1638–1715], and good pieces which are genuinely of the period fetch exceedingly high prices. The standard of craftsmanship during the whole of the period under review was, for the most part, extremely high, and cabinet-makers received royal patronage, and such distinctive titles as *Ébéniste du Roi.*

Furniture of the 17th century is usually elaborately and sumptuously decorated, the work of such important designers as JEAN BÉRAIN [*q.v.*] being used freely. Much use was made of exotic woods, and veneers and elaborate marquetry were employed with great effect. The use of VENEERS is further discussed under that heading, and also under MARQUETRY and PARQUETRY. Upholstered furniture was occasionally covered with tapestry from Beauvais.

André Charles Boule was made *Premier Ébéniste de la Maison royale* in 1673, and he, and his successors, decorated furniture with designs cut from sheets of tortoise-shell and brass. The sheets of both materials were clamped together, the designs being cut from both in one operation. The tortoise-shell was then fitted into the space cut from the brass in such a way as to form a single sheet which was used to cover the surface of the furniture. The waste remaining from this alternation could, of course, be used for the same design in reverse, the brass of the first sheet replacing tortoise-shell, and vice versa. This was called *contre partie* and used for less important things. The brass was often engraved with more or less elaborate designs which were heightened by having a little black pigment rubbed into the incised lines.

Great care is needed in purchasing anything decorated in this style. Many reproductions, inferior in the quality of materials and workmanship, were made during the 19th century, and these are quite common in Europe and the United States. Most Boule work is also decorated with ormolu mounts, and especial attention should be directed to the quality of these, particularly to such details as chiselling of the cast to remove any roughness due to the moulds and to sharpen the outlines. Mounts made in the 19th century are inferior in quality and workmanship.

Immediately following the death of Louis Quatorze we have the *époque de la Régence* [1710–1725]. Louis Quinze [1715–1774], great-grandson of the former king, was only five years of age when he succeeded to the throne, and for some time France was administered by the Duc d'Orléans. This period shows a gradual increase in the more elaborate kinds of ornament, and ormolu was freely used: Charles Cressent and Jacques Caffiéri, whose son modelled for the Sèvres porcelain factory, were noted designers of metal mounts for furniture, particularly in the ROCOCO STYLE (*q.v.*). Upholstered furniture was sometimes covered with Gobelin and Aubusson tapestry with designs after such artists as Watteau and Boucher.

The introduction of *vernis martin* (lit., Martin's varnish) belongs to the reign of Louis Quinze. Simon-Etienne Martin invented a varnish which was used to prepare panels for painting. The subjects for this kind of work were often taken from the paintings of Boucher, Lancret, and Watteau, all of whom had great influence on the decorative arts of the period, or from Chinese and Japanese lacquer.

Louis Seize acceded to the throne in 1774, but for some years before this the style associated with his name had increasingly superseded the scrollwork of rococo. The new style, at first restrained and relatively plain, and sometimes with elements of the rococo still to be seen, blossomed out after 1774 and often rivalled the earlier style in the richness of its ornament.

Legs of chairs became straight and tapering, with fluting

14 A pair of Chippendale armchairs in the Chinese style covered with contemporary Aubusson tapestry. Mid-18th century

15 A magnificent Charles II lacquer cabinet on a contemporary carved wood stand. One of a pair

16 A fine serpentine silver-table with a
pierced gallery, in mahogany. English,
mid-18th century

17 The Combe Abbey
mahogany library table
by Thomas Chippendale.
Mid-18th century

instead of the earlier scrolls. Gilt-bronze mounts were fashionable, the finest being the work of Pierre Gouthière. Increasing use was made of porcelain plaques inset into furniture, the best coming from Sèvres. *Vernis Martin* panels were still employed, but painted increasingly in the new classical taste. Upholstered furniture was sometimes covered with the tapestry of Beauvais or Aubusson, and often painted in white with ornament heightened with gold.

A commode with ormolu mounts
period of Louis Quinze

Immediately following the Revolution came the Directoire period, in which the neo-classical style was exceptionally severe. The First Empire, which succeeded it, is also noted for the use of Egyptian motifs which can first be seen just before 1800.

French furniture of the 17th and 18th centuries has been extensively copied and reproduced, the best of the reproductions being extremely faithful. Since it has always fetched very high prices, it is obviously a tempting subject for the forger. It is therefore advisable to buy only from experts. Like Sèvres porcelain, the frauds far outnumber the genuine specimens.

A few definitions are appended:

Armoire A large wardrobe. These range from the plain carved oak of Normandy to very rare specimens decorated in the style of Boule and made in Paris.

Bergère (Lit., shepherdess.) An easy chair.

E

Bonheur du jour A small writing table with drawers or cupboards over introduced about 1760, often with a marble top or with an inset Sèvres plaque. Pierced metal galleries were usually added.

Canapé A large sofa, often covered with tapestry.

Cartonnière A cabinet with drawers for papers.

Chaise-longue (Lit., a long chair.) A kind of sofa-cum-easy chair made for reclining in the day-time; sometimes made in more than one piece (the *duchesse brisée*).

Commode A chest of drawers decorated with ormolu mounts and in other ways. These usually have marble tops.

Console A small table often with a single leg designed to be partly supported by the wall. Console tables usually have a marble top.

Escritoire A writing cabinet or desk. It may have a fall-front or a cylinder front.

Étagère A small stand with several tiers for the display of *bibelots*.

Fauteuil An armchair with open arms, usually upholstered with silk damask or tapestry.

Girandole A candlestick with several branches.

Guéridon A carved gilt stand made to support candelabra. A small round table, often with a marble top.

Secretaire A writing cabinet.

Suite This was somewhat more extensive than the conventional English sofa and two armchairs. It comprised a *canapé*, two or four *fauteuils*, either four or six ordinary chairs (*chaises*) and often a *chaise-longue*, and a pair of *bergères*. Footstools were sometimes included.

Torchère A tall lamp standard.

Vitrine A cabinet with glass doors and sides for the display of porcelain and *bibelots*, sometimes decorated with *vernis martin* panels. Introduced late in the 18th century.

FURNITURE, ITALIAN   Imported Italian furniture is not plentiful in England, although elaborately carved and gilded specimens associated with William Kent are usually by Italian workmen.

Furniture in the rococo style, such as small commodes and cabinets with marble tops, sometimes completely gilded, came from Italy, and inlays of ivory, including engraved ivory plaques, ornamenting ebonized chairs and cabinets, are rare, but far from unknown here. In the 17th century the Italians made a specialty of ornamenting tables and cabinets with a mosaic of hardstone (*pietra dura*), and Renaissance coffers with elaborately painted panels by minor masters occur occasionally.

Reproductions of early work were made in large quantities during the 19th century, and the practice still continues.

GILDING   This is the art of covering materials with a thin layer of gold. Often the gold is in the form of leaves or sheets beaten to about one two-hundred thousandth of an inch, and this is then laid on the surface. Copper and bronze are gilded by covering the surface with an amalgam of gold and mercury, the mercury being driven off by heating. The process is extremely poisonous.

An amalgam of mercury and gold was used during the latter part of the 18th century for the gilding of porcelain. In appearance it is inferior to the earlier process, in which the gold was ground up in honey. The latter yields a dull gold slightly raised from the surface of the glaze.

Objects of wood and *gesso* are gilded by first painting the surface with a thin coating of gold-size, followed by pressing the gold-leaf into place. The work is then varnished. Usually wood is first covered with a thin layer of *gesso* – a kind of plaster of Paris.

In water-gilding the leaf is laid on a dry, sized surface with water and finished with a coat of varnish. Fire-gilding is the application of gold with mercury. Cold-gilding is done by dissolving gold in *aqua regia*, a strong acid, and then burning a piece of rag which has been dipped into the solution. The ashes are rubbed on to the metal, usually silver, leaving a thin deposit of finely divided particles of gold behind. Electro-gilding is a modern process in which the gold is deposited on the metal electrically. It dates from about 1840.

Silver, particularly, was quite often covered with gold (silver gilt). The colour, which is distinctly lighter than that of solid gold, makes confusion difficult; the process has the advantage of eliminating tarnish, thus reducing the need for cleaning. Care has to be taken in cleaning articles of silver-gilt since the gold is extremely thin. Soap and hot water is the best method. Even the finest silver polishes are abrasive, and will remove the gold eventually. Gold has often been used as an inlay in base metal. The designs are first cut into the metal with a graver which leaves the line somewhat wider at the bottom than the top. Gold wire is then inserted and hammered in, thus locking it into place. Much the same method is adopted with some kinds of silver inlay.

Electrum is an alloy of gold and silver – usually 50 per cent. of each. The colour is pale yellow, and resembles silver-gilt. It was used for overlaying wood and other substances by the Greeks and the Romans, and for jewellery. It has not been much used since.

GLASS   Although glass appears to be a solid, it does in fact belong to a class of substances known as "super-cooled liquids". It will flow extremely slowly under certain conditions, and a plate-glass window which has been installed for a long time will actually be slightly thicker at the bottom than at the top. For this reason it is possible to polish out surface scratches on old glass. If the surface is rubbed with a chamois leather impregnated with jeweller's rouge, using a certain amount of pressure, the surface can be made to "flow" slightly, thus eliminating the scratches.

Glass is made from a fusion of sand, soda, and lime under heat. When this mixture is melted in a crucible it forms a syrupy liquid that hardens on cooling without crystallizing, which is the reason for its transparency. The phenomenon is termed vitrification.

The formation of objects is usually done whilst the glass is in the syrupy stage, and a common method is to "blow" it. The tools of the glass-blower are still more or less the same as those used centuries ago – an iron tube (the blow-pipe), a pair of tongs, shears, and an iron rod (pontil). The pipe is dipped into the molten glass until a lump of sufficient size adheres, it being rotated meanwhile to keep the glass roughly spherical. By blowing through the tube the workman makes a bubble, which he proceeds to shape in various ways, some of which need a "marver", or iron table, on which the glass is rolled. By judicious reheating from time to time, the metal can be kept in a workable state for as long as may be necessary, and in this state it can even be cut with shears.

It can also be joined to other glass without trouble by welding.

Blowing, however, is not suitable for everything, and the use of moulds is an ancient practice. Often the glass is blown into the mould and finished by hand.

Two methods of making flat sheets are of interest to the collector, since both are no longer used and can be recognized fairly easily. The first involved the rotation of a large bubble of glass on the end of an iron rod to flatten it. This left a circular thickened area in the middle of the sheet. The second needed a blown cylinder which was cut down one side and opened out. Glass made in this way can be distinguished by the slightly uneven surface, to be seen with old mirror-glass, bookcase and cabinet glazing, and old picture glasses. The effect can be seen quite easily when the surface is looked at from a fairly acute angle.

It is desirable to say something about old mirror-glass. This can be recognized not only by the uneven surface but also by the wide but shallow bevels which were often used, and which are sometimes difficult to see. The glass was also much thinner than that in use for the same purpose today. The thickness of mirror-glass can be gauged by placing the edge of a coin against the surface, the distance between the coin and its image being the thickness of the glass.

Most old mirrors have defective silvering. They can, of course, be resilvered, but this would destroy the value. The better plan is to remove the glass altogether if the mirror is required for use, replacing it with new. The old glass should be carefully preserved, so that it can be put back if necessary. Original condition is important in the case of mirrors, and replacement by modern glass lowers the value considerably.

Decoration of glass falls under three main headings: (*a*) the use of glass itself in one form or another; (*b*) painting with enamels and lacquer colours, and gilding; (*c*) cutting, engraving, and etching.

Threads and rods of glass were often used when they were in much the same condition as soft candy. These could be applied in one way or another to the vessel, either for practical use as handles or as decoration, pure and simple. A glass rod in its soft state can be drawn out. It does not lose its shape, but its diameter is greatly reduced. Bundles of coloured rods were put together and drawn out in this way, and this technique was used to manufacture 19th-century glass paperweights.

Glass is coloured with metallic oxides of one kind or another. The addition of tin oxide renders it white and opaque, and other opaque colours can be made from a mixture of tin oxide and a colouring oxide. Clear glass is sometimes covered with a layer, or "flashing", of coloured glass, and patterns cut through the coloured layers to the clear glass beneath.

Glass can be decorated with enamel painting (*see* GLASS, ENAMELLED), and lacquer painting and gilding was sometimes applied to the *back* of a sheet of glass and protected from damage in one way or another. This is called *verre églomisé*.

Cut and engraved decoration is usually done on glass made from sand, potassium carbonate, and lead. It is heavier than the soda-lime variety, takes a higher polish, and reflects light much more efficiently (*see* GLASS, CUT).

Glass has been made from very early times. The origin may have been Egyptian, but the Syrians were also expert glass-workers. In Roman times the glass industry reached a high degree of technical skill, and specimens of Roman glass are not at all uncommon. Most show a well-marked iridescence on the surface as the result of burial, and almost all known examples have been excavated. Roman glass is particularly light in weight, and whilst important examples are highly valued, the poorer glass made for common use can be bought cheaply. Perhaps the finest existing example of Roman glass-work is the Portland Vase in the British Museum. This is made from blue glass under a layer of white. The decoration has been carved in relief by lapidaries.

Islamic glass made in Syria, Egypt, and elsewhere in medieval times is often valued very highly, and some of it is extremely fine, particularly the enamelled mosque lamps.

Venetian shipowners controlled the sea-routes to the Near East, and the art of glass-making was undoubtedly learned from Syria. The industry was well-established by the middle of the 15th century, about which time some remarkably fine goblets with enamelled decoration in the Gothic style were manufactured. By the 16th century a large export trade was in being, including the export of mirror-glass, and great technical advances had been made. A good deal of glass in the Venetian style, including diamond-engraved glass, was made elsewhere in Europe – Germany, France, Spain, and the Netherlands – during the 16th and 17th centuries. English examples of diamond-engraving are attributed to Jacopo Verzelini, a Venetian who may have come to England from Holland about 1571.

Apart from enamelled glass mentioned elsewhere, the Germans were glass-workers on a large scale, and much engraved glass was made at Nuremberg, Prague, and elsewhere during the 17th and the early part of the 18th centuries. A considerable amount of engraving was also done in Holland during the 18th century, often on English glass.

In England decorative glass was first made in quantity after the Restoration, and the work of George Ravenscroft, who started in 1673, is particularly sought. The principal interest in English glass during the 18th century centres on drinking glasses, particularly those with decoration having a Jacobite significance. Glasses made during the period are many and varied, and the stems were decorated in a variety of ways. The numerous air-twist and opaque-twist stems are especially interesting. English glasses with Dutch engraving are not uncommon.

Glass has been much copied and forged. Engraving of plain glasses with Jacobite and other emblems is common. Genuine examples are rare. Detection of the fraud depends principally on style.

The materials used to make the earlier varieties of glass usually contained traces of impurities of one kind or another. These coloured the glass very slightly, and it may be blue, green, grey, or yellow in tone. Completely clear glass is probably modern. Chemical methods can now be used to avoid such defects if it is to be used for an important purpose. Much cheap pressed and moulded glass still shows defects of colour. Early glass often had other minor defects like air bubbles trapped in the metal.

It is impossible for a glass vessel to survive without some signs of two or more centuries of wear. This can be seen in the form of multiple scratches on the base where it has stood on a shelf or a table. Dust is usually abrasive to some extent.

Forgers, of course, know all about scratches, and add them to new glass, but it is impossible to add them convincingly. Scratches made deliberately follow a limited number of directions. So far as accidentally acquired scratches are concerned, no two directions will be precisely alike. This can be seen under a powerful glass.

Old wine glasses, and much old glass besides, have a small rough mark in the centre of the base where it was joined during manufacture to the pontil. This pontil mark cannot be duplicated satisfactorily in glass made in any other way. The pontil mark on cut glass was sometimes ground out during the cutting process.

The new collector who is attracted to glass would be well advised to buy from specialist dealers, at least to begin with.

GLASS (CRYSTALLO CERAMIE) A process whereby small white decorative mouldings were incorporated into glass at the molten stage, the finished product being used for various purposes, such as paperweights. The motifs include busts and figures, flowers, crests, and so forth. The materials used were china clay and potassium silicate.

The manufacture was introduced by Apsley Pellat about 1819. A few examples were included in the Great Exhibition of 1851, but manufacture does not appear to have been continued thereafter.

The classical influence is usually to be seen in the form of these small mouldings, and both Josiah Wedgwood and James Tassie had some effect on designs.

Similar things were made in France about the same time.

GLASS, CUT The use of cutting and grinding to ornament glass goes back to Roman times, an important example being the Portland Vase in the British Museum. The earliest glass of this kind likely to be found by the collector, however, comes from Bohemia, where the industry was established in Prague at the beginning of the 17th century. The art reached England about 1675 and became extremely fashionable by the middle of the 18th century.

Vessels of all kinds are found with this sort of decoration, and the lead glass used for the purpose provided a metal which was particularly suitable. The many glittering facets which resulted from the cutting provided an effective decoration, and nowhere is this to be seen to better advantage than in chandeliers. They were made with many pendant drops designed to catch and reflect light, as well as with decorative glass candleholders. Some are also mounted with gilt-bronze.

Many such chandeliers have since suffered damage, accompanied by the loss of some of the drops. Those in very bad condition are often broken up and used to manufacture others, or to replace missing parts of those in better condition. Drops for this purpose can sometimes be purchased from antique dealers specializing in such things.

Damaged cut-glass is impossible to repair, but minor chips are sometimes ground out or disguised by new cutting. Such work is usually fairly obvious, and although it reduces the value to some extent, consideration should be given to the amount of such work and whether it interferes with the original design. Chips of some kind are almost inevitable in glass which has been used for two centuries.

Imitations of cut-glass made in moulds are very common. The easiest methods of detection are, firstly, the edges of the facets which are sharp and clear in cut-glass; secondly, the glittering aspect of reflected light from the facets is much reduced in the moulded version, the difference being similar to that between a diamond and paste, and, lastly, if the object is carefully examined, traces of the mould marks in the form of a fine raised line will be noticed. Moulded glass, unless of considerable antiquity, is of no serious value to the collector.

The usual method of cutting glass for decorative purposes is by the use of abrasive wheels, the commonest abrasive being wet sand which is applied with a revolving iron wheel. The various patterns used have, for their object, the reflection of light, and they are frequently very elaborate and needed a great deal of time and skill to complete. They are analogous to the facets cut on a diamond for the same purposes. The final polish was obtained by dipping the article into a solution of hydrofluoric acid, which is the only acid to affect glass.

Allied to this process is the practice of glass-engraving by means of very small copper wheels charged with an abrasive such as emery. Engraved work is usually of such decorative motifs as leaves, flowers, figures, and so forth. The engraved surfaces are left unpolished to form a contrast. Glass-etching, by means of hydrofluoric acid, is a method of decoration which is dissimilar to either of the two mentioned above. In this process the surface is protected from the acid by means of a suitable substance, and the pattern incised through the protective covering with various instruments. Exposure to the acid then removes glass from the parts of the surface now unprotected, leaving the pattern etched into it.

Cutting and engraving was not confined to glass. In Germany red stoneware from Meissen was decorated in this way by Bohemian glass-cutters, and porcelain with a coloured glaze was also engraved occasionally, the white body forming an effective contrast to the ground (*Schnittdekor*).

This technique is similar to one used by Bohemian glass-workers in which ordinary clear glass was covered by a "flashing" of (usually) ruby glass. Patterns were then engraved through the ruby "flashing" to show the clear glass beneath. Other colours (e.g. amber and blue) were also used for "flashing" in this way.

The technique of glass-engraving has much in common with the methods of working some hardstones.

GLASS, ENAMELLED   The addition of tin oxide to glass produced an opaque white substance which was also used occasionally to manufacture a porcelain substitute.

The use of enamels for decorating glass was known to the Romans, and specimens of Byzantine work of the kind survive. The enamel decoration of medieval Islamic glass from Egypt, Syria, and Mesopotamia is exceptionally fine, and the rare mosque lamps in particular fetch high prices.

Much glass of this kind was made in Germany and Bohemia, decoration frequently being in the nature of coats of arms and similar heraldic subjects. The big *Reichsadlerhumpen* (tall cylindrical beakers) are decorated in this way, with a central motif of the Imperial eagle, as the name implies.

Some less-sophisticated examples are decorated with peasant figures and inscriptions. Marriage beakers and similar things are not uncommon, and most belong to the mid-17th century. Enamelling of this kind was done by HAUSMALER (*q.v.*), and these glass-enamellers were responsible for the introduction of enamel colours for decorating porcelain and faience.

Enamelled glass was manufactured in Venice, the earliest known example probably dating from the 15th century, and a certain amount was done in England after about 1750. An opaque white glass was also used for the purpose.

Glass was sometimes painted with unfired lacquer colours which have usually yielded to time.

GLASS, ENGRAVED *See under* GLASS, CUT.

GLASS, IRISH Attempts have been made in the past to establish a steely-blue or grey tint in the glass as a mark of Irish manufacture. There can be no doubt, however, that this is usually erroneous, although a few of the less-important specimens may have this quality. Nearly all examples of good quality, however, have no special colour variations, and the best way of distinguishing glass made in Ireland is by the style.

Excellent work was done in Waterford, Cork, Dublin, and Belfast. Salad-bowls and water-jugs are among the most commonly surviving examples.

GOTHIC STYLE, THE Gothic was a movement away from the earlier Romanesque, which was in turn based on Roman architecture. It was current from the end of the 12th century to the Renaissance, but a revival of the style took place in the 19th century, and it has since been used, without much justification or excuse, for railway stations and town halls, as well as for ecclesiastical purposes.

Although the arch had been used by the Assyrians, it did not find favour with the Greeks. For the most part, Roman architecture is based on that of Greece, although the Romans used semi-circular arches, and vaulting which was the same, in principle, as the arch.

This division between the Greek and Roman (or classical) style and the Gothic is much more than architectural. It is to be seen in the arts generally, and it has a grammar of ornament entirely its own. For this reason the whole subject is one of considerable importance.

Primarily Greek architecture was based on the post and lintel (the columns and entablature), and the thrusts imposed by the weight resting on the columns acted vertically downwards, being transmitted by the columns to the foundations. These thrusts are called a "dead" load.

Gothic architecture, however, is based primarily on the arch, the overhead thrusts being transmitted diagonally downwards from the keystone to the springers, and thence – still diagonally – to the ground.

In earlier examples of the use of the arch these thrusts had been taken care of by walls flanking either side of the arch, which were sufficiently wide and strong to conduct the line of thrust down to the foundations; but only a part of the wall carried the actual thrust, and such walls inside a building tended to break up the structure into comparatively small, self-contained areas.

The Gothic architect devised methods of balancing one thrust with another in such a way that he was able to remove unnecessary partition walls, basing his springers on columns instead, and transmitting the thrusts across an arcade to the outer walls, where they were led to the ground by buttresses. As knowledge and skill progressed even the earlier massive buttresses were pared away to the essential minimum, and flying buttresses replaced them. There were, at the time, no ways of calculating such stresses, and the work proceeded by trial and error. From time to time buildings in course of construction fell down when the builders went too far, but a body of knowledge and experience was gradually built up.

The Gothic cathedral, therefore, is a structure in which the loads are balanced against one another, and are referred to as "live" loads. This, of course, is quite opposite to the classical principle of "dead loads", and, freed from such restrictions, the new style blossomed forth with towers and pinnacles, the weight of which was used to balance diagonal thrusts of one kind or another.

Additionally, now that walls were no longer essential for load-bearing purposes, the space they formerly occupied could be filled with stained glass, and this resulted in the series of magnificent windows to be seen in cathedrals and churches of the period.

Classical architecture is largely a matter of horizontal and vertical lines, with the main accent on the horizontal, since its width was greater than its height. It is static. Gothic architecture, on the other hand, is made up of vertical, soaring lines – one variety is referred to as Perpendicular – and is quite obviously dynamic.

These two quite different methods of building led to different ways of thinking about architecture, and about art

Characteristic Gothic ornament showing an heraldic lion and formal oak-leaves (*c.* 1475)

generally, and Gothic art shows radical departures from the accepted canons of classical art, with different motifs and different ways of using them.

Since that time it has been possible to see in most European art a constant conflict between the two principles, between the dignity and rigidity of classicism and the much more human and sometimes vulgar Gothic style.

Work in the late Gothic style was done by Urs Graf, Swiss mercenary, goldsmith, and engraver, and a selection of his engravings is reproduced in *Urs Graf*, by Major and Gradmann (London, 1942).

GRISAILLE, EN   Painting in shades of grey to imitate relief sculpture. The term is sometimes used of painting on faience and porcelain during the neo-classical period, but its origin is much earlier, and murals of this kind can be found as early as the beginning of the 17th century. Limoges enamels of the 16th century were similarly painted.

GROUNDS, COLOURED   See FONDPORZELLAN.

HALB-FAYENCE   See SGRAFFITO.

HAN DYNASTY (206 B.C.–A.D. 220)   The best-known examples of Chinese art of this period are the pottery tomb figures and vessels, the latter usually being of bronze form. A good green glaze was devised which often tends to become iridescent. Fine bronzes were still being made, although the best belong to the earlier periods. Bronze mirrors were made at this time, and later, in the T'ang Dynasty.

Silk was exported to the Roman Empire, and Hellenistic influence in the design of Han textiles, and occasionally in other things, is to be observed.

The period is noted for some exceptionally fine sculpture, and a few damaged examples of Han painting have survived. Jades are often of doubtful attribution, although amulets, and other articles of tomb furniture, are authentic.

HARDNESS OF MATERIALS   It is sometimes necessary to find the exact nature of a stone or crystal, and a rapid and reasonably certain way of doing it is to ascertain its relative hardness. A stone will always scratch another which is softer, or be scratched by one which is harder, and, bearing this in mind, it is possible to construct a table of various materials, the softest being at No. 1.

1	Steatite, soaprock, talc.
2	Gypsum.
2·5	Amber.
3	Alabaster.
4	Serpentine.
5	Coral.
5·5	Glass, lapis lazuli, obsidian.
6	Haematite, turquoise, opal, feldspar.

7   Agate, amethyst, flint, rock crystal, jade (nephrite and jadeite), chalcedony, cornelian.
7·5 Beryl, emerald, tourmaline, zircon.
8   Topaz, spinel, chrysoberyl.
9   Sapphire, ruby.
10 Diamond.

Jade is sometimes confused with steatite or serpentine by the uninitiated, but it will be obvious from this that whilst jade will scratch glass, both steatite and serpentine will be scratched by it. Differentiation is therefore quite easy. A steel knife-blade has a hardness of about 6, unless it has been specially hardened.

Much the same principle is sometimes used in testing PORCELAIN (*q.v.*).

HARDSTONES The term is usually applied to various forms of quartz used for carvings, inlays, jewellery, and similar articles. The term includes rock crystal, amethyst, rose quartz, agate, onyx, sardonyx, and cat's eye. The hardstones were frequently used by the Chinese, particularly during the 18th and 19th centuries, for small carvings which were fashioned by tools similar to those used for jade.

HAUSMALEREI An important part in the development of the decoration of faience, glass, and porcelain in Germany was taken by men who worked in their own homes. These were known as *Hausmaler* (lit., home painters). At Vienna they were called *Winkelmann*, a term which is somewhat less than polite.

The first record of *Hausmalerei* on faience can be placed to about 1660, when some extremely good work was done at Nuremberg by Johann Schaper. Specimens are now very rare. Work of the same kind was also done later in the century at Augsburg by Seuter and others.

At first white porcelain was sold freely to the *Hausmaler*, but, due to their habit of undercutting prices, and, in some cases, passing off inferior work as having been done by the factory, this practice was discontinued. Most factories, however, sold "seconds" or "wasters" to these "home painters", and, about 1760, Meissen instituted a system of making a cut in the glaze across the centre of the mark to indicate that the piece had been sold in an undecorated state.

The more important of the *Hausmaler* have been identified.

HERALDRY Some knowledge of heraldry is useful to anyone interested in antiques. Primarily it was a method of conveying, by the use of symbolic devices and colours, information about the bearer, his lineage, and achievements. Heraldic designs, of course, differ one from the other, and always remain the property of the owner. They cannot be used by anyone not entitled to them, and the only way in which they can be transferred is by legal succession. The devices are augmented and altered by events, such as marriage, during successive generations.

Usually, in medieval times, the devices were worn on the person embroidered on coats which covered the armour, from which the term *coat of arms*, and on the shield, whence *shield of arms*. The same insignia also appeared on pennants.

The practice of putting devices on shields and armour for the purpose of identification is very ancient, and was mentioned, for instance, by Homer. It was also widespread, and devices with a similar purpose were used in the Far East. Heraldry in the present sense, however, dates only from the Crusades. Undoubtedly it was first used for the purpose of identification in warfare, but it owed its subsequent popularity to the ease with which important persons could be identified in processions, tournaments, and so forth, even with the helmet vizor closed. Many of the devices adopted were allusive or emblematic. For example, the arms of Corbett had two *corbeaux*, or ravens, on the shield.

The use of these devices was regulated by heralds, and this is still done by the College of Heralds. Arms were granted by the king, and by feudal lords to their vassals. They were regarded as tokens of nobility, and the conferment of an entitlement to arms automatically gave the possessor a superior status.

The language by which the various parts of a shield of arms is described is complicated, and too long for discussion here. The reader is referred to the works mentioned in the Bibliography.

A helmet shown above the shield is an indication of status. Knights and baronets have a helmet with an open vizor, for instance, whilst esquires and gentlemen have a closed vizor. Peers, and a few others, are entitled to have their shield supported by two animals or human figures. These are known as *supporters*, and the grant of these was regarded as a great honour. Crests were originally worn on the helmet, and are

A royal coat of arms supported by Griffins. Continental

now represented above the shield of arms. They surmount a wreath or a coronet.

The shield of arms was used in the decoration of all kinds of works of art, and it provides an excellent method of ascertaining origin, and frequently the approximate date. Some of the books mentioned in the Bibliography give methods of tracing the better-known devices.

IMARI PATTERNS *See* CERAMICS – JAPANESE POTTERY AND PORCELAIN.

INVESTMENT, ANTIQUES AS AN The price of antiques is regulated almost entirely by supply and demand, and questions of value are uncomplicated by purchase tax and similar imposts. If there were no such thing as fashion it would be possible to buy any object of reasonable quality with the complete certainty that, sooner or later, it could be sold at a profit, since with the passing of time such objects become less in number. Even fashion cannot raise or depress prices permanently. The wheel always turns full circle, and nothing remains either fashionable or unfashionable indefinitely.

Three principal factors are responsible for the lessening number of antiques: accidental destruction and damage, natural deterioration, and acquisitions by museums. Important objects left to or acquired by museums are usually retained permanently, thus reducing the number for sale to private persons. Important collections are often left to museums, and this completely removes many important specimens from the market.

FASHION, which is considered under that heading, plays a part in deciding the value of a particular class of object at any given time. Obviously if a collection be formed when there are a large number of buyers top prices must be paid, and a subsequent decline in popularity will remove part of the value. This is offset, to some extent, by factors later discussed.

An affluent buyer, coming into a market which is temporarily unfashionable, will, if his purchases are on a sufficiently large scale, eventually force up prices, because other buyers will be attracted to the same things by his interest. At first sight this appears to work against him, but it must be remembered that many of his purchases will have been made before the market reaches its peak, and he succeeds, quite often, in acquiring a collection with a total ultimate value of much more than he paid.

The market in antiques is not a natural one. People can live without them, and it depends on the presence of a surplus of money over the amount required to ensure a reasonable subsistence level. It has therefore to be reinforced by the interest of a large number of buyers. Such buyers are steadily growing in number, because works of art and craftsmanship possess qualities which are desirable, and which are missing from the mass-produced articles of modern life.

The value of antiques as an investment is reinforced by that plague of modern society – inflation. Inflation has always been with us to some degree, but hitherto, except in such places as Germany in 1924, it has been a slow process. In medieval times a sheep could be bought for 6d. The difference between this and the price today is due to half a millennium of inflation. I think it fair to say that the price has risen at a

far more rapid rate in the last fifty years than it did at any time
in the preceding four hundred and fifty.

I am not sufficiently an economist to venture to discuss the
subject in detail, but it is hardly necessary. For our present
purpose inflation can be defined as a decline in the purchasing
power of money. This decline shows itself in increased prices
for goods and services. In this post-war era it is impossible to
see an end to the process, and although financial measures of
one kind or another are used to slow it down temporarily
when the hardest-hit section of the community becomes
sufficiently articulate, inflation is too valuable both to the
Government and to the majority for any serious attempt
to be made to end it. One of the reasons can be seen in
the low value of certain Government stocks, which will
eventually be redeemed in depreciated pounds, and which,
until very recently, were regarded as a proper investment for
trustees.

The effect of inflation is to make it unprofitable to hold
currency and the kind of stock referred to, and the last few
years has seen a strong movement away from them by wise
investors.

Antiques, on the other hand, appreciate in ratio to the
lack of confidence in the value of currency. This can well be
seen in the saleroom prices during the period of the 8 per cent.
Bank Rate of 1966–1967. Although the value of many com-
modities fell, the price of good antiques on the London art
market actually rose fairly steeply.

In addition, most antiques have an international value.
Such things as English and German porcelain, for example,
are even more highly valued in the United States than in the
country of their origin. Therefore, they are to a great extent
independent of such corollaries of inflation as the devaluation
of one currency in terms of another.

When the £1 was devalued from $4.04 to $2.80 the average
price of English antiques on the American market, after a
slight initial setback, remained more or less unchanged in
dollars. This meant that sterling prices in England rose to
a level which offset the reduction in the value of the £1 – a
free gift to the English seller which sweetened the bitterness of
the pill.

Of course, the same advantages are offered by such things

as gold and diamonds at present. Provided that no one succeeds in making diamonds, that de Beers keep their monopoly without serious competition from the U.S.S.R., and no new gold-mines of a size sufficient to disturb the market are discovered, then they will continue to have these advantages. Antiques, however, were made many years ago, and the number is always decreasing. No new sources can be discovered in quantity sufficient to disturb the market, and if all the museums in the world were to put their contents into the saleroom at once the market fluctuation would hardly be more than temporary. Reproductions have no serious market value, no matter how well they are made.

For the investment-buyer, however, a caution is necessary. Only the best is good enough. Mediocre examples are a gamble. Gambles have been known to succeed, but the risk is a big one.

INVOICES AND DESCRIPTIONS   After a good many years spent in buying antiques I have come to the conclusion that the standard of honesty in the fine art trade is very high. Nevertheless, it would be foolish to expect all dealers to be equally honest, and the buyer should, in common prudence, insist on a few precautions when buying from a source which is not well known to him. The most obvious precaution is the descriptive invoice. A dealer should not object to putting his description into writing on an invoice, nor to giving an approximate date of manufacture. If this is done, and his description subsequently proves to be incorrect, the article can be returned, and the money reclaimed.

Therefore, the buyer should insist on an invoice of this kind, and if the purchase is for a considerable amount the vendor can hardly complain at being asked to give a warranty in addition. "Warranted genuinely of the nature and period stated" covers the position adequately. A signature is essential.

It is as well to remember that even the greatest experts make mistakes. The fact that a dealer, or an auctioneer, makes an error in description is not evidence of dishonesty. Most dealers will rectify mistakes of this kind without question when they are pointed out, provided it can be satisfactorily agreed that an error has been made.

The buyer should beware of accepting the casual opinion of a friend that an object is not genuine. A dealer would not give a guaranteed invoice unless his knowledge and experience convinced him that he was right, and he is entitled to resent uninformed or ill-informed questioning of his opinion. If there is good reason to think a mistake has been made, then the best course is to discuss the matter in a friendly spirit with the seller. It is usually possible to agree on a course of action. The large museums will give an opinion on the date and provenance of objects gratis, but will not become parties to a dispute. The British Antique Dealers' Association are willing to arbitrate when one of their members is involved, and this is a course in which the buyer can have confidence. There are also independent experts who can be consulted at a fee which varies with circumstances.

The description on an invoice should always be read carefully. "In the style of . . ." does not mean the same thing as "of the period". "After" a particular artist is quite different from "by" him.

Much the same applies to auctioneers' catalogues. The large auction rooms, although they do not accept responsibility for errors of description, take very great pains to see that their descriptions are accurate. Cataloguing is often done by the foremost experts in a particular field.

It must be remembered that these catalogues mean exactly what they say – neither more nor less. The reader must be careful not to read into a description something which is not meant. For instance, a piece of Chinese porcelain might be described as bearing "the six-character mark of Ch'êng Hua" or the "Ch'êng Hua mark". This does not mean that the object was also made during the reign of Ch'êng Hua. The Chinese frequently use the date-marks of former reigns as a sign of veneration of early things. Where the date is undoubted, the description may conclude simply with "Ch'êng Hua", or with the much more definite "mark and reign of Ch'êng Hua".

Similarly "Dresden", under which misnomer Meissen porcelain often passes in England and the United States, does not necessarily mean that the object was made at the Royal factory at Meissen. It nearly always means that it was made or decorated in one of the factories or studios existing round the city of Dresden during the 19th century.

In each of the instances cited it will be seen that the lot has been accurately described. If the prospective purchaser cares to read more into it than has been said, this can hardly be the fault of the auctioneer. My remarks could, of course, be greatly extended, but the reader, by studying the catalogues, soon gets to learn the distinctive phraseologies.

These remarks, of course, apply to the large auction-rooms. Some provincial auctioneers are apt to be much more lax in their descriptions, and the old aphorism, *Caveat emptor*, applies with some force. Such auctioneers do a general business, and their knowledge is sufficient for what they do. They do not pretend to be specialists, and they cannot be expected to describe unusual objects adequately. Unless the buyer possesses sufficient knowledge to act on his own account, therefore, it would be safer to consult a reputable dealer.

The man who hunts for bargains, of course, cannot expect a descriptive invoice. If the seller knew enough to give him one he would be asking a much higher price, and to get an object below its current market value means that the buyer has to accept a degree of risk which varies according to his own knowledge. Despite assertions to the contrary, there is nothing immoral in bargain-hunting. I can see nothing against buying from an ignorant dealer at a low price if it can be done. The buyer who recognizes the greater value does so because he has spent time, money, and effort in acquiring the necessary knowledge and skill. The same course is open to the other party. The buyer, therefore, is taking a profit on his greater knowledge. Of course, where private sales are concerned, different criteria apply, since the seller is not a professional dealer, and could not be expected to acquire the knowledge and experience necessary to sell at a reasonable market value. Such people deserve special consideration.

ITALIAN COMEDY, THE A comedy performed by troupes of strolling players which was extremely popular throughout western Europe during the 17th and 18th centuries. It had no fixed form, and dialogue was improvised, although a scenario which laid down the main theme existed.

The characters are well known. Harlequin, Columbine, Pierrot, Pulcinella (Punch), and Pantaloon are extremely familiar. Less so are Dr. Baloardo, the Lawyer, Brighella, the Captain, Mezzetino, Scaramuccia (Scaramouche), the Lover, and his Inamorata.

These figures were the subject of paintings by such artists as Watteau, Boucher, and Fragonard, and were used by numerous engravers. They were modelled as porcelain figures and appear as porcelain decoration.

Augustus the Strong of Saxony was particularly interested in a company which he saw in Paris in 1687, and they were later invited to Saxony. J. J. Kändler of Meissen modelled an important series of Harlequins, and many of the best figures of Bustelli are based on the Comedy.

In England, Italian Comedy figures were especially made at Chelsea.

IVORY CARVINGS, EUROPEAN The art of carving in ivory has always been extensively practised, and a few examples still exist from Egypt, Assyria, Greece, and Rome.

Much work of the kind was done during medieval times, particularly such things as carved book-covers, pyxes, triptyches, altar-pieces, pastoral staves, and crucifixes. Most such work is carved in relief, with figures of the Virgin, saints, and other religious personalities. Not much work was done for secular purposes, although things of the kind exist.

By Renaissance times ivory was used as a medium by many Italian sculptors and the German ivory-carvers of Augsburg, Nuremberg, and elsewhere are well known. In the 18th century a few of them became modellers for porcelain factories, whilst ivory carvings were used as inspiration for some porcelain figures. Two names of importance are Balthasar Permoser of Dresden [1650–1732] and Simon Troger [*fl.* mid-18th century].

The carvers of Augsburg and Nuremberg made such things as vases, tankards, plaques, dagger-hilts, powder-flasks, and so forth, which can be seen occasionally. During the 19th century a good deal of ivory carving of religious figures was done at Dieppe, in France.

Prices are variable, but are usually good for anything done in the 18th century or earlier.

IVORY CARVINGS, ORIENTAL Carvings of excellent quality were done in Persia, but are not often seen. Characteristic miniature painting on ivory is a little more common.

Chinese ivory carving is not infrequent, and the best Chinese figures in this medium are very fine, and excel those of the Japanese. Apart from figures, elaborately carved screens and vases, as well as tusks, are usually decorated with pictorial scenes of figures in landscapes. Chessmen are often well-carved, and commonly surmount an intricately carved series of pierced balls, one within the other. These displays of virtuosity have no particular value in themselves. Ivory was used in conjunction with jades and hardstones as a decorative inlay.

The Japanese are also skilled ivory-carvers, and their work ranges from standing figures carved in a comparatively naturalistic style to the sometimes grotesque NETSUKÉ (*q.v.*). The Japanese tend to give their carvings rather more detailed treatment than the Chinese, and their use of animal subjects, and such things as insects and shells, is remarkable for its verisimilitude. Inlaying in ivory was especially practised in Japan (*see* SHIBAYAMA-WORK).

Much intricate work of little merit was done at Bombay and elsewhere in India.

JADE Most objects made of jade fall under one of four headings – Chinese, Indian (or Moghul), Mexican, or Maori. Occasional use of jade was made by the Russian Court jeweller, Fabergé. Chinese jade is by far the best known, and it comprises ritual objects of great antiquity and *bibelots* of comparatively modern manufacture.

The oldest Chinese jades are rarely older than the Chou Dynasty [1122–249 B.C.]. These are nearly always ritual objects, such as the *pi* – a circular disc with a central hole which represented Heaven, and was probably derived from the solar disc. Earth was represented by the *tsung* – a cylindrical tube squared on the exterior which sometimes bears the Eight Trigrams – a series of three broken and unbroken lines in varying order representing natural forces (wind, rain, and so forth – p. 174). A circular disc with a serrated edge (*hsüan chi*) was used for astronomical purposes. Some ritual jades were employed to prepare the corpse for burial, the orifices of the body being plugged with jade to keep out evil spirits. Various small amulets and pectorals were worn for other ritual purposes, and girdle ornaments and similar personal adornments have survived.

By the time of the Warring States and the Han Dynasty [206 B.C.–A.D. 220] we find that carving becomes more intricate, and small objects of adornment such as belt-hooks are known which are carved and engraved. From the Han period to the end of the Sung Dynasty [960–1280] some excellent work was done – figures of animals and fabulous monsters, vases and cups with animal handles, and vessels in imitation of bronze forms. Specimens are rare.

The carvers of the Ming Dynasty [1368–1644] were responsible for the large figures of horses and buffalo to be seen occasionally, and the earliest carved jade boulders probably belong to the Ming period. It is doubtful whether they are ever older. These boulders are irregular lumps of jade carved to represent a mountain on which are such details as pine trees, perhaps a small pavilion, and a figure or two, as well as the sacred fungus of longevity (*ling chih*).

The Ch'ing Dynasty [1644–1912] is a period of great virtuosity. Carvings are frequently intricate, and some vessels were hollowed out until their walls were almost paper-thin. Advantage was taken of pieces of parti-coloured jade to carve such things as insects on a leaf, the insects being of one colour, the leaf of another. Beakers of bronze form, and vases with free ring handles carved integrally, are sought, as well as such small pieces as belt-hooks and pendants. Inscriptions are not uncommon at this period. Jade table-screens, usually mounted in blackwood stands, belong to the Ch'ing period, as do most implements for the writer's table.

There are two principal kinds of jade – jadeite and nephrite. They are fairly similar in properties and appearance. Jadeite is slightly harder than nephrite. Both are extremely heavy. Chemically, they differ in the proportions of alumina (high in jadeite) and magnesia (high in nephrite).

Jade is almost infinitely variable in colour. Both black and white jade are known, as well as yellow, green, and even brown and red. Pieces showing more than one well-defined colour are not uncommon. Some colours are given exotic names by the Chinese. "Mutton-fat" jade is a light yellowish-white. Most jade is translucent, but an opaque ivory-coloured variety is sometimes referred to as "perished" or "burnt" jade.

Jade was prized by the Chinese for its resonant properties, and sounding stones were made of it. Some personal ornaments were made to chink as the wearer moved, the sound being regarded as pleasant and desirable.

Jade is principally worked by the use of rotating tools and abrasives. It ranks as a semi-precious hardstone, and can only be carved slowly and with difficulty. For this reason fine-quality jade objects are almost miracles of craftsmanship.

Before the 18th century all carvings appear to have been of nephrite, whilst Burmese jadeite became popular from then onwards. It is distinctly harder and more vitreous in appearance, nephrite being softer in colour, and with what has been well described as an "oily" surface. A bright emerald green, to be seen in later examples, is peculiar to jadeite.

There are other minerals which superficially resemble jade, and are sometimes offered as jade. Chloromelanite is comparatively rare, and is sometimes thus classified. Others, less close, are often confused with it. Steatite is sometimes labelled "jade" by the ignorant – a mistake which a brief cut with a knife would reveal, steatite being the softest stone in general use for carving. Serpentine is also sometimes confused with jade. The hardness test is the most useful (*see* HARD-NESS OF MATERIALS). It can be taken as axiomatic that if a substance can be scratched with a penknife it is not jade, whereas all minerals which can be classified as jade will scratch glass.

The Chinese carved many other semi-precious hardstones, usually of the quartz family, but these are sufficiently distinctive to make confusion unlikely.

Jades are nearly always difficult to date. Jadeite, of course, cannot be earlier than the 18th century, but this fact is not helpful when it is necessary to date nephrite. We have two main criteria which can be applied – the style and the apparent age of the material. The Chinese often repeated artistic idioms of previous centuries, and it is difficult for anyone but the expert to detect the difference. The material undergoes some changes with the passing of time, particularly if it has been buried. This is sometimes helpful, but it is rarely possible to say more than that a specimen has considerable antiquity. It would be impossible in a book of this size to enlarge on the methods of dating, but a few books are noted in the Bibliography which will help with this aspect.

The early jades are interesting to the student and the serious collector. The later examples are sought after as decoration, and are often more valued for the intricacy of the carving.

JADE, MAORI   Collecting Maori jade carvings has become more general in recent years with the increasing interest in primitive art. Greenstone – a type of nephrite – was used for axes. Some of these were intended for use; others for mounting in elaborately carved handles for ceremonial purposes.

The *tikki* – a kind of flat pendant depicting a distorted human form – is much sought by collectors.

JADE, MEXICAN   The jade-carvers of Central America attained considerable skill in working this material. The majority of surviving specimens are small personal ornaments, and occasionally masks. At present these are highly valued.

JADE, MOGHUL   Moghul jades are principally very thin, carved bowls, some of which are mounted with rubies. They are of jadeite, and usually extremely translucent. It is probable that some were made by Chinese craftsmen in India. Good specimens have considerable value.

KAKIEMON PATTERNS   *See* CERAMICS – JAPANESE POTTERY AND PORCELAIN.

KLEINPLASTIK   The term is difficult to translate, and means approximately small modelled sculpture. Small porcelain figures suitable for table decoration (and for the present-day collector's cabinet) were first made by J. J. Kändler during the early years of the 1730s. Prior to this date, most of the figures made at Meissen had been of extremely large size.

"KNOCKERS" "Knockers" are jewellery and antique dealers who operate by calling from door to door in search of something to buy, and their purchases are sold to larger dealers. Many "knockers" possess a wide, if superficial, knowledge of antiques generally, and they are able to assess the market price of most minor antiques within a fairly narrow margin. Mostly they are honest, although all of them will drive a hard bargain. The profession, like most others, has its black sheep, who are usually people merely trying to make easy money. The true "knocker" makes a business of it, and often manages to acquire a considerable amount of goodwill in a district by calling at intervals. The job is strenuous, but lucrative (*see* DEALERS and "RUNNERS").

LACQUER, CHINESE The art of lacquer has been practised in China from very early times, a few specimens from the Han Dynasty still surviving.

Lacquer is the natural gum of a tree, the *Rhus vernicifera*, which is coloured with various pigments.

Early lacquer with painted designs is not often seen, but the workshops of Canton made a good deal of it during the 19th century. A thin lacquer, used in the manner of paint, was employed on some Chinese furniture of no great value made at this time.

Large pieces of lacquer with incised and relief designs were used to make such things as screens, chests, and cabinets. Some of it is known as "Coromandel" lacquer, from the Coromandel Coast on the eastern seaboard of India whence it was shipped to Europe. Panels of this kind were also used in Europe for ornamenting furniture. The decoration is usually elaborate, being carried out in several colours with gilding, and the work was much prized in the West during the 17th century.

Carved lacquer is the most important variety, and reasonably good specimens are not infrequent. The earliest existing examples belong to the 14th century, but most of it was made during the reign of the Emperor Ch'ien Lung [1736–1795]. The most prized variety is the scarlet lacquer dyed with cinnabar. Yellow, black, brown, and green varieties also exist.

Lacquer was first applied to a foundation in successive layers until a sufficient thickness had been built up. The designs were then carved into it, and these carvings were often extremely intricate. Whilst most things of this kind are comparatively small – boxes, vases, miniature screens, and so forth – it was also sometimes employed for very large objects, the throne of Ch'ien Lung in the Victoria and Albert Museum being an example.

Usually landscapes, flowers, and similar Chinese motifs were depicted with great skill, and sometimes more than one colour can be observed in the same piece. This was done by super-imposing differently coloured layers one on another, and then cutting through to predetermined depths according to the colour required. Carved lacquer fell into disuse at the end of the 18th century, and does not appear to have been made since.

The imposing Coromandel screens usually fetch extremely high prices, and carved lacquer is principally valued according to the quality of the workmanship. Pieces of more than one colour are apt to be the most expensive.

LACQUER, JAPANESE Like that of China, Japanese lacquer has been made for many centuries, but few specimens of great antiquity have been exported.

Either cedar or magnolia wood is used for the foundation, and on this is painted a number of layers of lacquer. The surface is finally given a high polish with deer-horn ashes, a very mild abrasive.

Relief work is frequent. The practice of carving lacquer was introduced from China in the 17th century, but specimens are not very common, neither are they so intricately carved. Metallic powders, particularly gold, were extensively employed, as well as leaf-gold and mother-of-pearl.

Designs incised into the lacquer and subsequently filled with gold dust are a technique copied from China, and, like the Chinese, the Japanese also used lacquer for large pieces of furniture. Specimens are not uncommon in Europe, particularly stands in tiers, with shelves on different levels, and generally with one or two cupboards with sliding doors.

Most of the lacquer objects from Japan are boxes of one kind or another. Most frequent are the writing cases, and the *inrō*. The latter were attached by a silk cord to a NETSUKÉ (*q.v.*), and used to contain a seal (the word means *seal-case*) and also medicines of various kinds.

Most specimens are less than a century old, but the finer examples are usually of greater antiquity. Those more sketchily decorated are generally comparatively modern, the old work – even when the decoration is slight – being done with painstaking skill. Most of the decorative motifs are characteristically Japanese, more particularly in the quality of asymmetricality.

It is difficult to date most examples with accuracy, and quality of workmanship is the best guide to follow. Good Japanese lacquer, at the time of writing, is still comparatively inexpensive.

LONGTON HALL (STAFFORDSHIRE) PORCELAIN FACTORY This small porcelain factory was founded in 1751 by a partnership which included William Littler. It closed in 1758. At one time less was known of Longton Hall than of any other factory, but since the discovery of its site, and of many documents relating to its early history, by Dr. Bernard Watney, a great deal is now known about it. His book is included in the Bibliography.

The body of Longton porcelain somewhat resembles that of certain early Chelsea and Derby wares, but is much more apt to contain technical imperfections. The surface is often lumpy and slightly uneven, and black specks in the glaze and fire-cracks are common. The appearance of the glaze has been well compared to candle-grease.

Dishes, bowls, and jugs modelled in the form of leaves are a frequent Longton type. Most of the wares are unsophisticated, but very pleasing. Flower-painting is excellent, and some paintings of castles and *châteaux* are much prized. An underglaze blue used as a ground colour is known as "Littler's blue".

Longton figures are amusing, and often original, and the porcelain of this factory is highly regarded by collectors. Specimens are rare.

LOUIS SEIZE, STYLE OF (LOUIS XVI, 1774–1793)

First seen shortly before 1760, this style is the French equivalent of the Adam style in England. There are, however, notable differences, and after 1774, the year of the King's accession, ornament tended to become increasingly rich and elaborate under the influence of Marie-Antoinette.

LOWESTOFT (SUFFOLK) PORCELAIN FAC-TORY

This factory was founded about 1756 and, from the beginning, used a bone-ash body almost identical with that of Bow. The term "Oriental Lowestoft" is quite inaccurate, and refers to porcelain made in China for export to Europe. It has no connection whatever with the work of the East Anglian factory.

The body resembles that used for some of the later Bow service-ware. The glaze is slightly bluish and frequently specked. Much of the decoration is in underglaze blue, and the motifs are Oriental in derivation. Worcester porcelain of the humbler type was also imitated, and sometimes given false marks. Later enamel decoration of simple flowers, sprays and bouquets, was artlessly painted.

Production was mostly of service-ware, although a few simple figures have been recorded. Inscribed pieces – "A Trifle from Lowestoft" is typical – are comparatively frequent. Small tablets recording the name and birth-date of a child are a Lowestoft peculiarity.

MAIOLICA

See CERAMICS – ITALIAN MAIOLICA AND PORCELAIN *and* TIN-ENAMELLED POTTERY.

MARQUETRY

Inlays of coloured woods used to ornament furniture. Occasionally such materials as ivory and mother-of-pearl were also employed for the same purpose in conjunction with inlays of wood. For the method of cutting, *see* p. 128.

METAL-WORK

The use of metals of one kind or another for articles of utility and ornament dates from very early times. It is impossible to say when the use of bronze superseded flint and other hardstones in the making of implements, but certainly it was before 2500 B.C.

The metals known in early times were gold, silver, copper, tin, and lead. Iron was added to this list about 1500 B.C., when it first came into use, although, in the form of meteoric iron, it was undoubtedly known before this date as a curiosity.

Metals are rarely found in nature in a pure state. They were, therefore, subjected to the process of smelting in which the ore was exposed to great heat to separate the metal from substances with which it was combined. No doubt this led to the process of combining two or more metals to form a third which had slightly different, and usually more desirable, properties. Such combinations are known as alloys, and bronze is a typical example, being an alloy of copper and tin. It is a remarkable fact that neither copper nor tin were ever used to a noteworthy extent by themselves, even in the early period, and the Bronze Age is not preceded by a definite Copper Age. A few examples of unalloyed copper have been recovered, and the Celts occasionally made objects of Cornish tin, but such instances are rare.

Gold and silver were alloyed occasionally with each other to produce electrum, and slight additions of the so-called baser metals were sometimes added to harden them. Tin and lead were alloyed to make pewter, and copper and zinc to make brass. There is no doubt that brass was known to the Romans, and this is its earliest appearance. References to brass in the Old Testament are certainly mistranslations. Iron was never alloyed with other metals, although some iron contained a little carbon which converted it into a kind of steel, a much harder metal.

Metals were valued for various properties which they do not all share in common. Gold is very ductile – the opposite to brittle – and it could be drawn into fine wire or beaten into leaves. It also has the property of resisting corrosion to a marked degree, and for these reasons it is much valued. It is, nevertheless, extremely soft, and could certainly never be induced to take a cutting edge or to resist blows of any kind. Silver possesses much the same properties and defects, with the additional disadvantage that it soon oxidizes and acquires a black tarnish which needs to be removed at intervals. For this reason it was often gilded in one way or another, and it then

18 An important early ritual *kuei* with paw feet and handles in the form of archaic animal masks. Chinese, early Chou dynasty (1128–249 B.C.)

19 This large incense burner, of cloisonné enamel, is of exceptional quality. Chinese, 18th century

20 An ancient Egyptian bronze cat of the Saïte period (644–525 B.C.)

became silver-gilt. Other metals were gilded, either for the sake of appearance or to preserve them from corrosion.

Bronze was an excellent general-purpose metal. It was not particularly rare, and made sharp casts when poured into a mould. It could be shaped and tempered by cold-hammering, and would then take a cutting edge. Hammering consolidated the metal and made it harder, so that it could be used for helmets and armour. In addition to being malleable, it was also fairly ductile, and could be hammered into sheets. The sheets could be manipulated with small danger of breaking and tearing.

At first articles of bronze were formed by casting into a stone mould. This was followed by hammering, particularly in the manufacture of weapons. Early statues were formed from bronze plates hammered over wooden formers, the pieces being riveted together. At a slightly later date statues were cast over a clay core which was removed to leave a hollow cast. The "lost wax" method of hollow casting (described on p. 33) was an early discovery, and the Renaissance use of this method is described by Cellini (*Memoirs*).

Embossed decoration was done by hammering the back of a sheet of bronze on a yielding pitch-block, the pitch being melted off the finished work. This method was used by the Greeks and others, and some large and important work was made in this way which can be distinguished from cast work by the (often faint) impress of the hammer and other tools, and by the fact that the raised work on the front is faithfully followed by hollow work on the back.

A few things were made in pure copper during medieval times, and sheets of copper have always been used for roofing to a limited extent on important buildings. Lead sheets were similarly used for roofing and for decorative work on guttering, for water-cisterns, and so forth. Lead garden statues were cast, and lead was employed for fountains, since it stood exposure to the weather extremely well, and was unaffected by water.

Iron is both ductile and malleable when it is red hot. It can be welded when in this state by hammering, and joining is therefore fairly easy. This led to its use for grilles, ornamental openwork gates, balcony rails, and similar purposes. Beaten into sheets, it was used for plate armour, hinges, and many

F

other purposes. Tempered by fire, it took a sharp cutting edge, and therefore became popular for the manufacture of weapons and knives of all kinds. Tempering causes the metal to become harder but more brittle. Tempered swords would cut with great facility, but would break instead of bending. The art of sword-making has always been so to temper the metal that it could be given the sharpest possible cutting edge consistent with a freedom from excessive brittleness. Articles of iron and steel are always tempered to a degree which is best suited for the purpose for which they have been made. Those of my readers who have broken a penknife blade in trying to turn a screw have had practical demonstration of this fact.

Iron suffers from a liability to excessive corrosion when in contact with air and water, or, to put it more simply, it rusts. If it is not protected it will, ultimately, be converted completely into rust, and for this reason few really early objects of iron have survived. In a collection iron needs to be protected from rusting by a thin coating of vaseline or varnish.

My remarks so far apply to wrought iron – objects of iron formed by hammering. Cast-iron is a comparatively late development, first being made about the 16th century. It is somewhat inferior to cast bronze, since it is impossible to get a really sharp impression. Iron manufactured in this way is also extremely brittle, breaking easily if it is dropped or struck. Wrought iron, therefore, is superior for almost all purposes, although such things as cast-iron ornamental fire-backs are durable enough.

Methods of decorating metal are many and varied. Embossing (*repoussé* work) has already been described. Engraving, chasing, inlaying, and enamelling are mentioned elsewhere in this book (notably on pp. 98, 132, and 95). The term "damascening" is also applied to steel (usually sword blades) having a "watered" appearance which was achieved by repeated hammering, but it is more correctly used of inlays in gold and silver wire.

METAL-WORK, JAPANESE Japanese metal-work can be divided into two main classes – armour and weapons, and decorative and useful objects.

Good Japanese armour is not often seen in Europe in anything like a complete state, and those suits which are complete are usually inferior in quality and were intended for the "other ranks". Weapons, however, are somewhat more frequent. Sword and dagger blades are often finely decorated, and various small attachments (sword furniture) are worth collecting for themselves. The *kashira*, or pommel cap, and the *fuchi* which encircles the handle were often elaborately decorated, and the *tsuba*, or sword-guard, is of particular interest to the student of Japanese art.

Inlaying and damascening were frequently employed, and piercing was a common form of ornament. Engraving and chasing was done with great skill, and the subjects of decoration are many and varied. These items of sword furniture are usually detached from the swords, and a really good Samurai sword in a complete state is a rarity. A few fine specimens are signed by the maker.

Other Japanese metal-work is not uncommon in Europe. Various metals were used – iron, bronze, and silver – but the value of the metal is usually secondary to the workmanship.

The Japanese were highly skilled metal-workers, and particularly adept as engravers. A fault of most Japanese craftsmanship is a display of technical skill for its own sake, and this is no less noticeable in metal-work.

Things for household and personal use include mirrors, *saké*-kettles, and writing cases, as well as brush-cases and ink-holders. Vases are fairly common, and many of them were made for export. Enamel on a metal base is discussed under the heading of ENAMELS.

MEZZA-MAIOLICA   *See* SGRAFFITO.

MING DYNASTY, THE [1368–1644]   The Ming period is of considerable importance to the collector of the finer varieties of Chinese art. The dynasty was founded by the Emperor Hung-wu as the result of a successful revolt against the reigning Mongol house, and some distinct differences in the art of the period can be seen almost at once. Certainly it was well-marked by the time of the accession of Hsüan Tê [1426–1435].

The chief interest during the Ming period centres on its

pottery and porcelain. It is distinguished from the earlier periods by the much greater use of painted decoration. The development of underglaze blue and enamel colours in conjunction with a white body took place rapidly, and, whilst a few Sung types, such as the celadons of Chu Chou, continued to be made, they form a comparatively small proportion of the whole. In particular, the Imperial factories at Ching-tê Chên greatly increased in size and importance. During the earlier part of the period the underglaze blue decoration was particularly fine, and is now highly valued. Enamel colours are more frequent later, and by the reign of Wan Li [1573–1619] much of the blue-and-white was of minor importance.

Carved lacquer, the most important variety, was commonly made, and the finest work of this kind belongs to the Ming period.

Metal-work, and bronze in particular, is not of such importance to the collector. It is durable, and much more of it has survived. Moreover, there was considerable increase in the manufacture of commoner types. Dating is often difficult, and many things of the earlier periods were copied. Some of these copies were very close, and most of the apparently early bronzes which raise doubt in the mind as to their authenticity are probably Ming. Silver and gold vessels, of course, are often of great artistic importance, but these are particularly rare.

The use of *cloisonné* enamel on a metal base was introduced during the Yüan dynasty, but the finest specimens are probably referable to the middle of the 15th century.

Ming jade carvings are of good quality. As with bronzes, there was sometimes an archaizing tendency, particularly with smaller objects. Large carvings of horses and buffaloes are often exceptional in quality, and very highly valued. A few ivory carvings can be placed to this period with reasonable certainty.

Great caution is necessary in dating, and a date-mark should never be accepted as evidence of a Ming origin unless materials, style, and workmanship are all completely in agreement. Ming date-marks were extensively used by Chinese craftsmen during the Ch'ing period, and particularly in the 18th and 19th centuries.

MOSAIK PATTERNS Repetitive geometric patterns painted over a coloured ground. These were probably used in the first place to mitigate the effects of an unevenly laid ground, but later, particularly at Berlin and Meissen, such patterns were much used decoratively. The earliest occurrence on German porcelain was at Vienna. The scale patterns of Worcester are also similar in form and purpose to the *Mosaik* patterns of the German factories. They appear to be related to similar patterns to be found on Turkish faience and Italian *maiolica* of the 16th century. A faience factory at Berlin, where *Mosaik* patterns ere frequently used on porcelain, copied decorations appearing on Isnik pottery early in the 18th century.

MOTIFS OF DECORATION – ABSTRACTIONS

Arabesques A type of ornament so-called because it was assumed to have originated with the Arabs. Actually arabesques are Roman in origin, and are closely related to *grotesques* (p. 170). They consist of elaborate convolutions of various kinds (geometrical figures, fruit, and flowers interwoven in a fantastic manner) which were at first used for the adornment of walls and ceilings, and in painted form by Italian *maiolica* painters. They can be seen in French decorative art during the 17th and 18th centuries.

Baldacchini A kind of canopy often employed as a decorative motif by Jean Bérain, and especially to be seen on tapestries, faience, and other things in his style. *Baldacchini* were used over beds, and as a covered place for statues in churches. A portable variety covered newly crowned kings and popes in processions.

Cornucopia As the name suggests, this was a vessel shaped like an inverted horn, often overflowing with fruit and ears of wheat, symbolic of peace and plenty. Wall-pockets in this form were made by some of the 18th-century pottery and porcelain factories, and figures symbolizing Earth from a set of the Elements were sometimes provided with one.

Egg and Dart Bands A type of frieze ornament derived from the Greeks and used in neo-classical ornament. It consists of alternating oval (or egg-shaped) and tongue (or dart) shaped motifs in relief. There are a number of minor variations and elaborations on this basic theme.

Emblems The Greek gods had objects which were sacred

to them, or by which they were represented. Thus, the laurel was sacred to Apollo and the vine to Bacchus, whilst Mercury held a caduceus. From this it was a short step for the object to stand in place of the god, and it then becomes emblematic. Much the same things occurs in Christian art, a lamb frequently representing Christ, for instance.

Additionally, such things as groups of musical instruments were used to represent music, and a brush and palette symbolized painting. This kind of symbolism was carried to considerable lengths, and during the 18th century it was the practice to make figures and sets of figures representing such things as the Seasons, Continents, Elements, and so forth, the purpose of which could be deduced from the symbols carried by them. Thus, flowers represented spring; sheaves of corn, summer: grapes, autumn; and a brazier or fur-lined clothes, winter.

Key Fret   A geometrical border pattern much used in ancient Greece and in styles based on classical art. A simple version is as follows:

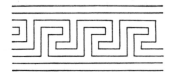

The Greek key fret, often used as ornament during the neo-classical period

Such patterns were also called "meanders". The motif developed independently in China, and can be seen on early bronzes.

Lambrequins   A type of ornament most commonly to be

An example of "Lambrequin" ornament used on early faience, porcelain, and other works of art

seen on certain kinds of French faience and early porcelain which was introduced by Louis Poterat of Rouen. It comprises pendant lacework ornament, drapes, and scrollwork adapted from such abstract ornament of the period as that used for bookbinding, lace-work, and iron-work (*ferronerie*). Swags of fruit and flowers were used in addition. *Lambrequins* adapted to a radial position are called the *style rayonnant*.

Laub- und Bandelwerk Literally, *leaf- and strap-work*. This was a popular kind of ornament on early German porcelain. It can occasionally be seen on German faience, notably that from Bayreuth, and on metal-work of the 17th and 18th centuries. *Laub- und Bandelwerk* is a characteristically baroque ornament. It took many forms, but essentially it is a symmetrical arrangement of interlacing scrolls and strap-work, with the occasional addition of conventionalized leaf-forms. On faience and porcelain it was carried out both in gold and in colours, the latter being the more usual. Engravers, such as Paul Decker, published books of designs for the use of craft-workers of all kinds.

An example of Laub- und Bandelwerk used on German faience, porcelain, silver, and other things of a like nature

Meander See KEY FRET, p. 166.

Trophies Originally these were the arms of a beaten enemy, which the Greeks hung on trees to celebrate victory. Later, weapons grouped together were used as the motif of much carved and painted ornament.

MOTIFS OF DECORATION – CARYATIDS
Sculptured female figures used in place of columns as supports
to parts of a building, particularly in Greece during classical
times. Later they were sometimes used as furniture decoration,
and in similar ways. *Atlantes* are male statues employed for a
similar purpose. They occur less frequently.

MOTIFS OF DECORATION – DOLPHINS The use
of the dolphin is very common. It first appears in classical
times, and is a frequent motif of Pompeiian wall-painting. It
is also to be found in Greek and Roman sculpture.

It was much used during the Renaissance, in ornament of all
kinds. It is common in porcelain, and often accompanies
tritons and nereids. An example of its use is the well-known
figure of Neptune with dolphin and trident, which was
copied by Derby from a Meissen original, and symbolized
Water in a set of the Elements.

The French title of *Dauphin* for the King's eldest son
means dolphin. The title came originally from the Comte de
Vienne Dauphiné, who presented it, with some property, to
the grandson of Philip VI. Dauphiné was one of the old
provinces of France, situated between Provence and Savoy.
This explains the frequent use of the dolphin in French
ornament.

MOTIFS OF DECORATION – EAGLES The eagle
is almost as frequently represented as the lion, and its use as a
motif of decoration dates back to early times. One has only to
mention its presence on the standard of the Roman legions.
In Christian art it is an attribute of St. John the Evangelist, and
is frequently carved in the form of a lectern. In classical
mythology it was the attribute of Zeus, and it carried Gany-
mede on its back. In both these rôles it is depicted in porcelain.

In heraldry the eagle is very common. The U.S.A., of
course, use it, and Germany, Austria, Prussia, France, and
Russia have all employed it at one time or another. The
heraldic double-headed eagle came originally from Byzantine
sources.

Eagles were used in the decoration of furniture during the
18th and early 19th centuries. They often surmounted Regency
mirror-frames.

MOTIFS OF DECORATION – FABULOUS MON-
STERS *Centaur* A mythical animal with the body of a
horse and the head and torso of a human being, usually male,
in place of the horse's head and neck. A classical motif which
often occurs later.

Chimera A winged lion, goat-headed lion, lion with an
additional head in the form of a goat, etc. Used for much the
same purposes as the griffin (*see* below).

Dragon, European The European dragon is a large animal
which owes something to the serpent and the crocodile. It is
no doubt related to the hundred-headed hydra which guarded
the Garden of the Hesperides. The dragon was addicted to a
diet of virgins and to ravaging the countryside, and was
usually slain by a hero or a god.

It was regarded by the Romans as a sign of warfare, and
occurs in the *Nibelungenlied*, in which it is slain by Siegfried.
The dragon occurs on English shields in heraldic form after the
Norman Conquest. In Christian art it usually represents sin,
and, for this reason, Satan. Sin is also represented by a serpent
with an apple in its mouth. It is probably most commonly seen
in representations of St. George of Cappadocia, but this legend
is even more dubious than most, and was probably derived
originally from St. Michael slaying Satan in the form of a
dragon.

Pistols with a dragon's head at the muzzle were called
dragons. The troops who carried these eventually came to be
known as *dragoons*.

The European dragon should be distinguished from the
Chinese dragon, which has the opposite connotation. This
appears quite frequently in European works of art based on
Chinese decorative motifs (*see* CHINOISERIES).

Two animals similar to the dragon are the *cockatrice* and the
wyvern. The former has a cock's head and comb, a tail ending
in a spear-point, and a bird's legs and claws. The latter is
virtually the same as the dragon, but has only two legs.

Griffin (Gryphos) The griffin is usually represented with
the body of a lion and the head and wings of an eagle. It
symbolizes strength and agility, as well as the destroying power
of the gods. First used about the 7th century B.C., it has been
employed as an element of decoration many times since then,
particularly in styles based on classical art. The Empire

style of the first decade of the 19th century is an example.

Grotesques Fantastic shapes which are usually a combination of human, animal, and plant forms. The origin is Roman, and grotesques of this kind are common at Pompeii. Raphael revived them after seeing some painting of the kind discovered in the ruins of the Golden House of Nero, and they were copied from him on to Italian *maiolica*. They were employed extensively by Renaissance craftsmen, and occur especially on Italian *maiolica*. They inspired the decorations of JEAN BÉRAIN (*q.v.*). Grotesque figures are mostly variations on such themes as a winged human female torso without arms and terminating in foliage, or in the hind legs of an animal. Masks were also treated in the manner of grotesques during the Renaissance, and undoubtedly owe something to Roman theatrical masks. Foliage sometimes takes the place of the beard for instance. Later grotesques from Urbino were lively and full of movement, the earlier variety tending to be static and formal.

Dolphins were sometimes given foliate tails, and in extreme cases, are represented by little more than the head, the remainder being foliate scrolls which follow the approximate shape of the body. (*See: Arabesques.*)

A grotesque of the kind extensively used as an ornament from the Renaissance until the first quarter of the 18th century

Medusa Heads The head of a woman, her hair in the form of writhing serpents. Perseus slew Medusa and presented her head to Athene as an ornament for her shield. The Medusa head was frequently used as an ornament for shields and breast-plates, but does not appear very often after classical times.

Sphinx The body of a lion with the upper part of a human figure. The early sphinxes are usually male. The female sphinx is slightly later, and the addition of wings was probably suggested by the Assyrian use of winged fabulous animals. The sphinx with a ram's head is seen occasionally.

Sphinxes were used during the Renaissance, and frequently employed in baroque designs. They can be seen on tapestries and pottery in the style of Jean Bérain, and ladies of the Court and actresses were sometimes modelled in this form in terra-cotta and porcelain in England and on the Continent.

Unicorn This animal resembled a horse, and had a single long, straight horn projecting from its forehead. It was particularly used in heraldry. A native of India, it was said that only a virgin could capture it. This was probably regarded as an excellent reason why no specimens could be seen in captivity.

MOTIFS OF DECORATION – LIONS The lion has been a popular element of decoration from the earliest times. No doubt this was due to an erroneous impression of its courage and ferocity, and it was credited with such human qualities as nobility. The lion was much used by the Greeks and Romans, and sometimes appears as a temple guardian. It was a frequent motif in Renaissance art, and from the time of the Crusades onward it was much employed as an heraldic emblem. In Christian art the lion is usually an attribute of St. Mark or St. Jerome, and Christ is represented as the Lion of Judah.

In heraldry the lion *couchant* represents sovereignty; *rampant*, magnanimity; *passant*, resolution; *guardant*, prudence; *salient*, valour; *sciant*, counsel; and *regardant*, circumspection.

The lion's head is also used extensively. With a ring in its mouth it becomes a knocker, a door-handle or a handle to metal vases and vessels. It is carved as an ornament on furniture, and is the subject of some cast ormolu mounts. Its paws are sometimes used as the feet of tables and chairs.

The panther and the tiger are much less often seen; the lynx-head was sometimes used as a gargoyle in Gothic times.

MOTIFS OF DECORATION – PLANT FORMS
Acanthus The acanthus is a plant which is comparatively common in Southern Europe. There are two principal varieties. The Greeks and Romans used the leaf in a formalized version for a variety of decorative purposes. The Roman version is the more realistic, the Greek and Byzantine being somewhat stiffer. It was extensively used from classical times onwards, even in Gothic decoration. It appears in the 17th and 18th centuries accompanying designs in the Palladian and neo-classical styles, and it was used to a lesser extent during the rococo period. It was also used in profile as a scroll.

Anthemion A formalized version of the honeysuckle originally derived from Greek sources and adapted as a frieze ornament on English neo-classical furniture and so forth. A version of it was popular as a border decoration for porcelain plates around 1800.

Bryony The tendrils and leaves of this plant are to be seen on some Hispano-Moresque pottery.

Hop The hop was frequently used as ornament on beer-mugs, jugs, and similar vessels from Staffordshire. It was also sometimes employed as decoration on silver drinking-vessels during the early 19th century, as well as being etched and engraved on ale glasses.

A version of the acanthus leaf used in ornament

Laurel Laurel was originally sacred to Apollo, whose priests wore chaplets woven from it. Statues of Aesculapius were crowned with it. It appears quite frequently as an element of neo-classical decoration in the 18th century, and has enjoyed a varying amount of popularity since classical times.

Olive The olive was sacred to Athene. Wreaths of olive

were awarded to victors in the Olympic Games. It was re-garded as a symbol of peace and in Christian art it is an emblem of the Virgin.

Palm The leaves of the palm were frequently used as decoration during classical times. They were awarded at the Olympic Games, and borne in triumphal processions in Rome. As a symbol of victory and peace, they appear in Christian art, and Gabriel holds a palm branch in representations of the Annunciation. Palm leaves, from classical times onwards, were often in the formalized version known as the palmette, which somewhat resembles the fingers of an outstretched hand. A half-palmette is a palmette divided vertically.

Rose Flowers are, of course, frequently used in all kinds of decorative art. The rose is very common, and is an attribute of several saints in Christian art. The rose and the thistle on engraved glass and pottery of the 18th century denoted Jacobite sympathies.

Wheat-ears Occasionally used decoratively. They appear in a carved form on the backs of some Hepplewhite chairs.

MOTIFS OF DECORATION – THE RAM   The ram's head was particularly employed during the neo-classical period. It appears as a furniture mount, as ornament to porcelain vases, and in many other forms.

MOTIFS OF DECORATION – SHELL ORNA-MENT   Nautilus shells were mounted as drinking vessels in silver and other metals in Germany, at Augsburg or Nurem-berg, during the 17th century. Added engraved decoration was usually heightened with black pigment, and may have suggested the later SCHWARZLOT painting (*q.v.*) on faience, glass, and porcelain.

Natural marine shells were used as ornament during the rococo period. Scallop shells formed the basins of porcelain table-fountains.

The pecten, or scallop, shell was employed as moulded decoration on English salt-glazed stoneware, and painted shells were a popular decoration on some kinds of porcelain (e.g. Worcester of the Barr, Flight, and Barr period) in the early 19th century. Natural shells were often collected and sometimes mounted in ormolu.

Furniture in the 18th century was often inlaid with scallop-shell ornament, which was also carved on the knees of cabriole legs and in other places.

MOTIFS OF DECORATION (ORIENTAL) – ABSTRACTIONS

There is space only for mention of a few of the more important of these. The Eight Trigrams represent natural forces – heaven, wind, earth, water, etc. The *yang-yin* with which they are associated is symbolic of the male–female principle. The Eight Buddhist Emblems are a series of eight stylized symbolic things – a flaming wheel, a conch shell, a state umbrella, a canopy, a lotus, a vase, a pair of fishes, and an endless knot – which are specifically connected with Buddhism and used as decoration.

The Hundred Antiques are a collection of instruments mostly used in the arts and sciences which have been adapted as decoration. The Eight Precious Things belong to this group – rhinoceros horn cups, a musical stone of jade, an artemisia leaf, a jewel, a coin, a painting, a pair of tablets, and a lozenge-shaped symbol of victory. Meanders and frets are used as border patterns.

Calligraphy is much used in the East. Chinese ideograms are frequently employed in this way, and are regarded as decoration in their own right. The Persian angular Kufic script and the more flowing *neskhi* script both appear as decoration on pottery, rugs, and many other things of the same kind.

The "Yang-yin" symbol in the centre, surrounded by the eight trigrams

MOTIFS OF DECORATION (ORIENTAL) – ANIMAL MOTIFS

Of the animals normally used by the Chinese as decoration, the *bat* represents happiness, and both the *stork* and the *tortoise* signify longevity. The *tiger* is found in China, and symbolizes military prowess. It also wards off evil spirits. The *hare* symbolizes the moon, and a *three-legged toad* has the same meaning. The Twelve Animals of the Zodiac are the *dragon, hare, tiger, fox, rat, pig, dog, cock, monkey, goat, horse,* and *snake.* Each year, month, day, and hour is associated with one of these animals. The Eight Horses of Mu Wang, an Emperor of the Chou Dynasty, are often used. *Fish,* frequently *carp,* as well as *duck* and *water-fowl* are common. The *deer* is shown with the *ling-chih* fungus, which symbolizes longevity.

MOTIFS OF DECORATION (ORIENTAL) – FABULOUS ANIMALS *Dragon* The dragon is the principal form of decoration on much pottery and porcelain, and other works of art and craft, from China and Japan. It is an ancient symbol, and although its aspect appears ferocious, the dragon has a mild and beneficent disposition. It symbolizes the Emperor, and is the Spirit of the Waters. It is also emblematic of spring. Dragons with five claws appeared originally on things for Imperial use, and with four claws or less for members of the Imperial Household and officials. The Japanese dragon nearly always has three claws.

Fo, Lion of Sometimes referred to as the Dog of Fo (or Buddha). These animals are usually represented in pairs, the male playing with a ball, the female with a cub. They are frequently seen in both pottery and porcelain as figures and as painted decoration. They are sometimes miscalled *Kylins* (*see* below).

A Chinese dragon of the Ming period. Later versions became more elaborate

Kylin (Ch'i-lin) This animal has the head of a dragon, a scaly body, deer's hooves, and a bushy tail. It has a short single horn in the centre of its forehead. Although it appears ferocious, it was, in fact, a creature of singular mildness, too gentle even to tread on living grass. It is very auspicious, and always appeared before some great event, one being seen before the birth of Confucius.

Phoenix (Fêng huang)   A symbol of the Empress. It represents spring, and is an auspicious symbol. It is often seen in porcelain painting together with the dragon. In Japanese it is the *ho-ho* bird.

T'ao t'ieh   A formalized animal mask much used on ancient Chinese bronzes, and on archaizing objects at a later date. *See* p. 41.

MOTIFS OF DECORATION (ORIENTAL) – FLORAL SUBJECTS   Very commonly represented is the *ling chih* fungus *(Fomes Japonicus)*, which symbolizes longevity. Deer often carry it in their mouths.

Flower symbolism is elaborate, and certain flowers are emblematic of the seasons and the months. The plum (or prunus) blossom symbolizes spring; the tree-peony, summer; the lotus, autumn; and the chrysanthemum, winter. The prunus in porcelain is often used against a background of blue divided by dark lines to represent the cracked ice of spring.

The bamboo, a plant of many uses, often appears, and symbolizes longevity. The lotus is associated with Buddhism, and Buddha and Kuan Yin are often represented seated on a lotus. The chrysanthemum appears in the T'ang Dynasty on bronze mirrors.

The peach, symbolizing longevity, is frequently represented. Less usual is the "Buddha's hand" citron, a fruit with finger-like appendages.

Flowers are also much used in Japan, where flower arrangement has reached the point of being a complete art. The chrysanthemum appears in a natural and a formalized version. In the latter form it is the Imperial Badge, or *mon*, and is analogous to European armorial bearings.

Flowers appearing on early Japanese porcelain were much used by European faience and porcelain painters during the 18th century. In Germany they were called *indianische Blumen*, since this type of porcelain was imported by the East India Companies.

MOTIFS OF DECORATION (ORIENTAL) – RELIGIOUS AND MYTHOLOGICAL PERSONAGES

Most frequently represented in Chinese art is Buddha, who is closely followed in the heavenly hierarchy, and in popularity, by the goddess Kuan Yin (Kwannon in Japan). The only figure of note associated with Confucianism who is used with any frequency is Kuan-ti, the God of War.

The Taoist god, Lao-tzŭ (Shou Lao) is very commonly represented, and can be recognized by a large and protuberant forehead. He is usually accompanied by the Eight Immortals. These are often made as figures and sets of figures, and are frequently represented as painted decoration on porcelain and in other ways. They are analogous to the Japanese gods of good fortune, which are headed by Jurojin.

Figure subjects are often drawn from literature. Poets and sages in a mountain landscape are a frequent theme, and occasionally it is possible to identify them, the T'ang poet, Li Tai Po, appearing in a number of forms.

Kuei Hsing, the distributor of literary degrees, who is sometimes painted on porcelain, has the face of a demon and rides on a fish-dragon.

MOUNTS, METAL Mounts to vessels made from a variety of different metals can be found from the 15th century onwards, and good mounted specimens are rare and usually valuable. The custom may have arisen in the first place from the esteem attached to the infrequent specimens of Chinese porcelain which found their way to Western Europe, since many of these were mounted in silver. A few examples of the 15th century are known.

By the end of the 16th century such things as Turkish faience from Isnik, German stoneware jugs from the Rhineland, and the English "Malling" jugs were receiving this kind of embellishment. A particularly fine example of Turkish faience with silver-gilt mounts is in the British Museum.

During the second half of the 17th century Japanese blue and white porcelain jugs from Arita and elsewhere, made in the forms of European faience and stoneware, were mounted in silver and pewter.

The 18th century saw a fashion for mounting Chinese vases and dishes in gilt-bronze, and these are highly valued. European porcelain, then a comparatively recent discovery, was also mounted in the same way, and ormolu sprays of leaves received the addition of modelled porcelain flowers and candle-holders.

Apart from pottery and porcelain, nautilus shells, coconut shells, boxwood cups, and ostrich egg-shells were mounted as drinking vessels. Vessels of leather – the "Black Jacks" – were mounted in the same way.

Prices for mounted pottery and porcelain are usually considerably in excess of the value of unmounted specimens. Care must be taken to see that the mounts are genuine, and made for the piece in question. Undoubtedly odd sets of mounts have been added to certain objects, but it is hardly conceivable that this could have been done without some kind of adaptation. This should be visible on careful inspection, although there are methods whereby mounts can be slightly "stretched", or increased in diameter, without affecting anything but the thickness of the metal.

NANTGARW (S. WALES) PORCELAIN FACTORY This small factory was founded by William Billingsley in 1813. Billingsley was a noted painter of flowers at Derby who had acquired or devised a formula for the manufacture of an extremely fine, if impracticable, soft porcelain body. This he proceeded to manufacture at Nantgarw. Kiln-wastage was extremely high, and little commercial success was possible, but a certain amount of superb porcelain was made, some of which was decorated at the factory, and some in London at the studio of Robins and Randall.

The factory was transferred to Swansea in 1814 with the co-operation of Lewis Dillwyn, the proprietor, and the character of the porcelain altered.

In 1819 Billingsley accepted employment with John Rose of Coalport, who thus obtained the Nantgarw formulae.

Nantgarw porcelain is extremely scarce, and good specimens are highly valued.

NEO-CLASSICAL STYLE, THE This began with the excavation of the ruins of Pompeii and Herculaneum. By 1755 a good deal of digging had been done and numerous works published on the subject. The most important were those of the Comte de Caylus and Sir William Hamilton (Ambassador to Naples). The publications of Johann Joachim Winckelmann, the German art-historian, also helped to popularize the movement.

Although a movement of this kind might have been expected to lead to a return to the somewhat severe forms of Greece and Rome, it was considerably modified by a number of outside influences, one of the more important being the publication of Goethe's *Die Leiden des jungen Werthers* (*The Sorrows of Young Werther*) in 1774. This excessively sentimental novel enjoyed wide circulation in Europe, and resulted in

A porcelain ewer derived from the Greek oenechoe, a classical mask at the base of the handle, and applied acanthus leaves at the base

a kind of hysteria almost without precedent in its time. Its attitude found fruitful soil in the rise of the *bourgeoisie* who, particularly after the Seven Years War, greatly increased in power and influence. Their tastes were catered for adequately by such porcelain modellers as Michel-Victor Acier at Meissen, and by such painters as J. B. Greuze and Angelica Kauffmann. The work of Greuze inspired several porcelain figure groups, and the work of the latter was copied on to porcelain as decoration on the Continent and in England, as well as on to furniture, wall-panels, and so forth.

In England the chief exponents of the style were the architects and decorators, the Adam brothers, and for this reason neo-classicism is often referred to as the Adam style.

The elements of the style itself are discussed elsewhere in this volume, particularly in the article on English furniture. The Empire (p. 123) and Regency (*q.v.*) styles are later modifications of neo-classicism.

NETSUKÉ   These small Japanese carvings have always been popular with the Western collector. All *netsuké* (properly so-called) are intended to be fixed by a cord to the *inrō*, or to a pipe-case or tobacco-box, to prevent them from slipping through the sash. The materials used were extremely varied, the commonest being polished wood, ivory, bone, and horn. The earliest are of wood, ivory being introduced in the 18th century. Signed specimens are not uncommon, but signatures do not always mean very much.

Netsuké are often carved with great skill and attention to detail. They are frequently used as an outlet for the Japanese sense of humour, which is acute and penetrating, and many of them are intended to be caricatures. The subjects are numerous, and can often be traced to folk-lore, religion, literature, and similar sources. A few show traces of European influence.

The *netsuké* is a kind of Japanese art well within the reach of the modest collector.

NEWHALL   (STAFFS)   PORCELAIN   FACTORY
This small factory took over the hard-paste formula from Richard Champion of Bristol about 1780. It made porcelain of this kind until about 1812, when it changed to the standard bone-china body.

The decoration, which at first leant heavily on Chinese patterns of the Mandarin variety, is rarely of good quality. Most of it is unsophisticated and intended for the cheaper market.

OKIMONO   Small ornaments used for decorating the Japanese house, or for religious purposes. The term includes small statuettes in ivory, metal, and other substances, incense-burners, and flower vases.

"ORIENTAL LOWESTOFT" A term applied, particularly in the U.S.A., to certain kinds of Chinese porcelain with European decoration which was painted in Canton for export to Europe.

The name was due, in the first place, to an error by William Chaffers, who assumed that porcelain of this kind was actually made and decorated at Lowestoft in Suffolk. There is no foundation for the supposition, and the class is much better termed "Chinese export porcelain".

Chinese export porcelain can be divided into a number of classes which more or less overlap. European forms, based on either European ceramics or metal-work, usually have decoration inspired by the same source. Services of one kind or another made for export frequently have armorial bearings. A much rarer class has such European decoration as Watteau subjects painted in colours, and the enamels are occasionally made to sink into the glaze in imitation of Western enamel-painting. Another class decorated in black with touches of red is strongly linear in drawing, and undoubtedly copied from European line engravings, and from the *Schwarzlot* decoration used on early German porcelain and on faience. A class decorated in black with Christian subjects, with a little gilding added, is known as "Jesuit" porcelain, from a presumed connection with Jesuit missionaries of the period.

European forms were used by the Japanese for porcelain painted in underglaze blue during the 17th century, the faience jug known as the *Enghalskrug* (narrow-necked jug) being among those selected for the purpose.

ORMOLU The term is an anglicization of the French *doré d'or moulu*, which means bronze mercurically gilded. It is also commonly employed for alloys of copper, tin, and zinc which are indistinguishable from brass.

Gilt-bronze was extensively used during the 18th and 19th centuries for ornamenting French furniture, and frequently for mounting such things as porcelain vases and figures.

The finest work of the kind is highly valued, and can be regarded as an important section of French applied art during the 18th century.

The usual way of making mounts in ormolu was by casting in moulds. Quality of workmanship can be judged from the care and skill used in cleaning up the casting and sharpening the moulded ornament with chisels and other metal-working tools. During the 18th century attention was lavished on details of this kind, but 19th-century castings are rarely finished with so much care. Comparison between 18th- and 19th-century mounts will usually show the essential differences in workmanship.

The addition of ormolu mounts to important specimens of porcelain and similar *objets d'art* increases the value considerably over unmounted specimens, provided that the mounts in question were made during the 18th century, and are of fine quality.

Porcelain flowers mounted with ornamental leaves and stems are sought after, and the material was used, in France, for making clock-cases and similar things, often with porcelain plaques inset. 19th-century examples of the latter are by far the most common.

In England furniture mounts in the French style were made both of gilt bronze and of an alloy similar to brass in Birmingham and elsewhere, and English brass-founders attained a high degree of skill in such work. Their casts are to be seen from mid-18th century onwards, although work of the kind was done long before, as witness the fine and intricate spandrels on early clock dials.

PALLADIAN STYLE This style was an attempt to revive the principles of Roman architecture as set forth by Vitruvius. The Italian architect, Andrea Palladio (1518–1580), was its best-known exponent, and it is he from whom the name is derived. In England Inigo Jones (1573–1652) introduced the Palladian style, and during the first half of the 18th century William Kent was among the designers influenced by it.

PARQUETRY Inlays of wood of the same colour. The design is usually geometric and the effect obtained by contrasting the direction of the grain of the wood. The use of rectangular wood-blocks for flooring is an example of parquetry.

PATINA One of the expert's most important assets is the ability to recognize the nature of patina, which is the change in the surface appearance of a variety of materials that can only come with age.

A good patina is always much prized, and it is the most difficult thing to fake. Variations in circumstances often produce a different kind of patina on what is fundamentally the same material. As an example, the patination which results from the burial of Chinese bronzes is quite different from that to be found on Egyptian specimens, largely due to the difference in the earth in which they have been buried.

It is not too much to say that much of the expertise which enables the experienced collector to differentiate between true and false is the result of a study of patination. Sun-bleaching on old furniture gives the wood a peculiar light colour which can come only with time. Likewise dust, the wear and polishing of centuries, and similar factors, leave traces which cannot be reproduced exactly by any known method.

The colour of old silver is quite different from that of new. This can well be seen if an antique specimen is put alongside an old one which has been subsequently electro-plated. The difference is extremely marked.

The recognition of these small but important points can be acquired only by the close study of genuine examples, but they are a vital part of the education of the connoisseur, and need to be given attention accordingly.

PEASANT WARES Used of pottery made by unsophisticated communities in contact with metropolitan civilization. For example, the wares of rustic communities for sale in local markets can fairly be described as peasant pottery.

PEWTER Pewter is an alloy of various metals in which tin predominates. The usual alloying metals are lead, antimony, copper, and zinc, but the proportions in which they were used vary widely. The finest pewter was made of tin with a proportion of copper. Pewter for plates was sometimes of tin, with a small quantity of antimony, bismuth, and copper, but the commonest alloy was about 75 per cent. of tin and 25 per cent. of lead, which is comparatively soft and inclined to be dark in colour. Modern pewter has to conform to various requirements regulating the lead content to avoid the risk of lead poisoning.

Pewter was much used for drinking vessels and table-ware before the manufacture of pottery on a scale sufficiently extensive to supply these needs. Since the metal has a comparatively low intrinsic value, no doubt more would have survived from medieval times but for its softness and liability to damage. As it is, most specimens belong to the 17th and 18th centuries, and anything earlier is very rare.

In England the manufacture of pewter was regulated by the Pewterers' Company, who instituted a system of apprenticeships and saw to the maintenance of quality in the metal used by its members. When an apprentice had been approved by the Company he was allowed to register his mark, or "touch", and this enabled articles of inferior quality to be traced to their origin.

"Touches" were first used about the middle of the 15th century, and their application was enforced by law in 1503. It proved impossible in practice to operate such a law, and, despite the persuasive influence of the Company, large quantities of unmarked pewter were made at all times.

Makers' marks were recorded on "touch" plates which were held in possession of the Company, but the registers which would have enabled us to link these with appropriate names have, for the most part, disappeared, some being destroyed in the Great Fire of London in 1666. With some exceptions, therefore, the marks cannot be used to identify makers.

The Pewterers' Company began to lose its hold on the trade during the 17th century with the rise to popularity of pottery and glass and their manufacture on an increasingly large scale. Later, various substitutes were introduced, such as the extremely fusible Britannia metal, made of tin, antimony, copper, and zinc, and Sheffield plate undoubtedly took some of the trade which would previously have been supplied by the pewterer. For these reasons, therefore, the craft was gradually extinguished, the last touch being registered in 1824. A type of pewter is still used for such things as tankards, but the alloy is very different from that of antique pewter.

Most pewter was made by casting in brass moulds, by hammering, or by spinning. In the latter process the metal was pressed on to a wooden former, or some similar tool, which was revolved in a lathe. Hammering both consolidated and hardened the metal.

Most surviving examples of pewter-ware are tankards, plates and dishes, measures, condiment-pots, spoons, jugs, teapots, coffee-pots, and beakers. Inkstands are comparatively uncommon, and the rare cast chimney ornaments in the form of figures are late, and may have been inspired by contemporary porcelain. Ecclesiastical pewter includes chalices, Communion cups, and flagons.

The styles used more or less followed those of contemporary silver, but at a certain distance and with much less refinement of decoration.

Except for rarities, objects in pewter are rarely expensive, and it is a fruitful field for the small collector interested in antique metal-work.

Articles for domestic use are also found in copper, and 18th-century copper work is not unusual. Spirit and corn measures are useful for flower vases, and an occasional old copper coal-scuttle in reasonable or repairable condition can be found.

PHOSPHATE TEST   To test porcelain for the presence of phosphates, put one drop of hydrofluoric acid on to an unglazed part. Leave for five minutes, and then wash the spot with a syringe into a test-tube containing a small quantity of warm ammonium molybdate in nitric acid. A yellow precipitate will form if phosphates are present. A wax taper is best for applying the acid. Porcelain glaze can be removed, if necessary, with a carborundum stone.

Hydrofluoric acid is a dangerous acid giving off irritating fumes. It attacks glass, and is therefore supplied in non-vitreous containers. The bottle should be stored in a safe place (preferably a locked cupboard), and it should not be stored near glass, since a slight leak of fumes past the stopper will affect the surface of any glass near it. After its use porcelain should be well washed to remove all traces of acid.

Acids of any kind should not be used without immediate access to running water. The first-aid treatment for spilled acid is copious flooding with water to remove it, either from the skin or from any other surface. Hydrofluoric acid will attack glazed sinks unless it is copiously diluted and washed away with running water.

This acid is also used by fakers to remove sparse decoration from old porcelain so that it can be redecorated with more valuable designs.

PINXTON (DERBYSHIRE) PORCELAIN FAC-TORY   This small factory, established in 1796 by William Billingsley, was built on the estate of John Coke. The porcelain is somewhat similar to that of Derby, but often of better quality. Much of the decoration was of slight floral sprigs, with some landscape painting which was probably done by John Cutts. Billingsley left in 1804, but the factory was continued by Cutts until 1812.

PLAQUES, PORCELAIN AND POTTERY   Plaques of porcelain, often extremely well painted, were used to ornament furniture, clocks, sedan chairs, and similar objects. The fashion existed from the last half of the 18th century onwards into the 19th. The French factories, in particular, specialized in this kind of work because the ormolu used for decorating furniture could also be made to hold the plaque in place. To a lesser extent the German factories made similar things, and cabinets in the *Biedermeier* style thus decorated can be seen from time to time.

In England the Wedgwood factory made many jasper and basaltes ware plaques of all sizes for the same purpose, but the English porcelain factories did comparatively little work of this kind.

Plaques painted as a *chef d'œuvre* or a test-piece are often signed and dated.

PLYMOUTH (DEVON) PORCELAIN FACTORY   This factory was founded by a Quaker apothecary, William Cookworthy. The independent invention of hard-paste porcelain in England was the result of many years of experiment by Cookworthy, who started to manufacture it on a commercial scale in 1768. He was inexperienced, and found the task of operating a factory too onerous. It was, therefore, transferred to Bristol in 1770 and subsequently taken over under licence by Richard Champion.

The body is extremely hard, but full of such minor defects as fire-cracks. "Smoke-staining" was common, and bowls, cups, and saucers usually show a well-marked spiral "wreathing" in the body. The wares, in fact, have a primitive appearance.

Decoration was often in a blackish-blue, and enamel colours were used on some of the later pieces. Bird painting in enamels of excellent quality has been attributed to M. Soqui, a French painter from Sèvres who also worked at Worcester. Much porcelain was left undecorated. Figures often closely resemble those made at Bow and Longton Hall, and it seems certain that moulds from both these factories were, in some way, acquired by Cookworthy. Mr. Tebo, a Bow modeller, worked for him.

Plymouth porcelain is scarce, and prices are usually high.

PORCELAIN, HARD, MANUFACTURE OF Chinese porcelain of the Ming Dynasty [1368–1644] and later is made from *kaolin* (china clay) and a fusible feldspathic rock known as *petuntse*. The rock was ground to powder and mixed with the clay to form the body. It was also applied in powder form to the surface to form the glaze. The *petuntse* vitrified in the kiln, the more refractory clay helping the object to retain its shape.

The Chinese secret was not discovered until the first decade of the 18th century at Meissen in Saxony, the discovery being due to the researches of Ehrenfried Walther von Tschirnhausen. About twelve years later another factory was started with a similar formula at Vienna, and by mid-century, or slightly afterwards, the factories of Nymphenburg, Höchst, Frankenthal, Berlin, Fürstenberg, Ludwigsburg, Ansbach, Kelsterbach, and Fulda were all in production. The formula was adopted at Sèvres about 1770, and was subsequently extensively used in Paris and elsewhere. A factory was established in England at Plymouth in 1768 which was subsequently transferred to Bristol (*see* above). A small quantity was also made at Newhall in Staffordshire.

Hard porcelain has been the preferred body on the Continent since the 18th century, most of the early soft-paste factories using it only because they were unable to acquire the hard-paste formula. It has, however, met with little success in England, and since the early part of the 19th century the standard body has been the so-called bone china, which is the hard-paste body modified by the addition of bone-ash. Bone china is a hybrid which has few of the charms of soft porcelain, and still fewer of the advantages of hard. It has, however, achieved considerable commercial success as a suitable material for table-services, and as such it is exported in immense quantities to North America, as well as being the standard material on the home market. It is not manufactured on the Continent, where the hard porcelain body is now universal.

PORCELAIN, SOFT, DISTRIBUTION OF MANU-FACTURE   The first soft (or artificial) porcelain was made in Florence at the end of the 16th century, and is referred to as Medici porcelain. Surviving specimens are very few in number, and are extremely highly valued, as much as £1,200 having been paid for a plate.

In 1664 there is a record of an attempt to establish a soft porcelain factory in Paris, but no specimens survive. Porcelain was made at a factory at Rouen during the last quarter of the 17th century. The first production in quantity, however, was at St. Cloud, and the factory appears to have been well established by 1700. This was followed by Chantilly (about 1725), Mennecy (about 1748), and Vincennes (effectively about 1745) transferred to Sèvres (1756). The manufacture of hard-paste porcelain was started about 1770, and soon became the standard French body.

Soft porcelain was manufactured in Italy. The principal factories are: Nove (Venice), 1728; Doccia (Florence), 1735; Capo-di-Monte (Naples), 1743. The latter factory was transferred to Buen Retiro in Spain about 1760.

Basically, the bodies used at all these factories were similar, and it was in England that substantial variations on this formula were first introduced.

The porcelain of Chantilly and St. Cloud was at first imitated by Chelsea and Derby, and the Longton Hall formula was substantially the same throughout its life. The knowledge appears to have been brought by migratory workmen from France. The modification of this formula by the addition of bone-ash was introduced at Bow in 1749, adopted by Chelsea about 1755, Lowestoft about 1757, and Derby in 1770. It subsequently became even more widely used, and its manu-facture did not entirely cease until 1820.

A group of factories making a porcelain compounded of

china clay and soaprock forms a separate and important group. This formula, much closer to hard porcelain than any other, was first used at Bristol about 1748, Worcester in 1752, Liverpool in 1756, and Caughley in 1772. It was finally discontinued at Worcester about 1830.

PORCELAIN, SOFT, FORMULAE Imported Chinese porcelain had a particular quality which caused it to be highly valued – that of translucency. Without some kind of coherent body of chemical knowledge, however, it was impossible for European potters of the 16th and 17th centuries to analyse this porcelain to find out why it was translucent, and they were compelled to proceed by analogy. The most common translucent substance known to them was glass, but glass cannot be formed in any of the ways used by the potter. The transition from a solid to a syrupy liquid is fairly abrupt, and it cannot be worked or modelled except at a comparatively high temperature, whereas the potter is accustomed to modelling plastic clay.

The expedient of grinding the glass to powder and mixing it with clay was therefore tried. Clay is refractory and melts only under the most intense heat, and this method enabled a translucent body superficially resembling Chinese porcelain to be made.

The origin of these experimental attempts to imitate Chinese porcelain is unknown, but during the 16th century Persian potters appear to have experimented with clay mixed with glaze material which yielded a slightly translucent body somewhat resembling a crude soft porcelain, and the Florentine potters may have owed something to their efforts in this direction.

European soft porcelain was at first invariably of clay and ground glass, but the English factories introduced two major modifications around 1750 which were not used outside England. The first was the inclusion of bone-ash, which, to some extent, sacrificed appearance and quality for greater ease of working. The presence of bone-ash can be detected by the PHOSPHATE TEST (*q.v.*). The second was the use of steatite or soaprock instead of glass.

It will be seen that all these bodies have one thing in common with hard porcelain, i.e. clay. The other ingredients are variable.

Although soft porcelain is physically softer than hard, the terms actually refer to the firing, and not the hardness of the body. True porcelain is given a hard firing at a greatly increased temperature. The actual figures are about 1,100 degrees Centigrade for soft porcelain, and 1,450 degrees for hard.

Soft porcelain was finally superseded because of its extremely critical temperature range. Slight increases above the optimum temperature resulted in severe warping and even melting of the body, and decreases led to incomplete vitrification. Both bone-ash and soaprock porcelain gave a slightly greater latitude, but all these bodies were finally discarded because of the large number of kiln "wasters" resulting from their use.

PORCELAIN, SOFT, RECOGNITION OF The ability to differentiate between soft (or artificial) and hard (or true) porcelain is very important to the collector of ceramics. The principal tests which can be applied easily are listed below:

(1) Soft porcelain can be cut with a file. A small file of triangular section is needed, and the angle should be drawn across the unglazed base gently but firmly. Only a small cut is necessary, and if the file can be felt to "bite" instead of sliding over the surface, the test is complete. Deep file cuts are unnecessary, and do not add to the information gained. Often a cut from a previous test will be noticed, which makes repetition superfluous.

(2) Soft porcelains often have air bubbles trapped in the body. Particularly is this the case with plates and dishes. Held to the light, these appear as bright circular patches – the so-called "moons" which are especially frequent in early Chelsea. These are indicative, but not, by themselves, conclusive. They can be seen occasionally in early hard porcelains, particularly Meissen.

(3) Fire-cracks and warping are both fairly common faults. They also appear, but less frequently, in some early hard porcelains. Fire-cracks are not accidental damage, and are only a detraction in the sense that a specimen is more desirable without them. They are not justification for rejecting a specimen as damaged. The term "age-cracks" sometimes applied to them is a misnomer, since porcelain does not

develop cracks with age except from accidental damage. Warping is much more common with soft porcelains.

(4) Much soft porcelain is slightly porous. A little stain or ink touched on an unglazed part is often difficult to remove. On hard porcelain it will wipe off at once. Occasionally under-fired specimens of soft porcelain will absorb ink like blotting-paper, but this is unusual. Dirt on the base of a soft porcelain object is often difficult or impossible to remove. Dirt on hard porcelain will wash off at once.

(5) The body of soft porcelain was fired first and the glaze added afterwards. The body and glaze of hard porcelain was fired in one operation. On the former, therefore, the glaze is thicker, richer, and inclined to run in drops, to pool in hollows, to crack, and to craze. Where it is thickest it is often greenish in colour. It can be seen as a perceptible layer of glass over the body. Hard porcelain glazes are thin and glittering.

(6) The glaze is softest on soft porcelain, and will often show multiple scratches from wear and tear.

(7) Enamel colours usually sink into a soft porcelain glaze at least to some extent. Enamels on hard porcelain will lie on top of the glaze, often palpable to the finger-tips.

(8) Where there is a chip, soft porcelain will exhibit a granular texture akin to fine sugar. Hard porcelain chips like glass.

QUALITY Few words are more controversial than this one. To the buyer of antiques and works of art, however, few words are of greater importance.

Quality has two aspects, aesthetic and monetary. Discussion of the aesthetic aspect is probably the least rewarding and the most controversial. Books have been written on it, a few of which have something sensible to say. In the paragraphs which follow I shall be mainly concerned with quality as it influences monetary value, leaving its aesthetic aspects to those who feel inclined to venture into such uncharted waters.

Purists object to the coupling of works of art with money. I am quite unable to understand their prejudice. Figures mean quite a lot to the knowledgeable.

If someone tells me that a Meissen group by Kändler sold in Sotheby's for £100 I ask, "What was wrong with it?" If, on the other hand, an English delft plate is mentioned as selling for the same price, I comment, "It must have been a fine specimen." The figures, coupled with the nature of the object, have told me a great deal about the quality without ever seeing the things themselves.

Of course, experience is involved in either interpretation. I know that bidders in a saleroom such as Sotheby's are shrewd men whose assessment of values is to be trusted, and I know that a fine Kändler group will always make many times £100. On the other hand, knowledge of market values assures me that only an exceptionally good delft dish would make anything like £100. The figures are a convenient shorthand which relieves both parties from the necessity of describing objects in detail.

The dislike of the mention of prices is probably a nostalgic and snobbish relic of the days when people could still buy works of art without thinking of the cost. Today, although the enjoyment remains, it has to be tempered with the desire to make a reasonably safe investment as well. The tax-gatherer has seen to it that no money is left over with which purchases can be made without counting the ultimate cost.

All estimations of quality are relative, and they vary from one individual to another. There can be no estimations in relation to an absolute standard, since this does not exist. Attempts have been made from time to time to fix absolute standards, the art of Greece, for example, being at one time regarded as the highest point of excellence, other things being valued according to the closeness of their approximation to its principles. The art of the Aztecs, or of the bronze-founders of Nigeria, would emerge rather badly from such a comparison.

The fact that there is not, and cannot be, an absolute standard of excellence of this sort means that each work of art has to be judged in relation to other things of the same kind. Of course we must have some fixed points, although these vary from one generation to the next, which accounts for trends of fashion and fluctuations in saleroom prices for particular classes. The problem can be made a little clearer by representing it diagrammatically in the form of a scale. At one end of the scale we put the first of our fixed points – a work which is, by general agreement, the best of its kind. At the other end we put the worst, estimated in the same way. If, for example, early Chelsea porcelain is in question, we might

21 An English
silver-gilt dish with the
arms of George I

22 A dish of painted
enamel on copper with a
ruby back, from Canton,
China. 18th century.

23 A pair of silver
sauceboats by William
Kidney, 1739

24 An octagonal silver
sugar-box and cover.
London, early 18th
century

25 A Queen Anne
silver-gilt monteith, or
wine-glass cooler,
hall-marked London,
1707

put, at one end of the scale, the famous early group of Lovers, and at the other end one of the cruder *putti* of the same period, thus:

The Lovers ____|____|____|____|____ The *putto*
£4,000   £250

We can then mark off the scale and locate other figures at the various points along it according to our estimation of quality. In doing so we consider such factors as modelling, subject, rarity, colour of the paste, technical points such as presence or absence of fire-cracks and warping, and general condition. We are then left with a rough estimate of quality according to location at various points along the scale. This will be fairly accurate for practical purposes, and if we mark in saleroom prices, starting at £4,000 for the Lovers, and going to £250 for the *putto*, we shall find that they agree tolerably well. Of course, as soon as we move on to another kind of antique we shall have to construct another similar scale.

We can take the process a step further and construct a scale of relative values for the work of the various 18th-century factories, taking the work of Chelsea as the highest and Caughley as the lowest, thus:

Chelsea ____|____|____|____|____ Caughley

Somewhere between the two extremes will be located the other factories, based on such criteria as originality of design, general excellence of craftsmanship, rarity, and so forth. If, once again, we fill in an average of saleroom prices we shall find a considerable measure of agreement.

Of course, I do not suggest that one should normally proceed to erect scales of measurement of this kind, but the method does, in the initial stages, help the beginner to make estimations rationally, and will reduce the problem to an orderly process which may not always be strictly accurate when judged by the yard-stick of prices, but it will approximate far more closely than reliance upon such dangerous guides as the presumed possession of a "flair". There is no such thing as a "flair" for quality or anything else. What the observer sees in action is the result of hard toil and sweat in learning as much as possible about the particular kind of object. It is a matter of observation that most people, in trying to estimate quality, employ a great deal of irrational prejudice. As an example, I knew a man who could never see anything good in Japanese art because he had been a Japanese prisoner of war. This is understandable, and a great deal more definite than many of the trivial reasons which lead people to praise or condemn, but it is not a rational way of estimating quality.

The beginner will see, if he tries to construct a few scales of this kind, that it is vitally important to know not only the best but the worst, as well as quite a lot about the things which come between. No estimation made without experience is likely to be worth anything. A man who has seen only one piece of jade in his life cannot tell whether the carving is good or bad. If he has seen two pieces, one will be better than the other. He has started to estimate quality. By the time he has seen, and studied, a hundred pieces of all kinds, his opinion is likely to be sound. When he has studied a thousand he can fairly claim to be an expert.

Generally, and as a very approximate guide, the two principal points are quality of craftsmanship and quality of materials. Good craftsmanship was rarely lavished on poor materials, and the two things will usually be related. To this might be added the advice *Always buy the best you can afford.* The best is the safest investment.

My remarks on VICTORIANA (*q.v.*) on a later page have some bearing on the subject at present under discussion, and it is suggested that the reader turns to them.

RÉCHAUD   *See* VEILLEUSE.

RÉGENCE STYLE, THE   The term refers to the period [1710–1725] of the minority of Louis Quinze. It is not often used, and it cannot be defined with any kind of exactness. The transition from the earlier baroque to the later rococo started about this time in France, and some modifications of the baroque can be noticed. Ornament increased in elaboration, and was less symmetrically disposed.

REGENCY PERIOD, THE   This term in the English decorative arts is applied, more often than not, to a period extending from about 1800 to 1837. This, of course, takes in part of the reign of George III, the Regency, and the reigns of George IV and William IV, finishing with the accession of Victoria.

Strictly, the Regency period should start in 1811, when the Prince of Wales became Regent, and stop in 1820, when he acceded to the throne. It seems best, however, to regard it as a convenient term for the productions of the first quarter of the 19th century.

The style itself is principally a reflection of the Empire style of France which grew out of the earlier neo-classical, and many elements of neo-classicism were retained. Thus we find the use of such motifs as urns and swags continued from the 18th century, as well as the acanthus leaf and things of this kind. Painted panels based on the work of Angelica Kauffmann and others were still sometimes used for furniture, and her work was also copied on to porcelain. The use of lion-paw feet and lion masks on furniture belong to the period, and the earlier dolphin and eagle motifs were repeated. The monopodium, or single leg surmounted by a human or animal head and torso, is peculiarly Regency, and such motifs as winged sphinxes and scarabs testify to the interest in Egyptian art and history which was made fashionable by Napoleon's Egyptian campaign. Caryatids and Greek columns can be seen, and inspiration was drawn from Greek vase painting.

The rare use of Gothic motifs was probably due to the popularity of the Gothic novel, to the work of Augustus Charles Pugin, the father of Augustus Welby Pugin, and the influence of Beckford's Fonthill Abbey. The style can be seen occasionally in such things as long-case clocks, some of which have a lancet-shaped hood.

Furniture inlaid with brass was fairly common, although the use of ormolu mounting never achieved the same popularity in England as in France. About the same time a certain amount of furniture ornamented in the manner of André Charles Boule was made in London in the Edgware Road.

The first sign of the revived rococo style can be seen about 1810, principally in silver, and furniture of this kind was being produced by 1825. The style was much used by the china manufacturers to whom it was probably suggested by a similar revival at some Continental factories. Such things are greatly inferior in design to 18th-century rococo porcelain.

REPAIRS AND RESTORATIONS   Every work of art or craft deteriorates from the moment it is finished, however slow the process may be. Sometimes the process may be speeded by accidental damage, but inevitably the day arrives when the question of repair or restoration has to be considered.

Whether to restore, and by how much, is a vexed question. In my opinion it is legitimate to put an object back, as nearly as possible, into its original condition, *if* this can be done without affecting the remainder. For instance, to put another leg on a chair which has only three is sensible, but to French polish the whole chair to give all the legs the same colour is indefensible. Much better that the restoration be obvious than that invisibility be attained by such means. Likewise, it is legitimate enough to replace the arm of a porcelain figure, but to smother the surface with paint to disguise the extent of the repair, and – worse still – to finish by spraying the glaze with cellulose acetate varnish, is a very dubious practice.

Skilled restorers who do not indulge in these practices are few, and they are getting fewer. They are necessarily men with a very high degree of skill in several associated arts. The best of them can produce restorations which without resorting to questionable practices of any kind are indetectable to the eye.

Such men are worth finding, and if their work is apt to be expensive, it must be remembered that what seems to be a comparatively simple job is often difficult and time-consuming. In fact the jobs which appear the simplest are often the most difficult. A repair amid a mass of complicated ornament easily passes unnoticed.

So far as dirt is concerned, there can be no two opinions. It should be removed if it is safe to do so. But the PATINA (*q.v.*) on bronze, for instance, should not be confused with dirt. Whilst it is an accretion which is the result of time, it is also evidence of age, and it is due to definite changes in the metal. It would, therefore, be impossible in any case, to restore the object to its original condition.

The best way of finding a restorer is by recommendation. It would be risky to give important work to someone unknown and untried, and amateurs with a taste for craft-work are inclined to set up in business as repairers, particularly as china-repairers.

Dealers can usually arrange for work to be done by some-one of standing, or can make recommendations.

RHODIAN WARE   *See* CERAMICS – TURKISH POTTERY.

ROCKINGHAM (YORKS) PORCELAIN FAC-TORY   A 19th-century porcelain factory situated on the estate of Earl Fitzwilliam was started in 1807 and closed in 1840. It manufactured a good quality bone-porcelain, and was responsible for many of the early 19th-century tea and dessert services in the revived rococo style. Some good ground colours were used, and landscape painting was of excellent quality.

ROCOCO STYLE, THE   The origin of the rococo style is often awarded to a Paris architect, goldsmith, and *orne-maniste*, Juste-Aurèle Meissonier. His work became extremely popular, and the characteristic scroll-work of the style was largely designed by him.

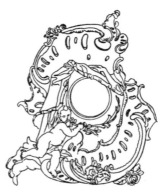

A porcelain watch-holder showing the characteristic asymmetrical scroll-work of the rococo style which can also be well seen in such things as mirror frames, *c.* 1755

The influences which helped to form the style were many. Undoubtedly some part was played by the popularity of Oriental arts and crafts, and their effect on the prevailing baroque. Water was also a common theme in the early days of rococo, and shells and other marine subjects – rocks, and things of this kind – were frequently used. One of the masterpieces of rococo art, the Swan service, made by the Meissen factory for its director, Count von Brühl, was almost entirely concerned with aquatic motifs.

Rococo crossed the Channel fairly speedily, and the work of Paul de Lamerie in silver is almost entirely in this style. The

English porcelain factories worked in it from the beginning, shortly before mid-century. Whilst nearly all the more important work of Meissen is baroque, the factory at Nymphenburg, near Munich, assisted by the superb modelling of Franz Anton Bustelli, played a part in creating the important Bavarian rococo style.

The tendency of the rococo artist was undoubtedly to subordinate form to ornament, and this can well be seen in some of the German porcelain figures and groups of the period. In porcelain the characteristics of the style are the scrolls and flourishes added to the bases of figures, and the asymmetrical scroll ornament surrounding decorative painting. In furniture these points are not so apparent in many things, but can be especially well seen in mirror-frames. The asymmetricality of the ornament is an important feature.

Rococo started about 1725, and gave place to the LOUIS SEIZE STYLE (*q.v.*) shortly before 1760. The latter is at first a modification of the earlier motifs due to the growing popularity of classical art. Rococo finally disappeared about 1774 in France, somewhat earlier in England.

A revival took place during the early years of the 19th century, both in England and on the Continent. This revived rococo, however, was a much debased version of it, and such things are not worth serious attention.

RUGS   *See* CARPETS.

"RUNNER"   The "runner" is a little higher in the social scale than a "knocker". He buys from and sells to dealers, taking a modest profit in so doing. His markets are more certain, and he performs a valuable service in taking things which a dealer finds difficult to sell and placing them where they are wanted. His constant contacts with his customers enables him to know within a little what they can sell, and what they need (*see also* DEALERS and "KNOCKERS").

SAXE, PORCELAINE AU   Just as the English have always miscalled Meissen porcelain "Dresden", the French have always referred to it as "*Saxe*". "*Saxe au point*" refers to *die Punktzeit*, the period during which a dot was used between the hilts of the crossed-swords mark, and *Saxe a l'etoile* to the Marcolini period when a star (or asterisk) was placed in the same position.

SCAGLIOLA Literally, splinters. An imitation marble invented by Guido del Conte of Modena in the early part of the 17th century. Essentially it is a kind of plaster mixed with weak glue, into the surface of which has been embedded the *scaglioli* of marble, granite, spar, and other substances of a like nature. It was used architecturally, and for such purposes as a substitute for marble table-tops.

SCHWARZLOT This kind of decoration on faience, glass, and porcelain is predominantly in black enamel, although touches of iron-red were sometimes used, particularly for flesh tones.

Decoration in this style frequently resembles an engraving, and was probably suggested by the custom of adapting engravings to work in other media. It was first used for painting on glass, and its application to faience was due to Johann Schaper in the middle of the 17th century. It became popular, and it was used on porcelain during the early part of the 18th century, particularly at Vienna, where the best work was done by Jakob Helchis, and by the Augsburg *Hausmaler*. It was also used at Meissen during the early period.

Similar work was done in China during the 18th century for export and is usually termed "Jesuit" porcelain.

SGRAFFITO Literally "scratched" decoration. The term is usually applied to pottery which has been washed over with slip through which the decoration has been incised to show the body colour beneath, but other kinds of *sgraffiti* exist. The term is sometimes applied facetiously to untutored scratching on lavatory walls, and similar *sgraffiti* are to be found in the ruins of Pompeii, proving that the habit is of considerable antiquity.

SHEFFIELD PLATE This substitute for silver has always been of great interest to collectors. In 1743 Thomas Bolsover of Sheffield discovered a process whereby two flat pieces of silver could be soldered on to either side of a much thicker piece of copper, the bar then being passed between heavy steel rollers and flattened into a sheet. The copper, therefore, is the filling in the sandwich, with a sheet of silver foil on either side. The thickness of this sheet varies between $\frac{1}{16}$ and $\frac{1}{32}$ inch, and it was at first shaped by methods appropriate to the silversmith.

Sheffield plate does not bear the standard silver-mark because it is not silver. Very close approximations to it were later devised, and these can be deceptive at a glance. The remedy is to examine them carefully. Before 1784 only workmen's marks were applied, but by an Act passed in this year manufacturers were allowed to use marks, provided these were registered with the Assay Office. Marking, however, was not compulsory. The marks were often put in inconspicuous places.

If the nature of the material is in doubt the simplest way of making certain is to look at the foot-ring of the article or any sheared edge which can be observed. If the object is Sheffield plate this will be fairly obvious under a magnifying glass, not only from the brownish gleam of copper between the two sheets of silver, but from the foil-like nature of the silver itself. Electro-plating, introduced about 1840, has a different appearance, the silver being deposited particle by particle and becoming much more an integral part of the base metal.

At most appropriate places fairly successful attempts were made to disguise the presence of copper, sometimes by adding ornament in silver. Even on the foot-ring itself efforts were made occasionally to disguise the sheared edge with silver wire, for the manufacture of which a machine was patented in 1779.

Wear and cleaning succeeds ultimately in getting through the silver to the copper beneath. Such pieces are sometimes restored by electro-plating, which can usually be recognized by a spurious brightness of the surface. Silver used for the manufacture of Sheffield plate was alloyed with brass, and is therefore of a slightly darker colour than ordinary silver. Additionally, an examination of the foot-ring will reveal that the tell-tale sheared edge has been covered with deposits of silver. A little experience, together with a knowledge of the processes used, will render the various differences fairly obvious, although a good magnifying glass is usually an indispensable aid to examination.

Sheffield plate had more or less ceased to be made by about

1850, its place being taken by electro-plating on copper and other alloys. Most such plating was done on nickel-silver, hence the "EPNS" common on much plated ware – electro-plate on nickel silver. The process was introduced by Elkingtons of Birmingham in 1840.

Most of the oldest specimens of Sheffield plate were made by methods appropriate to the silversmith, coffee-pots, for instance, being cut out of the flat plate with shears, and the seams hammered. Modern wares in imitation of it are often spun, without seams. Unless an old piece has been subsequently electro-plated, it is usually possible to detect seams on close examination if they are present at all, although they are usually inconspicuous.

It was not, of course, possible to cast Sheffield plate, since the nature of the material precluded this method of working, and any cast ornament present must either be of silver or of some base metal resembling it, and silver was quite commonly used for additional cast ornament to the best Sheffield plate. What at first sight appears to be engraved work is usually flat chasing, or an indented pattern done with punches and a hammer. The work is inferior to engraving. True engraving was sometimes done on a plaque of silver let into the plate for this special purpose.

The first use for the new plate by Thomas Bolsover was for the manufacture of buttons, but Matthew Boulton established a factory in Soho, Birmingham, in 1762 and produced many articles usually made of silver. The process was further industrialized by the invention of machines for stamping out ornament during the 1760s, and the quantity manufactured increased rapidly. Shapes often tend to be simpler than those of silver because simple shapes were more easily adapted to machine production. The new plate was also much in demand among people who could not afford silver. Almost all varieties of 18th-century silver were copied in Sheffield plate, most of it in the neo-classical and Empire styles (*q.v.*).

SHIBAYAMA-WORK Dōshō Shibayama was a Japanese ivory-carver of the early part of the 19th century. He added decoration in mother-of-pearl, coral, metal-work, and other substances to his carvings, and the generic name of Shibayama-work has been given to things of this kind. His own work was of excellent quality, although sometimes decorated to excess. Imitations are the most commonly seen.

Work of this kind was used to decorate furniture and specimens of good quality are comparatively uncommon in England, although rather less so in France.

SILVER AND GOLD Objects of silver and gold were highly valued by the Romans, much of the finer work being by Greek craftsmen. Like most things of the kind, however, this work has long since found its way to the melting-pot, and the few objects which remain have, for the most part, been excavated.

Drinking vessels of one kind or another are probably the most frequent survivals, but such things as silver mounts for furniture and chariots, horse-trappings, small votive objects, and statues have also been recovered.

The decay in the art of fine metal-working began in Rome during the 3rd century A.D., when much plate was melted during the unrest of the period.

Some important Byzantine gold and silver work is in existence, dating from the 4th to about 11th century A.D. The Emperor Arcadius had a massive gold throne and a chariot of the same metal in the 5th century, whilst silver furniture decorated the houses of the nobility and the wealthy. Apart from the addition of precious stones, Byzantine craftsmen used *niello* – a black composition used to fill engraved lines – which was later employed fairly commonly in Russia. ENAMEL (*q.v.*) was also applied to gold and silver work.

From the 11th century onwards many churches were decorated with fine metal-work of all kinds, and even such things as altar-fronts were sometimes made of gold. Secular craftsmen took the place of the monks during the 13th century, and were patronized by princes and the nobility. Such work reached its height with Benvenuto Cellini, who, in 1545, became goldsmith to Cosimo de Medici, and who wrote a treatise on the art of the goldsmith. Very little can now be traced to his hand with any kind of certainty.

Much interest has always centred on the work of the goldsmiths and silversmiths of Augsburg and Nuremberg, who were, at first, much influenced by those of Italy. The names of many of the finest craftsmen are known. The father of Albrecht Dürer was a goldsmith from Hungary who came to Nuremberg in 1502. Although the best work was done in the 16th century, the work of both these centres continued to be important during the 17th century, and fine specimens are always sought after. The famous silver furniture of Louis Quatorze was melted in the 1680s.

At the end of the 17th century and during the first quarter of the 18th, much excellent work was done at Dresden, encouraged by the Elector Augustus the Strong, who had a notable collection of gold and silver in the baroque style, much of it executed by the Court goldsmith, Johann Melchior Dinglinger.

The neo-classical style in silver is probably to be seen at its best in France during the reign of Louis XVI, and French goldsmiths, particularly Juste-Aurèle Meissonier, were largely responsible for creating the rococo style, although Paris silver of this period was largely melted in the 1750s.

Much Continental silver of all kinds was melted down during the Seven Years War, and again during the French Revolution, when, in particular, an enormous quantity of ecclesiastical plate was sent to the Mint. The armies of Napoleon were also responsible for looting the Treasuries of a number of Continental countries. Spain, in particular, suffered in this way, objects of gold and silver being broken into pieces by the troops for easy transport to the French Mint.

SILVER, ENGLISH It would be unprofitable in a book of this kind to devote a great deal of space to silver made before the Restoration. During the Civil War much plate was melted down for purposes of coinage, and specimens are therefore rare. Those which escaped this fate are mostly fine pieces which, even then, were thought too important to destroy. Belonging to this category are some important Hanaps, or standing drinking cups, and these are very rare and valuable. The conversion of plate into coinage was by no means unusual, much the same thing happening in France during the early years of the 18th century, and the intrinsic value of the metal is one of the reasons why more old silver has not survived.

Of surviving examples of pre-Restoration workmanship, drinking cups are by far the more common. The earliest were bowls made of wood, termed "mazers", but wood was not particularly suitable for making drinking vessels, and no doubt those of silver were kept when the rest of the family plate went to the Mint. Another thing to survive, although very rarely in sets, is the apostle spoon. These were made as christening presents, and were either thought too small to be worth melting or were held back because of some kind of sentimental attachment. A complete set contains thirteen spoons, including one representing Christ, and the handle of each is surmounted by a figure. They can be identified from their attributes. Spoons with the figure of a saint as a finial are often miscalled apostle spoons, regardless of the figure represented.

Spoons appeal to many collectors, and there is a great variety from which to choose. The Commonwealth spoon has a stem of rectangular section ending without ornament. The style was probably copied from France. These were followed by spoons which had a rounded end notched into three lobes, known as trifid handles. Many spoons have a pointed continuation of the stem on the back of the bowl to act as reinforcement which is called a rat-tail. These apart, there was a wide variety of spoons for all purposes – caddy spoons, mustard spoons, strainer spoons, marrow spoons, and so forth. The Georgian strainer spoon had a pierced bowl and a long, slim, pointed stem for clearing teapot spouts. Punch ladles are an extension of the spoon, having a deep bowl, with a long handle made of wood or whalebone. Some have a coin let in to the bottom. The fork was not common until after the Restoration, and it is a fairly rare item until the 18th century.

Salts have always been important items of table furniture, and often much skill was lavished on them. The large standing salt used until the Restoration is particularly handsome. Those made afterwards are usually smaller, being low and plain in form, whilst the small bowl-shaped salt on three feet became more or less the rule by the reign of George II, both in silver and later in a version made from enamel on copper from Staffordshire. Blue glass liners were introduced about 1770, and pierced designs through which the glass could be seen became popular at the same time.

Early sugar-casters are a desirable item. These were introduced about 1690, and the tops show a variety of elegant piercings.

Richly decorated silver work was done during the reign of Charles II, and such objects as toilet-services, and even furniture covered with wrought silver, can be seen. Examples of fine quality are at Knole, in Kent. Such large pieces as wine-cisterns and fountains were made at the same time and later, an example of the reign of George II being reputed to hold sixty gallons. Its weight was 8,000 ounces.

Punch-bowls came into use for brewing and serving punch. The "Monteith" had a scalloped edge shaped to fit the foot of punch glasses, and was used to cool the glasses. The punch ladle already mentioned was used to serve it. Even inns during the reign of William and Mary used silver tankards, and the demand for silver became such that it was profitable to melt down coinage for the metal. To prevent this the Britannia standard of 11 ounces 10 pennyweights of silver in the pound troy was introduced in 1697. This appears to have had the desired effect by 1720, since it was discontinued in that year, although it has occasionally been employed since.

Tea-equipages came into use with the increasing popularity of the new beverage. A few cups were made of silver (handle-less, like the china tea-bowls of the time), but they were impractical and too hot to hold. They were therefore soon discontinued. From this time onwards the English may be said to have had a Tea Ceremony of their own almost rivalling in its conventions that of the Japanese.

The earliest teapots were made soon after the Restoration, becoming reminiscent of the stoneware pots of Yi-Hsing in form. They were not frequently made until the beginning of the 18th century, when a particularly elegant pear-shaped body makes its appearance. This had no added ornament. Plain globular pots followed, but by 1735 embossed designs were being used, the embossing becoming more definitely rococo in style until the ADAM STYLE (*q.v.*) came into favour. The neo-classical period shows considerable divergence from the earlier designs, an oval body with a straight spout being perhaps the most common form. Decoration was at this time usually engraved and chased.

The tea-service was provided with a cream jug and a sugar-basin. The early cream jugs were pear-shaped, without feet, but jugs on three small feet were introduced soon afterwards. The neo-classical period favoured the helmet shape, which is, perhaps, the commonest survival.

With the rise of porcelain to favour after the 1750s tea-services of silver began to go out of fashion, although they were still regarded as necessary for special occasions.

Tea-caddies are an interesting adjunct to the rest of the tea-service. A typical Queen Anne caddy is rectangular in shape, usually holding about $\frac{1}{4}$ pound of tea. They were made in sets of two or three to hold different blends, and cases with locks were provided for them. The cases were made of wood, sometimes covered with tortoiseshell or shagreen, and quite often a space was provided for a bowl for blending. Such cases, when they have the original fittings, are sometimes highly valued. Vase-shaped caddies, oval or rectangular in section, became popular in the 1740s, and were ornamented in the rococo style. Those made during the neo-classical period have characteristic shapes and ornament.

Tea-urns or kettles were popular from the middle of the 18th century onwards. Like the samovar, they had a tap from which the tea could be drawn, as well as a stand and a spirit lamp to keep the contents hot.

Coffee-pots were sometimes made *en suite* with the tea-service. They first appear towards the end of the 17th century. The earliest specimens are in the shape of a truncated cone, with a conical lid and a straight spout. It followed much the same style in decoration as the teapot.

During the early period the handles of teapots, coffee-pots and chocolate-pots can sometimes be found at a right-angle to the spout instead of opposite to it. The chocolate-pot had a small aperture in the lid through which the contents could be stirred, otherwise they are difficult to distinguish from coffee-pots. The position of the handle is of no particular importance in distinguishing the purpose for which a vessel was made.

Salvers, waiters, and trays are not uncommon. The early examples had a high central foot, whilst those made later often had three or four small feet under the rim. Moulded and gadrooned borders were used during the Queen Anne period, whilst trays of mid-18th century had borders similar to those carved in wood on Chippendale tables and trays. Ornament, when present, is chasing and engraving, with, usually, a cast border. Armorial bearings are frequent.

Cake, bread, and sweetmeat baskets are elegantly pierced, or made with silver wire. They were in favour from about 1750 onwards, and have a swing handle. Coasters (decanter stands) were made with similar pierced work, and vine-leaf ornament was frequently added. These were originally in sets of eight.

Sauceboats were in fairly common use after about 1720. Early specimens had a spout at either end and two central handles – a type which was made in Worcester porcelain during the early period. A pouring lip at one end and a handle at the other came into use about the middle of the 18th century.

The complete dinner-service in silver was, of course, only for the wealthy, and it did not become widely fashionable until the 18th century. Such services did not long survive the introduction of porcelain and cream-ware for everyday use, and soon were relegated to those state occasions when people were prepared to eat uncomfortably in the interests of display. Plates are not now so much in demand as large dishes. Soup and other tureens are large and imposing pieces of silver, usually of great weight and consequently fairly expensive. They vary considerably in shape and decoration and follow the prevailing fashion in design. The sauceboat later became the sauce-tureen, from which the sauce was ladled instead of poured. The change was probably due to the fact that the sauceboat could not easily be adapted to the neo-classical style.

Épergnes, or centre-pieces, are now very rare and extremely valuable. They are exceedingly large and solid, and were equipped with receptacles of all kinds, later examples providing places on which to hang pierced baskets. They have their counterparts in porcelain in the elaborate centre-pieces made at Meissen and elsewhere.

Drinking vessels of one kind or another are always popular among collectors. Porringers (so-called) and caudle-cups are very scarce and expensive. The porringer was a cup with handles on either side in use during the latter part of the 17th century. It is frequently decorated with embossed and chased ornament, usually floral and foliate, and very occasionally with an early type of *chinoiserie*.

Caudle-cups, or posset-cups, were made to contain caudle (a sweet gruel made with spiced wine or ale) or posset (a mixture of hot spiced milk and wine or ale).

Before the manufacture of wine-glasses became common,

silver wine-cups were used. Wine-coolers were introduced during the Restoration, and are usually massive. Of later wine-coolers, those by Paul Storr are often handsomely decorated, but inclined to be ornate. A number of small accessories associated with wine- and punch-drinking include the wine-funnel and the lemon-strainer, as well as wine-tasters. An item frequently collected is the wine-label, of which specimens are to be seen in silver, in enamel, and in Sheffield plate. These small articles vary in shape, and were engraved with the name of the wine or spirit and hung round the neck of the decanter. Examples before the reign of George III are rare.

Tankards for drinking ale replaced the earlier jugs of Rhineland stoneware in the 17th century. The earliest are usually plain, or with slight decoration, and are straight-sided in the form of a slightly tapering cylinder. The flat cover is provided with a thumb-grip for opening. "Peg" tankards were used for communal drinking, the pegs measuring the amount of ale to be consumed by each of the drinkers. This is the origin of the expression "to take down a peg". The tankard of baluster form appeared shortly before mid-18th century, and was provided with a domed cover. The straight-sided tankard also remained in use.

Ink-stands were known as *standishes*, whether in silver or porcelain, and the expression is still sometimes used. Apart from receptacles for ink, pens, and so forth, they had also a pounce-pot with a sprinkler top for the sand used to absorb the wet ink before the invention of blotting-paper.

Candlesticks exist in considerable diversity of form. The early form of candlestick – the pricket – had a spike on which the candle was impaled, but these were more often of wrought iron than silver. Most of them are either table-candlesticks, or chamber candlesticks which have a handle for carrying. Wall-sconces in silver are very rare. Candlesticks first became popular towards the end of the 17th century, although the rushlight still persisted among the poorer classes well into the 18th century. Multi-branched candelabra are also comparatively rare, and, particularly when in pairs or sets, are highly valued. Fluted columns, and similar forms, became popular during the neo-classical period, and they were occasionally provided with an extension which carried several nozzles on branches. Candle-snuffers, which also provided the means for cutting the wick, had trays which are now often missing, or are to be found separately.

The potato-ring came into use in Ireland about mid-century. The hall-marks are not infrequently defective. The manner of use is debatable, but they are often extremely well decorated.

The form of ornament most popular after the Restoration was embossing. Chasing and engraving were also employed. The motifs were floral and foliate, with animals and birds in addition. The work was ornate and elaborate, and Dutch influence predominated. Perhaps to the same source may be traced the *chinoiseries* derived from lacquer, the Dutch being extensively engaged in the Far Eastern trade. Armorial bearings are not uncommon.

These styles gradually fell into disuse, and plain silver, which had been a little unfashionable during the second half of the 17th century, became the vogue. From the reign of Queen Anne, the Huguenot silversmiths in particular produced much plain silver which is exceptionally fine in quality, and by the reign of George I this was the rule. The plain surface lent itself to engraving, armorial bearings, and such things, being well executed, and surrounded by ornamental designs. Flat chasing was also used for border patterns on a considerable number of later specimens, salvers especially.

The styles of this period were gradually modified. At first, work derived from the rather more elaborate RÉGENCE STYLE (*q.v.*) supplemented the fashion for plain silver, and, under the influence of Paul de Lamerie and others, this merged into the fashion for rococo. The characteristic scrollwork and asymmetrical ornament of this style appears during the 1740s, and is at its height during the 1750s and the early part of the following decade. Embossing was again used, and *chinoiseries* once more became fashionable, the designs of the engraver, Jean Pillement, being used both for silver and porcelain. Rococo scrollwork was also engraved as a surround for armorial bearings.

The introduction of the neo-classical style can first be noticed during the early years of the 1760s. Greek and Roman shapes were adapted to those of contemporary silver. The usual neo-classical motifs – rams' and lions' heads and floral swags – were freely used, as well as fret borders and classical meanders generally. The Adam brothers designed for the silversmiths of the period, and, at a slightly later date, the work of John Flaxman (who also designed stoneware for Wedgwood) was translated into silver by Paul Storr and others. Storr worked mainly for Rundell, Bridge, and Rundell, who were silversmiths to the Prince-Regent. Their name appears on much fine plate of the time. Generally, the Regency period contains little domestic silver that is noteworthy, whilst practically nothing of merit appears after 1840. Victorian silver is artistically negligible, and unworthy of the attention of the serious collector.

When the hall-mark is clear the dating of silver is comparatively easy, but many hall-marks have been partly obliterated by years of cleaning, and in other quite legitimate ways. When this happens, dating must be done by style of shape and ornament, assisted by the shape of the shield surrounding the original mark if this is still reasonably clear. Small objects, of course, were not always hall-marked, and some received only the single mark recording the Assay Office.

Many objects of silver, tankards and salvers especially, were engraved with the arms of the owner, and these can often be identified (*see* HERALDRY). Arms are not necessarily contemporary with manufacture, and it is possible to remove the original engraving and substitute a fresh device. This, of course, is quite legal. Arms, therefore, are sometimes a poor guide to date.

Where fraud is suspected, the position of the mark may assume importance, and divergences from the normal should be questioned.

The following brief list of the more usual positions may be helpful. It must be emphasized that divergencies are not definite evidence of fraud, but indicate that especially careful examination is needed.

SIDE (NEAR TOP)	BOTTOM
Tankards (early)	Tankards (later)
Porringers	Trencher salts
Caudle-cups	Jugs
Coffee-pots	Dishes,
Teapots (rarely)	Punch-bowls
Chocolate-pots	Coffee-pots

SIDE (NEAR TOP)	BOTTOM
Sauceboats	Teapots (usually)
	Chocolate-pots
	Sauceboats
	Saucepans
	Casters
	Tea-caddies

The side mark is more likely to be used on an early piece, the bottom mark on later examples. An instance of this is the coffee-pot, but no definite rule can be laid down. Bottom marks are sometimes in line, but later examples may have them arranged radially. The maker's mark always appears either at the beginning or the end, since this was done by the maker, whereas the other punches were added by the Assay Office. Candlesticks are marked on the side at the bottom. Spoons (early) are marked on bowl and stem. Spoons (from the last decades of the 17th century) are marked on the stem only. Covers to tankards and such things, which do not form an integral part of the piece, are marked separately. This also applies to detachable candle-nozzles.

Pieces which have liberally embossed decoration may have the marks fairly well hidden by such work if it is contemporary. When silver was embossed at a later date, pains were frequently taken to avoid the mark.

Although a good deal of English silver was sent to America during the 18th century, much work of excellent quality was also done in Boston, New York, Philadelphia, and elsewhere. Boston silversmiths were already working during the latter part of the 17th century. Many New York silversmiths were Dutch settlers and their descendants, and the craft was well established by the end of the 17th century. Philadelphia had a number of silversmiths of repute by the middle of the 18th century, and their work was much in demand. The best known American silversmith is Paul Revere.

Drinking-vessels of one kind or another are the most frequent among early American wares, the various kinds of service-ware becoming commoner as the middle of the 18th century is approached. Styles much resemble those of contemporary English silver, although forms are apt to be plainer and simpler, with less elaborate ornament. New York silver shows a considerable amount of Dutch influence. Generally, prices in the U.S.A. are somewhat higher than for comparable examples of English silver, which is much less scarce.

There are no assay marks on American silver; the silversmith added his own mark or device, and during the 19th century marks resembling English hall-marks were applied.

Some terms used in discussing ornament are defined below:

Cast Ornament cast in moulds and affixed with solder. Such things as teapot spouts and handles are often cast.

Chasing See *Embossing.*

Embossing *Repoussé* work. The process of raising ornament in high or low relief with punches and a hammer, usually with a pitch-block as a base. Embossed work is raised from the back, chasing is ornament indented *from the front.*

Engraving The art of drawing on metal by means of an incised line. Much of the work is done by a tool of lozenge section called a *graver* or *burin*. A *scorper* removes metal in depth.

Flat-chasing A type of decoration which somewhat resembles engraving in appearance produced by hammering punches along the surface. The difference is that an engraved line is defined by the removal of metal, whereas a flat chased line is indented.

Stamping Ornament stamped out in a press and affixed with solder. This, of course, is mass-produced work, and relatively unimportant.

SILVER (HALL-MARKS AND VALUES) The assay or hallmarks to be found on silver within the range of most collectors are listed in Appendix IV.

Both silver and gold are comparatively soft metals, and need to be alloyed to give them strength and toughness. Obviously the proportions of added base metal must be controlled, otherwise there would be unlimited opportunities for fraud. At the present time gold is valued in the region £12 per fine ounce;* the value of alloying metals is fractional. An extra ounce of alloy in a piece of gold plate, therefore, would mean an additional profit of £12 to the maker, since

* I.e. un-alloyed.

the value of the metal, as well as that of the workmanship, is taken into account in fixing the price.

To preserve the fixed standards all articles of silver or gold have to be presented, after making and before being offered for sale, to an assay office which determines the proportion of alloying metal. If this falls within the permitted standard a series of punch-marks (known as hall-marks) are put on to the piece which form the buyer's guarantee of quality. If the piece submitted falls below the standard it is broken up before being returned to the person submitting it.

Each assay office has a device by which it can be identified. Birmingham, for instance, uses an anchor, whilst in London this is a leopard's head inside a small shield. The London leopard has varied slightly from time to time. Until 1822 it wore a crown.

The lion *passant* is used on all gold and silver marked in London as a sign that it meets the required standard. The same mark is used at the provincial offices, some exceptions being Edinburgh (the thistle), Glasgow (a lion *rampant*), and Dublin (Hibernia). From 1697 to 1720 a finer silver standard (known as the Britannia standard) was introduced, and the leopard's head and the lion *passant* in London were then replaced by a figure of Britannia and the lion's head *erased*.

From 1784 to 1890 a tax was levied on gold and silver plate, and the payment of this tax was acknowledged by the addition of the head of the reigning sovereign as an extra stamp, making five in all.

The maker's mark appears on silver and gold plate from about 1363. The first marks were some kind of device. The premises of merchants and craftsmen were often given devices and names during medieval times of a kind which now survive only in the naming of inns and public houses. The practice was related to that of HERALDRY (*q.v.*).

At a later date the initials of the goldsmith's name replaced the device, and from 1697 to at least 1720, and in some cases until 1739, the first two letters of the maker's surname were used instead. These marks are listed in the monumental work of Sir Charles Jackson (*English Goldsmiths and Their Marks*), which is an indispensable aide to the serious collector of gold and silver plate. This has now been reprinted in an inexpensive edition (£6 10s. at the time of writing).

The practice of adding a mark to record the date of assay was introduced about the end of the 15th century. For this purpose twenty letters of the alphabet are generally used, omitting j, v, w, x, y, and z, although this is not invariable. As can be seen from Appendix IV, the *form* of the letters is changed at the end of each period, and the shape of the shield containing the letter is also altered. Date-letters are changed on 30th May of each year, and from the combination of the *type* of letter and the *shape* of the shield the year of assay can be discovered. Not infrequently marks on old silver have been worn away to some extent by generations of cleaning, but an examination of the combined marks usually makes it possible to ascertain the date within a little, even when the date-mark itself is not clear.

Troy weight is used in weighing gold and silver. The troy ounce is equivalent to 31·1035 grammes, and is slightly heavier than the ounce avoirdupois. There are 12 ounces to the troy pound.

The cost of articles of old silver must always be at least the current value of the metal used to make them. In selling scrap silver and gold some allowance must be made for brokerage, and the dealer will not offer full market value of the metal. He must also make some allowance for the alloy in calculating value. Thus, for every pound of silver scrap by weight, there will, at most, be only 11 ounces 2 pennyweights of silver which is recoverable.

In valuing other kinds of silver the current price for the metal can be taken as a basis, and to this is added a varying amount per ounce for such intangibles as quality of workmanship, rarity, condition, and so forth. Age does not add much, if anything, by itself; a piece of 17th-century silver which is in very bad condition, and fit only for scrap metal, will only be worth scrap price. The status of the maker is important. Prices for well-known makers of high repute are usually considerably higher than for those makers less well known. Two examples of this may be found in Paul de Lamerie and Paul Storr. Other factors are occasionally present. The silver of Nicholas Sprimont is highly valued, partly for his connection with the Chelsea porcelain factory. Fashion, too, plays a part, and not infrequently results in higher prices. This may be a fashion for a particular period or type of silver, such as the plain silver of Queen Anne, or the popularity of a certain maker. An example may be sought in the values attached to the work of the woman silversmith, Hester Bateman, in the United States, although her work is not noticeably better than some of her contemporaries.

Later additions usually reduce the price catastrophically. Plain silver of the period of William and Mary or Queen Anne which is usually valued highly fetches little or nothing above the price of Victorian silver if the embossed rococo decoration of the 1840s has been added subsequently.

Purchase-tax, although it is not levied on old silver, affects the price to some extent, particularly in the case of the less important things. Quite obviously, if it is impossible to buy modern silver under a figure which represents the cost of the metal, plus workmanship, *plus tax*, then the price of comparable antique examples will also be increased in ratio.

Auction-sale catalogues often give the weight of the article being offered. The weight, of course, cannot be given unless the article is entirely of silver. Such things as candlesticks are frequently loaded in the base to safeguard them from being knocked over, and the weight of silver then has to be estimated by the purchaser. At one time it was customary for the bidding at auction to be *per ounce*.

The serious collector needs a spring balance with which silver can be weighed, although dealers in old silver will give the weight as a matter of course.

SILVER (REPAIRS AND ALTERATIONS TO) The following remarks apply also to articles of gold. It is necessary for both collectors and dealers to be very cautious when repairs or alterations to articles made of silver are in question. These are subject to several Acts of Parliament. The most important are the Plate (Offences) Act, 1738, The Silver Plate Act, 1790, The Gold Plate (Standard) Act, 1798, The Gold and Silver Wares Act, 1844, Gold and Silver Wares Act, 1854, Hall-marking of Foreign Plate Act, 1904, The Forgery Act, 1913, and the Hall-marking of Foreign Plate Act, 1939, as well as numerous references to silver and gold plate in more general Acts and several Orders in Council. Both gold and silver plate, unlike most other things, have an intrinsic value which is apart from the workmanship, and damaged silver and gold articles which are beyond repair can be sold for their value as metal. This value varies somewhat from time to time according to circumstances, but in these inflationary days it is far more stable than that of currency and increases with the devaluation of money. At present bullion prices are being held at an artificially low level. Both silver and gold are important, therefore, and need special protection. This protection is conferred by the system of hall-marking [*see* SILVER (HALL-MARKS AND VALUES)] and by precautions which are taken to discover and suppress spurious examples.

The position may be summarized briefly as follows:

It is illegal to add metal to wares previously marked, either with the intention of increasing the weight or altering their character, unless the modified object is submitted to the Assay Office for the addition to be hall-marked. In some circumstances the piece will be marked as new ware. The permission of the Goldsmiths' Company must be sought before alterations or additions are made, and the standard of silver must be equivalent to that of the original object. Similar permission must be sought before later additions are removed, especially if they have been marked.

Hall-marks may not be deliberately obliterated, counterfeited, altered, or transposed. (The latter refers to the occasional practice of removing a mark bodily from an unimportant piece and adding it to something of apparently greater importance, usually a modern forgery.) If a person possesses such a piece knowingly, and without reporting it to the Goldsmiths' Company, it is a felony punishable by up to fourteen years' penal servitude. If he attempts to sell it, then he is guilty of the crime of "uttering", and the penalty is the same. Nevertheless, in case my readers feel that it is too dangerous to possess silver, it is a relief to remember that the operative word is "knowingly", and there is no likelihood of anyone who has been deceived into buying a piece which has been tampered with spending an appreciable part of his life in jail. He is, however, required, upon discovery of the tampering, to co-operate with the authorities in trying to trace the person responsible.

It is as well to remember, however, that if the collector wants to have something altered or restored, and the work necessitates the addition of an appreciable quantity of new metal, then an inquiry at the Goldsmiths' Hall will relieve him of both responsibility and anxiety.

It is not an offence to decorate plain silver, provided no metal is added. Hence the 18th-century silver in circulation which has been decorated in the 19th century with Victorian *repoussé* ornament in a bastard rococo style. Equally, it is not an offence to remove decoration, provided no substantial amount of metal is taken away. Therefore, there is nothing illegal about removing an inscription. Repairs, likewise, are not illegal, and if done by an expert are sometimes difficult to detect. To alter the character of a piece – to make a mustard-pot out of a small mug, for instance – is always illegal.

The detection of such alterations is not always easy. Breathing on the polished surface causes it to mist over, and the difference between the original surface and the part which has been altered often shows up plainly. Soldered joints are usually quite easy to see. Sulphur vapour is even more effective. Examination of the metal with the thumb and finger, or, in the case of a tray, by depressing with the thumb, often reveals thin places, and this is usually a sign of a removed inscription. Discoloration of the surface is sometimes the result of the application of heat which is essential to carry out most repairs.

Electro-plating is sometimes used to disguise repairs, and the difference between this and the surface appearance of old silver is obvious. It has a spurious brightness and evenness which it is difficult to pass. Gilding is sometimes used for the same purpose, the articles being sold as silver-gilt.

Repoussé work is sometimes hammered out to restore the original plain form, but the result is disastrous to the shape.

The Worshipful Company of Goldsmiths, whose address is the Goldsmiths' Hall, Foster Lane, London, E.C.2, are always ready to advise both dealers and private persons on questions relating to gold and silver objects in their possession.

If a ware of a fineness below the permitted standard is submitted to them it is broken up, and the value of the metal returned to the owner. For gold, the standard is 9, 14, 18, or 22 carats of pure gold in every pound troy [*see* TROY WEIGHT under SILVER (HALL-MARKS AND VALUES)]. For silver, the standard is 11 ounces 2 pennyweights or 11 ounces 10 pennyweights in every pound troy. The latter is the Britannia standard introduced in 1697.

218 The Antique Collector's Handbook

If ware is submitted which does not conform to the hall-marking laws the Wardens will, if possible, recommend ways of bringing it within the law. These a dealer must accept. A private owner need not do so, but he will then be cautioned not to sell the piece in question. If marks are spurious they will be obliterated and the piece remarked. Questions will also be asked about its origin. Unmarked ware must either be marked with the year of assay or remain in private ownership.

Foreign plate which is more than 100 years' old is exempt from assay or marking, and certain types of Oriental ware, which may be sub-standard, are also exempt, particularly if they are inlaid with metal other than gold or silver.

Information on specific points should always be sought from the Goldsmiths' Company, who are the final arbiters in cases of doubt. Dealers who are members of the British Antique Dealers' Association may apply to the Secretary for information.

SLIP AND SLIP-WARES Slip is clay diluted to the consistency of cream. It can be either white or coloured.

It is sometimes used as a wash to rectify faults of body colour. Designs are incised through a contrasting slip into the body beneath (*see* SGRAFFITO ware), and it can be dotted and "trailed" like icing on a cake with very similar tools to those used by the cook (e.g. English slip-ware).

White slip can occasionally be confused with tin-enamel when a lead glaze has been subsequently added.

STONEWARE Stoneware is a ceramic substance midway between soft earthenware and porcelain. It is fired at a temperature high enough to vitrify it to some degree, but not, except in rare instances, to the point of translucency.

In China it preceded the discovery of porcelain, and most of the classic glazes of the Sung Dynasty cover bodies which are by strict definition, stoneware and not porcelain. Later, the Chinese manufactured porcelain almost exclusively, but a few stonewares, such as those of Yi-Hsing, were still made and often exported to Europe.

The stoneware of the Rhineland forms an important group of wares, and the later red stoneware of J. F. Böttger at Meissen in the first place imitated that of Yi-Hsing.

Much European stoneware was glazed with salt. A shovel-ful of salt was thrown into the kiln during firing. The heat split it into its component sodium and chlorine, the former combining with the silica in the body to form a thin glaze the surface of which is slightly pitted like the skin of an orange. Occasionally a little red lead was added to the salt, which increased the thickness and brilliance of the glaze and elimi-nated the pitting. Stone-china, manufactured by Miles Mason and others during the early part of the 19th century in Stafford-shire, is a type of stoneware. Stoneware is now used principally for articles of utility, but the salt-glazed work of Dwight and others during the 17th and 18th centuries is particularly important.

STYLE IN WORKS OF ART   "Style" is a word much used in discussing problems of attribution, but it is extremely difficult to define adequately. Every period has its own idiom, and most works of art not only bear the impress of the per-sonality of the man who made them but of the period in which he lived.

The expert in the attribution of pictures quite often works with the aid of such things as an extensive collection of photographs of detail, since most artists have a typical way of handling certain small points. Even such small details as brush-marks are peculiar to the individual painter. There are also other idiosyncrasies, such as the hands in portraits by Lely, which are highly characteristic.

Paintings, however, bear the very personal stamp of their creator, and such points rarely assist us to any extent in evaluating such things as pottery, silver, and furniture. Nevertheless, there are still many factors which can be used for this purpose.

Perhaps the easiest example is the 19th-century copy. During most of the 19th century a repellently sentimental approach can be noticed in many European works of art and craft which are genuinely of the period, and the imitator of earlier things found it difficult to keep this out of his reproduc-tions. Forgeries of Italian *maiolica*, particularly portraits of women, often have this quality in the drawing which is entirely missing from Renaissance works. Another example, not difficult to see, is to be found in the 20th-century copies of the Victorian pottery figures known as "flatbacks". These are reproduced today, and are often cast in the old moulds, but the painting of the faces is invariably 20th century in style, as a comparison with a Victorian original will show at once.

In its application to forgeries the question of the idiosyncratic style of the artist can well be seen in the forgeries of van Meegeren if they are examined side by side with his normal work. The face of *Christ at Emmaus*, the best known of his forgeries, is precisely the same in construction as that of a woman which appears in a genuine example of his normal work, and the same face is not uncommon in other works by his hand. To this extent, therefore, this particular facial structure can be regarded as characteristic of his style. The most curious aspect of all van Meegeren's forgeries, in fact, is their relatively slight resemblance to the genuine work of Vermeer, and their easy acceptance is completely inexplicable on rational grounds.

It must be remembered that all artists and craftsmen were surrounded by the artistic idiom of their time, and they accepted it naturally and completely. Obviously they had no knowledge of later styles, and, although they could observe the styles and idioms which had gone before, they could only copy or adapt pre-existing works.

An excellent comparison is to place a piece of silver decorated with genuine rococo motifs beside one decorated in the revived-rococo of the Victorian period. Most obvious will be a direct copy of an 18th-century piece. This was difficult to do, and was rarely attempted. When it was done it appeared laboured and spiritless. If, on the other hand, the piece is a free adaptation there will be many obvious differences, because the man who made it was working with a knowledge of the neo-classical and Empire styles, and the others which had intervened. The original impetus and meaning of rococo was lacking, and the use of the style had, in fact, become a mere exercise in manual skill.

A copy can never have the value of an original work. The intellectual concept which created the original belonged to the artist alone. No one capable of doing good original work could ever find satisfaction in making a copy of that of someone else.

To use style as a method of judgement means that it is

necessary to study genuine examples until small variations become noticeable. The more obvious reproductions will then be immediately rejected. Vessel-shapes, for example, persisted in China for thousands of years, yet each period exhibits some subtle variation from the original shape which dates a specimen inevitably.

It is important to develop a sense of perspective in time. A work of art obviously cannot have neo-classical elements and yet belong to the rococo period. It is either as late as the neo-classical elements suggest, or else done much later by someone who was careless about details.

Four Chinese jars of (*from left to right*) the T'ang, Sung, Ming, and Ch'ing dynasties respectively, showing changes in the basic form in the course of 800 years. Such points are of great assistance in dating

It is, of course, impossible to do more, in so small a space than to indicate a few of the aspects of stylistic methods of dating, but many more will suggest themselves to the serious student.

SUNG DYNASTY, THE [960-1279] Between the fall of the T'ang Dynasty in 906 and the beginning of the Sung period in 960 a period of internecine strife intervenes. The Sung Dynasty itself was a period of great social and cultural advancement, however, and the arts were particularly encouraged. Painting is especially important, although undoubted examples in the West are almost non-existent.

The ceramics of the period are also important. Many of them have a stoneware body covered with a feldspathic glaze in a variety of fine colours. Perhaps the best-known group is the celadons – glazes varying in colour but usually green, or brownish green – which have always been in world-wide demand and in medieval times were used as gifts between princes. Chün ware – a lavender-coloured glaze suffused with purple – is much sought after in Europe, although it is not so highly esteemed by the Chinese. Translucent porcelain is at its best in the white Ting ware, to be found with moulded designs or with extremely fine incised decoration. The latter is the more valuable.

Although most Sung ceramics were decorated with coloured glazes, and impressed, incised, or carved designs, some excellent painted decoration (usually of simple floral subjects) was done at Tz'ŭ Chou, and these form the earliest painted wares of China.

Sung sculpture is much prized for its simplicity of form, which is the key-note of the work of the period. Most jades are of somewhat doubtful attribution.

During the Sung period emphasis was on form and colour rather than on decoration. Ceramics in particular have become much more common in Europe during the last few decades, and they are now more widely known and appreciated. Many of the Sung stonewares were reproduced during the Ch'ing period, but in a porcelain body. Although this is usually washed over with brown pigment to simulate stoneware at the foot-ring, a small chip will reveal the difference even if this should not be immediately obvious.

Good Sung works of all kinds usually fetch excellent prices on the art market.

SWANSEA (S. WALES) PORCELAIN FACTORY
The Nantgarw factory was transferred here in 1814. Excellent porcelain was made, some of it to a similar formula to that of Nantgarw, but much in a body devised by the proprietor, Lewis Dillwyn, which contained soaprock. Painting of fine quality was done by Thomas Pardoe, William Weston Young, Thomas Baxter, and others. Swansea porcelain is much sought by collectors.

T'ANG DYNASTY, THE [618–906]
This was an extremely fruitful period in Chinese art. For the first time for centuries China was united under a stable government, and conditions made it possible for a great expansion in the production of works of art and craft to take place. Many things

have been excavated within the last few decades from T'ang tombs, and the characteristic products of the period are now relatively familiar in the West.

Undoubtedly the best known are the pottery tomb-figures which re-create the social *milieu* because of their great variety, covering almost every aspect of life at the time. They are remarkable for their naturalism, and this was a comparatively new departure in Chinese art. The greater freedom from artificially imposed restraints and conventions led to such things as the use of lively wheel-thrown forms in pottery which owed little or nothing to the art of bronze-casting. Earlier vessels had often been based on bronze forms, and frequently were close approximations. The brilliantly coloured glazes, too, gave T'ang pottery a less sombre dress, more particularly in the use of splashed or dappled colours. It was during this period that both the celadon glaze and translucent porcelain were introduced. These were both remarkable technical and artistic achievements.

The arts of painting and sculpture are equally remarkable, although examples are exceedingly rare. Much sculpture was inspired by Buddhism, and the same note of realism is struck, instead of the more formal treatment of earlier periods. Few examples of painting, either mural or on silk, now survive, but those which do show similar tendencies.

Jades which can perhaps be referred to the T'ang period are rather more numerous, but certain attributions are almost impossible, and, so far, little has been excavated which gives any kind of reliable assistance.

Some excellent silver work was done, much of it inspired by Persian metal-work. Bronze vessels are not so fine or important as those of the earlier period, the peak being reached in the Shang-yin and Chou periods, but bronze mirrors, often inlaid or otherwise decorated with gold and silver, are exceptionally fine in conception and execution, and are not infrequently to be found. The very rare figures of animals are equally interesting, and some reflect the style of the pottery tomb figures.

Foreign influences are fairly numerous. Both Persian and Greek influence appear in pottery and metal-work, the latter being the delayed result of the conquests of Alexander the Great in the Middle East.

TAPESTRIES Tapestries are principally in demand as wall-hangings, and are extremely effective decoration, particularly in high rooms and in conjunction with French furniture.

Most textile fabrics consist of a warp, or series of vertical threads, interwoven with a weft of horizontal threads which pass alternately over and under the warp from side to side. The weft in tapestry-weaving, however, is made up of a series of short stitches which produce the pattern. In this it is unlike embroidery, in which the stitches are superimposed on a warp and weft woven in the usual way.

This note on the subject is confined to a consideration of European tapestry weaving. The principle was employed in the Middle East in making rugs (the Kilim and the Soumac, for instance), but these are comparatively rare.

Most tapestries are extremely large and were woven in sections on a loom, the part not in use being kept on rollers at top and bottom which were put under slight tension to keep the warp threads in position, and which were moved as the work proceeded.

Two methods were used – the low warp, in which the loom was horizontal, and the high warp in which it was upright. Generally, most Flemish tapestries are low warp, most French tapestries high warp. Wool was the principal material used, although others were employed occasionally, including gold and silver thread.

Tapestry-weaving in Europe did not become common until about the 14th century, the so-called Bayeux Tapestry being embroidery. In the 14th century, however, tapestries were made extensively in Flanders, principally at Arras and Bruges. From the few examples which now survive, often in fragmentary condition, it seems evident that the early designs were based on contemporary mural painting by Van Eyck and others. The finest work was done before the 16th century, but examples are extremely rare and valuable.

Arras was so well known for tapestries that at one time it was almost a generic term for tapestry in general, and was so regarded by Shakespeare. The remark of Polonius to the Queen is well known:

"Be you and I behind an arras then"

and in a later scene Polonius hides behind an arras and is slain by Hamlet's rapier thrust through it. The town was taken by Louis XI in 1477, and the manufacture of tapestry was transferred to Brussels.

The first reliable record of tapestry manufacture in France is in 1539, when Francis I founded a factory at Fontainebleau. Several workshops were soon operating in and around Paris, and in 1603 a family of dyers named Gobelin established themselves as tapestry weavers in the Faubourg St. Marcel. This, and some of the other workshops, were brought together by Jean Baptiste Colbert, the Minister of Louis XIV who established the Manufacture royale des Meubles de la Couronne with the aid of Charles Lebrun, Court Painter to the king, and arbiter of fashion in the arts in 17th-century France. This manufactory supplied furniture, tapestries, jewellery, paintings, and such things to the Court, and was established on the site of the original Gobelins factory. Lebrun was the first Director.

During this period many tapestries of the finest quality were woven. The influence of painting became especially strong, and most things of the period are copies of easel-pictures of one kind or another. Many of the early designs were based on the work of Raphael, whose work was used for the same purpose by some of the later Flemish tapestry-weavers.

After the end of the 17th century the factory came under the influence of a number of directors, of whom the most notable was Jean Baptiste Oudry. Hardly less important was François Boucher, who provided many mid-18th-century designs.

The treatment changed in accord with the fashions of the times, and during the early years of the 18th century the designs of JEAN BÉRAIN (*q.v.*) were much used. We find, also, such exotic subjects as *chinoiseries*, and fantasies of a like nature. A new departure was the use of designs representing the wall of a room with a central medallion of a picture hanging on it which we probably owe to Boucher.

During the 17th and 18th centuries the subjects included motifs drawn from the Bible, from mythology, and from history, ancient and contemporary. The factory also made tapestry for upholstery, and, after 1826, also carpets in a tapestry-weave. A few such carpets to special order were made in the 18th century.

The factory at Beauvais was established about 1665 under

H

the direction of Louis Hinart, with the assistance of Colbert. After Hinart's retirement in 1684 he was replaced by Philip Béhagle, under whose direction the factory flourished. Particularly fruitful was an association between Béhagle and Bérain, and the latter's characteristic grotesques and *baldacchini* appear in much of the work of the period.

Béhagle died in 1705, and in 1711 the enterprise was taken over by the brothers Fillieul. They met with great difficulties, and it came into the hands of de Merou in 1722. The appointment of Oudry as designer in 1726 greatly improved the position, and in 1734 he took over the factory in association with Nicolas Besnier. Oudry was later appointed inspector to the Gobelins factory also, and he is one of the great names in 18th-century French tapestry. Much of his own work was landscape and animal painting, and he put his skill to good use in the design of tapestries with hunting subjects. Some of his work was much copied later. Boucher also contributed many designs to Beauvais.

In 1754 the factory came under the direction of André-Charles Charron, who was subsidized by the French Treasury. Oudry continued to help with the work until his death in 1755.

The following period shows many pastoral subjects in keeping with the fashion of the day, but the manufacture of wall-hangings was greatly reduced during the Revolution and after. Like the Gobelins factory, Beauvais is now a national enterprise. Much tapestry was made for upholstery, many such things being a reduction of larger works. Carpets were also made.

The workshops at Felletin probably date from medieval times, and those at Aubusson from somewhat later. During the 17th century much work was done, hunting scenes and religious subjects being especially favoured. The work of other factories was also copied, and from 1665 the mark MRD or MRDB (Manufacture royale Daubusson) was supposed to be woven into each piece, although this was not always done. The best work probably dates from after about 1735, and in 1760 cartoons by Oudry were received from Beauvais. Designs were contributed by Boucher, particularly of *chinoiseries*, and the work of Lancret and Vernet was also used.

The workshops made tapestries for upholstery, carpets with a heavy tapestry weave, curtains, *portières*, and similar things.

Much furniture tapestry and many carpets were made during the 19th century.

A small amount of tapestry was made in England during the 15th and 16th centuries, although most was imported from Flanders. Cardinal Wolsey, for instance, bought more than a hundred pieces of Brussels tapestry in 1522.

The manufacture of tapestry on a somewhat larger scale was started at Mortlake, near London, in the reign of James I, and Charles I caused weavers to be brought from Flanders to work here. The director was the painter, Sir Francis Crane. Some examples are initialled FC, and others have woven in them "Car. Re. Reg. Mortl" (Carolus Rex Regnans Mortlake). Manufacture was finally given up at the close of the 17th century.

Tapestries were made during the 16th, 17th, and 18th centuries in Italy, at Florence, Venice, Turin, and elsewhere, and a papal factory was established during the 18th century in the Vatican.

Very high prices are realized for early tapestries, although these tend to ease as the 18th century is approached. For 18th-century work price mainly depends on quality and size. Extremely large tapestries, which are difficult to display, are likely to be lower in price than smaller examples. Prices for Mortlake tapestries are variable, the best being given for those with other than religious subjects. This applies to tapestries in general, and religious subjects are not much in favour. On the other hand, good tapestries after designs by Boucher are always in great demand. Tapestries, of course, are made of wool, and demand the usual protection accorded to all wool textiles against moth.

TIN-ENAMELLED POTTERY   When tin oxide is added to glass it becomes white and opaque. Glazes of this kind are used on certain kinds of pottery (faience, *maiolica*, and delft), and they have the appearance of being painted with white decorators' enamel. Since the tin-glaze is generally used over a buff body, the effect is fairly obvious.

Tin-enamelled wares are usually decorated in colours applied directly at the same time as the glaze (high-temperature colours, or colours of the *grand feu*), or with colours painted over the glaze after it has been fired (enamels, "muffle" colours, or colours of the *petit feu*). The addition of a clear lead glaze was sometimes made. In Italy this was known as *coperta*, and in Holland as *kwaart*.

Tin-enamel glazes are of great antiquity, the earliest use being referable to Assyria at the beginning of the first millennium B.C. They were rediscovered by the Persians, and brought to Europe by way of Moorish Spain in medieval times.

The term *maiolica* is employed to describe the wares of Italy, and sometimes more loosely wares in the early Italian style. Faience is usually applied to tin-enamelled wares made in France, Germany, Scandinavia, and Spain, and delft is used alike of such wares made in Holland and England.

Manufacture was very widely distributed during the 16th, 17th, and 18th centuries, but it fell into disuse thereafter (*see* FAIENCE-FINE).

TRANSFER-PRINTING   A method of decorating pottery, porcelain, and enamels by the use of paper transfers.

The invention of the process is attributed to John Brooks about 1753, and it was first used at the Battersea Enamel Works, at Chelsea, to a very limited extent, and slightly more often at Bow. Its first use on any considerable scale on porcelain was at Worcester, where the most notable practitioner of the art in the 18th century, Robert Hancock, went in 1757.

Sadler and Green of Liverpool claimed the independent discovery of the art, and they decorated much cream-ware, and some porcelain, from Staffordshire and elsewhere. It is possible that the process was also discovered independently on the Continent by Anders Stenman of Marieberg (Sweden) and Adam Spängler of Zürich.

The later process of bat-printing employed "bats" of flexible glue instead of paper transfers. These prints were done in the stippled style of Bartolozzi. Transfer-printing in gold was invented by Peter Warburton in the 19th century.

"Outline" transfers filled in with enamel colours by hand were done at some of the porcelain factories, and transfer-printing in colour can be seen on porcelain made at Liverpool during the 18th century. Transfers from lithographic stones came into use during the 19th century.

The transfer-printed wares most usually collected are of those subjects engraved by Robert Hancock on Worcester porcelain, and prices vary somewhat according to the rarity of the subject, as well as condition. A standard work on Hancock is noted in the Bibliography.

TROMPE L'ŒIL A term invariably used in connection with painting in one medium or another. It must be done with such realism that it looks to be the object delineated. To this end various tricks of perspective and shadowing are used.

An example is the *décor bois* sometimes used on faience and porcelain in which the subject is an engraving pinned to a piece of grained wood.

ULTRA-VIOLET RADIATION The use of ultra-violet light in the examination of works of art of all kinds is now so widespread that a discussion in some detail is justified.

Ultra-violet light is radiation of a wave-length too short to be seen by the human eye. The most usual source is a quartz tube in which radiation is excited by passing an electric discharge through mercury vapour. This provides an intense visible illumination, bluish-white in appearance, which is also extremely rich in invisible ultra-violet rays. It is necessary to screen off the visible part of the illumination, and this is done to a great extent by interposing a filter of suitably dyed glass. In practice, a certain amount of red and violet light still passes. It is only possible to get completely invisible radiation in specially made laboratory apparatus, but the visible light usually passing does not noticeably interfere with results in most cases, and can in others be an asset.

In the more usual type of apparatus the mercury vapour discharge tube is arranged in such a way that radiation is directed through a glass filter. Usually this filter is made from Woods glass, which contains about 10 per cent. of nickel oxide, together with a small quantity of copper oxide added to eliminate red light. The filters of American lamps are made by Cornings.

Examination is carried out in a darkened room. Results may be divided approximately into two kinds – a genuine fluorescence and a reflection of the small amount of visible light passing the filter. The latter may or may not be accompanied by a variable degree of fluorescence, and in some cases it may modify or mask a true fluorescence.

Fluorescence is exhibited when ultra-violet radiation falls on certain materials. It differs from phosphorescence only in the sense that it does not persist when the exciting radiation is removed. When short waves of this kind fall on a particular substance the wave-length is transformed sufficiently for them to become visible. Fluorescent substances are often present in traces in some materials which, because of this, exhibit fluorescent effects. Some substances, on the other hand, not only do not fluoresce themselves but have the property of "quenching" fluorescence in others.

If a work of art made from a substance which is fluorescent is added to with a non-fluorescing material, or with one which fluoresces differently, the extent of the addition is immediately apparent, since the two parts will be of differing colours. This has especial application in the case of old pottery and porcelain, where any repairs, no matter how well done, are usually fairly obvious. Paint and varnish fluoresce in a completely different manner from a ceramic glaze.

Recently a method of repairing old pottery and porcelain has been used which involves spraying the entire object with cellulose acetate varnish. This, of course, makes it very difficult to gauge the *extent* of the repair, since the whole of the surface fluoresces, usually with a yellowish-white colour. This fluorescence, however, is so unlike that exhibited by ceramic glazes, which are usually a shade of violet, that the tampering is obvious, and such an example is better rejected altogether. Varnish of this kind can be removed with amyl acetate or acetone.

Overglaze enamels which have flaked are sometimes restored with paint. Ultra-violet light shows these additions quite clearly.

So far as glass is concerned, early 18th-century Continental glass often exhibits marked orange fluorescence which may be due to the presence of uranium oxide. The same effect is to be seen with some kinds of modern laboratory glass. English and Continental lead glass shows traces of reflected violet light from the visible radiation passing the filter, but otherwise there is nothing to be seen. Deposits on the surface of the glass may fluoresce to some extent. Very little work has been done on the application of ultra-violet radiation to glass, but where the fluorescence of a specimen differed from that of an undoubtedly genuine example of a similar type, it might be a forgery. Fluorescence, however, is due to trace-elements in the materials used, and such a test could be conclusive only if it could be assumed that both examples ought to have come from the same factory or batch of material.

Ultra-violet light has given excellent results in the examination of sculpture and stonework, more particularly in the case of marbles, alabaster, and limestone. Marble is a crystalline form of limestone, and old marbles undergo degenerative changes with age and weathering which start on the surface and penetrate inwards, forming a kind of skin. Often this is due to aerial-borne sulphur, the lime carbonate being converted into lime sulphate. It is necessary to check the kind of fluorescence to be expected from genuine examples before proceeding to an examination of suspected objects, but it is obvious that any alteration to an old carving, or the most skilful repair, would necessarily show as a difference in fluorescence. Reference can always be made to buildings of a known age comparable to that of the specimen under examination, and which is constructed of the same kind of stone. Rorimer, in the course of his experiments, found that freshly cut marble had an intense purple appearance under ultra-violet light, whereas old marble surfaces had a mottled white appearance. Jade is also said to fluoresce with a uniformly intense colour when newly cut, older specimens exhibiting a colour more nearly akin to old marble. In my experience this generalization holds good for jadeite, but not for the earlier nephrite.

Ivory has been found to show a purple colour when newly cut, whereas old ivory has a yellow tone. The scraped surface of old ivory showed violet against the original yellow. The first may be due to surface impregnation with fatty substances from frequent handling, fats and soaps always fluorescing brilliantly with a colour which varies from white to yellow.

Enamels, more particularly the painted variety, are often restored with oil or cellulose paints, and this is always obvious under ultra-violet radiation.

Prints and drawings can often be examined in this way with

profit. For example, holes in water-colour drawings are often ingeniously repaired with paper patches, but the likelihood of the old paper and that used for the repair having the same fluorescence is remote. Such things as fox-marks removed by bleaching often show up remarkably well, and erased signatures, altered dates, and so forth can be detected with some facility. The apparatus is often used by criminal investigation departments for this purpose. Old paper fluoresces very much more than new, and comparison of an attested specimen with a suspected forgery can be very revealing.

The practice common among medieval scribes of erasing writing in order to use the surface afresh can always be detected, and often the original writing can be read.

Furniture, textiles, and such things can be examined in this way, and new work will often show considerable differences from old.

So far as oil-paintings are concerned, X-rays are frequently more revealing than ultra-violet radiation. Overpainting can often be detected by the latter method, however, and oil varnishes can often be distinguished from spirit varnishes – a fact which has been used in the detection of such things as faked Stradivarius violins.

Signatures on oil-paintings have often been examined in this way. There is a case of a painting attributed to Pissarro, and bearing a signature asserted to be his, that – under ultra-violet radiation – revealed the signature of another artist which had been removed, the slight traces of paint remaining being fluorescent.

Although the results of examination by ultra-violet light need to be interpreted by the eye of experience in some fields, there is much to be learned from it, and the apparatus is almost indispensable to the serious collector or to the dealer.

There are a number of standard types of equipment on the market, the best-known being the Hanovia Models 11 and 16. A cheap and efficient source of ultra-violet radiation for less important work can be speedily constructed from the "Osira" lamp, which resembles an electric light bulb. The source of radiation is contained within the glass envelope, which is made of Woods glass. It needs to be wired in circuit with a choke and a capacitator. This is marketed by the General Electric Company.

VALUATIONS FOR INSURANCE The basis for valuation for this purpose is what it would cost to replace the article in the least favourable circumstances. A collector may have bought a Chelsea figure at the bargain price of £10, but if it would cost him £100 to buy another from a West End dealer, then this is its correct value for insurance purposes. He is not obliged to take £10 and then to hunt for a similar bargain.

Insurance companies usually insist on a professional valuation to safeguard themselves from fraudulent claims, and it is equally in the interest of the insured party to have such a valuation, since it minimizes the risk of disputed claims.

Insurance companies sometimes put restrictions on their policies in cases where the risk is higher than usual. For instance, they usually refuse to insure valuable porcelain against breakage unless it is kept in a locked cabinet. They may demand special locks or burglar-alarms where there is a collection of valuable silver or jewellery. These restrictions are reasonable and, if they were contested, the company (if it accepted the business at all) would be compelled to increase its premiums to cover the additional risk involved.

Insurance companies vary somewhat in their reactions to insuring works of art. Some have had more experience than others of this class of insurance, and they are usually the best to deal with.

VALUATION FOR PROBATE At death a valuation of the effects of the estate is made to form a basis for negotiation with the Estate Duty Office. If the property is to be retained unsold for a period of years this valuation (if accepted) is used to assess the duty payable. If the property is sold the actual selling price is taken instead of the valuation.

The basis for such valuations should be what the property would have been likely to fetch had it been sold at auction in normal circumstances *at the date of death*. Any subsequent appreciations or depreciations should be disregarded.

Work of this kind is usually done by chartered auctioneers and estate agents, and items of more than £50 in value are separately itemized. For most purposes auctioneers and estate agents in good standing are very satisfactory as valuers for the purpose, but they are not always so satisfactory when the valuation of works of art is necessary. If, therefore, an unduly high value appears to have been put on any particular object, and the duty payable is likely to be high, then it is often advisable to get another opinion.

It would, of course, be distinctly inadvisable for a trustee or a beneficiary to accept probate valuation as a fair index of value in the case of works of art without being separately advised.

VALUE OF WORKS OF ART   The notes below are intended to give the reader general guidance on this difficult point, but should not be regarded as a substitute for proper legal advice in cases of dispute.

Value has been defined by an eminent legal authority as what a willing buyer will pay to a willing seller, and it is impossible to improve on this as a general principle. Nevertheless, like so many pronouncements of its kind, by trying to be all-embracing it inevitably excludes unusual circumstances, and these are the stuff of which law-suits are made.

The value of a work of art rests to some extent on its aesthetic merit, but a bad picture by a well-known hand is likely to fetch much more in terms of money than a masterpiece by a minor artist. On purist grounds this is indefensible, but the position exists and has to be accepted. Therefore, the date and provenance of a work of art are both important.

If a seller approaches a dealer knowing what he is offering, and what market conditions are likely to be, then both parties are evenly matched. It remains only for the seller to recognize that the dealer must have a reasonable margin for profit on the transaction in order to live, and to pay the expenses (often heavy) of his organization, as well as some reward for the fact that he may have the article for a long time before selling it, and for the risk that he may not succeed in selling it at a profit at all.

The situation is more difficult when the seller is unsure of his ground. Obviously he will not put temptation in the dealer's way by saying, "Give me what you think it is worth", and he attempts to extract information from the dealer as to the nature and value of the article. Manifestly, this is unfair. Dealers are fully aware of the risks they run in making offers and discussing the nature of an article. The seller all too often take the view that if an object is worth £100 to one dealer it is worth £110 to another. Therefore, most dealers will refuse to make offers unless they are well acquainted with the seller, but will ask him for his price.

A dealer is under an obligation not to misrepresent the facts. If, for example, he is offered a Chelsea porcelain figure worth £200 he cannot say that it is "Derby" and worth only £50. If he buys it on this basis the bargain can be set aside. The dealer, therefore, may not mislead the seller, although he can refuse to make any comment at all.

If the seller asks a foolishly low price – £10 for an article worth £1,000 – the position is different. It is doubtful whether the seller could recover anything, but the dealer would certainly have to satisfy himself that he was not being offered stolen property. If, in fact, it later proved to be stolen, then the bargain would seriously prejudice the dealer's position if it could be proved that he was well aware of the value of what he was buying.

If a valuable article is sold at less than its true worth, and both parties are mistaken as to its nature and value, then, in some circumstances, the contract of sale can be set aside.

Fortunately there is a way of avoiding such difficulties. Most dealers are also prepared to value objects for a fee which is reasonable in relation to the services they perform. Usually, if the item is subsequently offered to them, the valuation fee is remitted.

Of course, these remarks apply principally to dealings between strangers. Dealers make special arrangements for customers well known to them, since their association is a matter of mutual benefit, and negotiations are conducted on a basis of good faith.

It is fair to both sides in a matter of this kind to point out that the expert dealer, as distinct from one who buys anything saleable at auction and adds what he thinks the object will bear as profit, spends most of his life in studying his market and the objects in which he deals. Therefore, when approached for advice and assistance he is entitled to be paid for his services in the same way as any other professional man. Most collectors respect this point of view, but a thoughtless minority trespass on the dealer's time and good nature by expecting free valuations to enable them to offer objects elsewhere.

A point which often puzzles a would-be seller is the difference of opinion on questions of value between one dealer and another. The difference principally arises from the reason for which the valuation is sought. Frequently, where valuations are for insurance purposes, there is little difference of opinion. When it is a question of buying one dealer may have a much more favourable market for a particular object than another, and is therefore willing to pay more for it. Another may only be in a position to buy it as a speculation. For this reason the definition of value already quoted is probably the one which best covers all circumstances.

So far as the scale of charges for valuations is concerned, this varies considerably according to the work needed to be done, the reason for it, and the total amount of the valuation. When very large amounts are in question special arrangements could probably be made.

The Royal Institute of Chartered Surveyors and the Chartered Auctioneers and Estate Agents Institute recommend 5 guineas per cent. on the first £500 and 2½ guineas per cent. thereafter to value furniture, fixtures, trade stocks, and so forth, and 5 guineas per cent. on the first £100, 2½ guineas per cent. on the next £400, and 1½ guineas per cent. thereafter for the valuation of furniture and effects for probate and similar purposes. Of course, in cases where an unusual amount of work or research is required special fees may be charged. In such cases the work is given to experts in their particular field, and although their charges are high, they do not accept a commission in which they have no chance of success. They are therefore likely more than to save their fees.

The principles of valuation of specific objects are referred to in somewhat more detail elsewhere, and the reader is advised to consult the KEY TO THE CONTENTS which precedes this book, but a few general remarks which bear on the subject are appended.

A point of some difficulty is the question of *age*. In estimating value age is of comparatively little importance beside such factors as quality. Few things are older than some of the excavated pottery from Cyprus, but the market value is very low for anything but a high-quality specimen.

There can be no doubt that the principal factor is demand, followed by QUALITY (*q.v.*), condition, rarity, and age, in that order. Since demand is usually for the best quality which can be afforded these two factors are necessarily linked.

For this reason a good valuer is necessarily a good judge of quality. The value of an article of poor quality is not a *little less* than one of high quality of the same kind, but a *great deal less.*

Condition is also important. When perfect condition is allied to good quality the price will be high. Nevertheless, it must be recognized that there are things where perfect condition is virtually unobtainable, and too much stress need not be put on minor damage when the quality is otherwise good.

So far as the finer points of valuation are concerned, a number of factors need to be considered which affect the price an article is likely to fetch. A recent important sale of comparable objects, for example, will have the effect of increasing value, whilst rarity which is so excessive that examples are infrequently for sale may actually depress market value, since buyers will not be interested in isolated objects about which little is known, and which must stand by themselves. This remark does not, of course, apply to rarity within a particular group, which will usually increase price. For instance, a Chelsea figure of which only one example exists if it is otherwise desirable will fetch a higher price because of its rarity.

When all is said and done, although these remarks may assist towards an assessment of value, there are almost as many assessments as there are valuers. The only test which approaches finality is to offer the object in a saleroom. Even this is only valid for that particular moment in time. A different sale, and different presentation, might yield an entirely different result.

VEILLEUSE Literally, a *night-lamp* (German, *Nachtlampe*). The *veilleuse* is also known as a *réchaud* (a food-warmer). It consists, usually, of five parts – the base, a cylindrical body with handles and air-vents, a container for food, a cover, and a lamp (the *godet*), which was placed inside to act as a source of heat. The lamps are usually missing.

In the 18th century these were always food-warmers so far as Continental productions are concerned, but shortly before 1800, and thereafter, the food-container was often replaced by a teapot. The *veilleuse* can be found in both pottery and porcelain, the latter often being well decorated, the lamp illuminating the painting.

The most frequent 19th-century examples are in the form of a tower with battlements which are usually elaborately painted in the style of the period. The *veilleuse* in the form of a figure – the *personnage* – is also a 19th-century production. Great ingenuity was often used in the manufacture of these, the hat, for instance, forming the cover of the teapot, one arm being the spout, and another the handle. The best come from the factory of Jacob Petit. They are at present being imitated.

VENEERING   The use of thin sheets of rare and expensive wood to ornament furniture. These were glued over a carcase of cheaper or more durable wood. The work can be carried out in one wood only, e.g. satinwood, or in a number of woods of different colours, as in marquetry. Veneered furniture was made extensively during the latter part of the 18th century. It needs particular care in centrally heated atmospheres.

VICTORIANA   Because Victorian things are sometimes the subject of a minor flutter in the dovecots of fashion, and are even spoken of by some people as the antiques of tomorrow, a few words on the subject may be helpful to the neophyte collector.

It is not snobbish to decry Victoriana, neither are people who express their distaste for the period taking a purist attitude. It is disliked by such people (among whom I am numbered) because it is, for the most part, neither art, nor craft, nor their legitimate offspring.

The industrializing process which started in the 1750s had gained considerable ground by the end of the century, and the Napoleonic Wars, by creating a *nouveau riche* class, succeeded in debasing taste to an extremely low level. Nevertheless, the effect at this time was not so bad as it later became. During the REGENCY PERIOD (*q.v.*) a certain amount of good taste restrained the worst aspects of industrialization. Designers were, to some extent, still subject to the discipline of the neo-classical style, which was then in its later phases.

Neo-classicism, however, by admitting the sentimental approach (first to be seen in Goethe's *Sorrows of Young Werther*), carried within it the seeds of its own destruction, and this sentimentality gushed forth in full flood by the time of the Great Exhibition of 1851.

Moreover, the arbiters of taste in the 18th century had been a cultured aristocracy. The craftsman worked for these people, and had been guided by them. Now he worked for a *bourgeoisie* many of whom lacked a cultural background, and whose only entitlement to the prerogative of acting as arbiter of taste was that they could afford to pay.

Thus we find early neo-classicism merging into the florid Empire style, the Gothic and the rococo revived in a debased version without the social implications which made them acceptable in their period, and, ultimately, every conceivable style and technical trick current in Europe during the preceding five hundred years laid under contribution, usually with an excess of ornament which was often machine-made.

The days of the craftsmen who worked for men of taste were over. In their place was the factory which sought only to make its products look as though they had cost the owner a lot of money. It is obvious that ornament was valued for its own sake as imparting additional value to an object from the wreckage of the fine 18th-century plain silver which the Victorians have left us as a legacy. The vandalism which caused bastard rococo designs to be hammered into it under the firm conviction that this tampering was adding to its artistic merit is a crime for which the 19th century cannot be forgiven.

Towards the end of the century a few people who realized to what depths taste had sunk attempted to adjust the balance. Some, like William Morris, tried to return to the earlier methods of the craftsman. Others copied and adapted 18th-century furniture and this survives today in large quantities, sometimes called in the antique trade "second period Chippendale".

Furniture made in imitation of William Morris was referred to as "art". An advertisement in the back of a South Kensington Museum *Handbook* for 1877 mentions "art" furniture, "art" curtains, "art" cretonnes (for covering furniture?), and "art" carpets. Illustrating the advertisement is a centre-piece – a villainous glazed cabinet, described as "Old English" – filled with "art" decoration which beggars description. The drawing-room suites advertised as being in stock for selection are referred to as Queen Anne, Chippendale, Louis Seize, etc., and the dining-room suites as Gothic, Early English, and Elizabethan. These things were said to be of a "superior class", and from the publication in which it appeared the advertisement was obviously intended to reach a public with some pretensions to taste.

In the same *Handbook* another firm solicits inspection of its stock of Indian handicrafts, including Indian furniture. This is completely covered with crude carving in every available space, the only uncarved part of a chair, for instance, being its upholstered seat. Another firm advertises cheap and artistic porcelain from Persia and India (where none was made), and China and Japan. Prices range from 6d. to 100 guineas. The accompanying illustrations seem better calculated to act as an emetic than as a persuasion to buy.

Good taste has been aptly defined as a sense of what is appropriate. The oft-quoted 19th-century porcelain figure of Venus with a clock in the middle of her belly is a classic example of the inappropriate.

The Victorian manufacturer bludgeons our sensibilities in a manner almost unique in the history of arts and crafts. Perhaps he was, to some extent, excelled by Indian arts and crafts of the same period, and it is possible that the possession of an Indian Empire may have had some effect on the taste of the public here. The Indian Art Gallery advertises, in the publication already mentioned, such things as salvers of steel inlaid with gold, and zinc inlaid with silver, together with an assortment of Indian necklaces, gem bracelets, Lucknow silver bangles, and various items of pottery from Delhi, the Punjab, and elsewhere, all of which were popular with the middle classes of 19th-century England.

In the middle of a jaundiced survey of modern productions I sometimes reflect that the improvement in popular taste over that of the last sixty years or so of the 19th century and the first decades of the 20th is already so marked that there is room for hope for the future. Victoriana may, from time to time, be fashionable in a limited circle, but the taste for it is an attitude, not a conviction, and it will never be worth anything substantial on the art market.

WEDGWOOD The firm of Josiah Wedgwood & Sons

26 An Aubusson carpet of
the Empire period

27 A jug of Bohemian glass, imitating the appearance of jasper. Early 19th century

28 A *Reichsadlerhumpen*, or beaker, of German glass enamelled with the arms of the Electors of the Holy Roman Empire. Early 17th century

29 A goblet on a white twist stem, enamelled with armorial bearings, by Beilby of Newcastle. *c.* 1762

30 A mantel clock made in London, the ormolu case inset with enamel plaques signed by W. H. Craft. *c.* 1790

31 A bracket clock signed by Joseph Knibb, London, and made during the first quarter of the 18th century

32. Hercules and Anteus. A late-16th-century bronze of the school of Giovanni da Bologna

Ltd. of Barlaston, Stoke-on-Trent, was founded in 1759 by Josiah Wedgwood, who had, at first, been in partnership with Thomas Whieldon. In 1769 he entered into partnership with Thomas Bentley (Wedgwood and Bentley period) which lasted until the death of the latter in 1780.

Wedgwood was the largest maker of pottery in Staffordshire in his day, and the tradition has been carried on by the company. They still make many of the wares introduced during the 18th century, and in particular the well-known blue jasper.

The first wares definitely attributable to Wedgwood are some teapots and teaware in the form of cauliflowers and cabbages covered with good green and yellow glazes, which he made while associated with Thomas Whieldon. The production of a type of red stoneware followed (*rosso antico*), together with the development of an earlier Staffordshire earthenware body at first known as creamware, and later, when it had received the approbation of Queen Charlotte, as "Queen's ware". This achieved an enviable reputation in England and on the Continent (where it was called faience-fine), and it was decorated in colours and with transfer-prints.

This was followed by a hard black stoneware known as basaltes, black porcelain, or Egyptian ware, which was much used for all kinds of decorative purposes, including vases, medallions, plaques, and figures. Painting in enamels (encaustic painting) in imitation of Greek vases was also done on this body, and later, during the 19th century, some effective painting in the *famille rose* palette is to be seen.

Best known is probably Wedgwood's fine stoneware called jasper. This was a completely new invention at the time, and was first made in blue with relief ornament in white. Later the range of colours was considerably extended, even a black jasper being made occasionally. The earliest blue jasper is "solid", i.e. coloured throughout. After about 1777 the colour was applied on the surface only.

The jasper body was used for many important things, including a copy of the Portland Vase which was especially lent by the Duke of Portland for the purpose. A great variety of objects were made in jasper, including plaques with relief ornament for ornamenting furniture and similar purposes, cameos, portrait medallions, candlesticks, vases, watch-cases, shoe-buckles, chessmen, snuff-boxes, opera-glasses, and tea-ware for special occasions. Figures are rare, and usually support vases. Latterly they have been recognized ornamenting mantel-clocks by Vulliamy.

Porcelain has been made from time to time, beginning in 1812, but the company have generally concentrated on cream-ware and the fine stonewares associated with their name.

Among notable artists to work for Wedgwood in the 18th century are numbered John Flaxman, John Bacon, William Hackwood, George Stubbs.

Wedgwood's wares have been much copied in England and on the Continent.

Old Wedgwood has always been a particular favourite among collectors, both here and in the United States, and prices remain extremely stable. Most expensive are the coloured jaspers, blue being the commonest. Most jasper-ware is in two colours – the ground colour and a white relief, but three or more colours are fairly well known, five-colour jasper being very rare. Good specimens of basaltes ware and *rosso antico* are in demand, but generally prices are lower than for the coloured jaspers. So far as creamware is concerned, price depends on decoration and rarity. Plates are probably the least valuable, but well-made pierced specimens or pieces from known services often fetch good prices. Jelly moulds in creamware are particularly rare.

WOOD-CARVINGS Wood-carving of all kinds has been practised since very early times. Egyptian work of this kind has survived, and both the Greeks and the Romans used carved wood extensively.

During medieval times wood was much used for building, and ornament was frequently carved on it. Examples of such work divorced from its architectural setting can be seen occasionally.

Much work of the kind was done for ecclesiastical purposes, and, apart from altars and shrines, figures of saints to be set in the shrines were often carved with great skill, and painted and gilded. The Spaniards were especially noted for this kind of work.

In Italy during the Renaissance, as well as richly decorated furniture, such special things as marriage caskets were often elaborately carved and inlaid, the carved work sometimes being of bone or ivory as well as wood. Interesting small sculpture in fruit-wood and boxwood by Stefano Maderno and others belongs to the 15th and 16th centuries and later.

German wood-carving, some of great importance, was done at Augsburg and Nuremberg, and in England Grinling Gibbons [1650–1721] did excellent work and founded a school which continued his style. The magnificent porcelain figures of Bustelli were probably first carved in lime-wood.

During the last few decades much interest has been taken in wood-carvings from Africa, New Zealand, Polynesia, and other primitive sources. Examples produced before any considerable contact had been made with Western civilization are often of value as works of art. Things made in native villages especially for the tourist, and for shipment to Europe, have rarely either merit or value.

The woods usually favoured for free carving are box, lime, and pear, and these are also used for printing-blocks. They are comparatively free from a well-marked grain. So far as architectural carvings are concerned, the wood was selected for its primary purpose as structural timber and its use for carving necessarily had to be subordinate to this.

A good deal of excellent wood-carving has been done on picture frames, and a well-carved frame is highly valued. They are usually carved from pear, or some similar wood, and are overlaid with a thin layer of *gesso* (a kind of paste made from whiting and glue) which was then covered with gold-leaf. Inexpensive picture-frames are made from machine-cut ornament treated in the same way, and some are made entirely from moulded *gesso* on a wooden base, and finished with gilding. These have no special value.

WOODWORM IN FURNITURE Stories about the use of the shot-gun to simulate worm-holes in furniture are probably apocryphal, but *Anolium punctatum* (the furniture beetle) is certainly the enemy of the collector.

Pieces of furniture which appear sound enough to the eye are occasionally honeycombed with passages under the surface of the wood to an extent where it will crumble to powder if pressure be applied. Except in the case of some kinds of walnut furniture, however, this is uncommon.

The larvae of the beetle leave a very small circular hole of entrance on the surface. One such larva by itself is not likely to do grave damage, but any such hole suggests the need for careful investigation. If the piece is tapped with the knuckle and fine sawdust is seen the worm is still active. Holes of this kind are often filled with beeswax and similar kinds of "stopping", and they are not always easy to detect.

Occasionally old wood in which worm has been active is used to repair furniture, or even to make up a spurious object. It is therefore a good plan to look for holes which have been cut through lengthwise by the saw, and which appear on the surface as the section of a tunnel. When this is seen the whole piece demands very careful investigation. Worms always penetrate from the surface inwards. They do not make half-tunnels opening on the surface.

Mahogany, oak, and the harder furniture woods are rarely affected very seriously. A few worm-holes can sometimes be seen, but they do not affect the structural stability of the wood.

Walnut and soft woods are the most likely to be seriously damaged.

WORCESTER PORCELAIN FACTORY   This factory had its origin at Bristol in 1748, and was transferred to Worcester in 1751. Among the moving spirits may be numbered Josiah and Richard Holdship and Dr. John Wall.

Worcester used a porcelain made from clay and steatite (or soaprock). The porcelain was of excellent quality, and particularly valued because it would not crack in hot water – a fault to which some of the other porcelain of the period was prone. In the early period it was decorated in underglaze blue, and enamel colours, with patterns derived from Chinese sources. In 1757 Robert Hancock, the engraver, brought the art of transfer-printing to the factory, and much work of this kind was done.

In the 1760s many good coloured grounds were devised – powder-blue, green, turquoise, and others, and decoration of fine quality was done by the miniaturists, Jeffryes Hamett O'Neale and John Donaldson. A ground pattern of overlapping scales in several colours, but principally in blue, was used in conjunction with reserved panels in which flowers and birds were painted.

Much Worcester porcelain was painted by an English outside decorator, analogous to the German *Hausmaler*, named James Giles, who had a studio at Clerkenwell.

After 1783 the factory was owned by Thomas Flight of London. A rival factory started by Robert Chamberlain was particularly successful, and the two were amalgamated in 1840. A small factory owned by Thomas Grainger, and started in 1812, was also absorbed.

Worcester porcelain has always been highly valued, and it does, in fact, hold its value remarkably well, being less subject to fluctuations of taste and fashion than that of any other English factory.

YÜAN DYNASTY [1280-1368]   This was founded by Mongol invaders led by Genghis Khan, the best-known Chinese Emperor of the house being Kublai Khan.

Most of the ceramics and other works of art are a continuation of Sung styles, with an increasing tendency towards flamboyance. Celadons of the period are not uncommon, and the first porcelain painted underglaze in blue and in copper-red dates from this time. The use of figure subjects in painted decoration also appears to date from this period.

English Porcelain

FACTORY MARKS

△   CHELSEA 1745–1749. Incised. Known in under-glaze blue.

Chelfea 1745   CHELSEA 1745. Incised.

    CHELSEA 1749. In underglaze blue.

    CHELSEA 1750–1770. Raised on medallion, red, blue, lilac, brown, and gold.

    CHELSEA 1770–1784. Red and gold.

    DERBY ?1750. Incised.

1750   DERBY 1750. Incised.

WD-Go   DERBY c. 1760. Incised.

DERBY   DERBY c. 1764. Mark of Richard Holdship on transfer-printed mug.

    CHELSEA–DERBY 1777. In gold.

    DERBY 1780–1784. In blue or purple.

    DERBY 1784–1810. In red, blue, and gold. Incised on base of biscuit figures.

Derby 1795–1796. Duesbury & Kean.

Derby 1820–1848. Bloor period.

Derby. Copy of Meissen mark.

Pinxton. In gold.

Pinxton. In red.

Pinxton. Workman's mark. In red.

Bow 1749–1753. Incised.

Bow 1749–1753. Incised.

Bow 1749–1753. Incised.

Bow 1758–1775. In red. Possibly a Giles mark.

Bow 1755–1760. In underglaze blue.

Bow 1758–1775. On figures. Usually in blue.

Bow 1758–1775. In underglaze blue. Mostly on figures.

Longton Hall 1750–1758. In blue.

Lowdin's (Lund's) Bristol *c.* 1750. Workman's mark.

Bristoll 1750	LOWDIN'S (Lund's) Bristol 1750.
	WORCESTER 1751–1760. Workman's mark. In red.
	WORCESTER 1755–1760. Pseudo-Chinese mark.
	Chinese characters meaning "Great Ming" for comparison.
	WORCESTER 1755–1795. In red, blue, gold, and black.
	WORCESTER 1757 onwards. On blue-printed wares.
	WORCESTER 1755–1783. In underglaze blue.
	WORCESTER 1755–1783. In underglaze blue.
	WORCESTER. Pseudo-Meissen mark. Used from 1757.
Flight	WORCESTER 1783–1792. In blue.
FLIGHTS	WORCESTER 1783–1792. Impressed.
Flight	WORCESTER 1789–1792. In red and blue.
D.F.B.	WORCESTER 1807–1813. Impressed.
Chamberlains Worc	WORCESTER 1800–1820. Chamberlain's factory.
	CAUGHLEY. In underglaze blue.
	CAUGHLEY. In underglaze blue.

S	CAUGHLEY. In underglaze blue.
SALOPIAN	CAUGHLEY. Impressed.
2	PLYMOUTH 1768–1772. In blue, red, and gold.
X	BRISTOL (Champion's factory). In blue enamel.
ₓX	BRISTOL (Champion's factory). Pseudo-Meissen mark. In underglaze and enamel blue.
B_6	BRISTOL (Champion's factory). In blue enamel.
SWANSEA	SWANSEA 1814–1817. Impressed. A similar mark known painted in red and other colours.
NANT-CARW **C.W**	NANTGARW. Impressed.

ARTISTS' MARKS

Z B ZACHARIAH BOREMAN. On a Derby mug *c.* 1780.

𝒮 JOHN DONALDSON. On a Worcester vase *c.* 1765–1770.

✱ ISAAC FARNSWORTH, repairer. On Derby *biscuit* figures and groups.

△ JOSEPH HILL, repairer. On Derby *biscuit* figures and groups.

onεωαᎸ JEFFREY O'NEALE. In a disguised form as part of an inscription. Chelsea *c.* 1754.

T° TEBO 1749–1780(?). The mark of a migratory repairer who worked at a number of factories. Impressed into body.

APPENDIX IA
Wedgwood

WEDGWOOD
WEDGWOOD

Mark upon Queen's Ware from 1769 until the present, and upon ornamental jasper, black basalt, and terra cotta, from 1780 until the present. Recently the words Etruria and Barlaston and the name of the pattern have often been added.

Mark found inside the plinth of old basalt vases and sometimes on the pedestal of a bust or large figure.

Mark placed round the screw of basalt, granite, and Etruscan vases.

**WEDGWOOD
& BENTLEY**

Wedgwood
& Bentley

Marks used from 1769 to 1780. After Bentley's death WEDGWOOD only was used. Found on busts, vases, figures, plaques, medallions, and cameos.

WEDGWOOD
(in red or blue)

Mark upon bone china or porcelain 1812–1815, printed in red, blue, or gold.

WEDGWOOD
BONE CHINA
MADE IN
ENGLAND

Mark upon fine bone china from 1878 until the present, printed in sepia and other colours.

OF ETRURIA
WEDGWOOD
MADE IN
ENGLAND
BARLASTON

Mark upon Queen's Ware from 1840 to the present, with the name of the pattern often added.

NOTE: THE SQUARE FRAME IN THESE ILLUSTRATIONS DOES NOT APPEAR ON THE WARE.

Continental Porcelain Marks

FRENCH AND BELGIAN PORCELAIN

 S?C
T

Saint Cloud: In blue. Used separately, but known in conjunction. The latter mark sometimes incised.

Chantilly: In red or blue. The usual mark, with several variations.

D.V.

Mennecy: in blue, red, black, and incised.

Sèvres: Mark for the year 1753. Nearly always in blue enamel.

Sèvres: Mark for the year 1788.
The Royal Monogram of the crossed L's was in use at Vincennes before 1753. The letter in the centre of the Monogram was added from 1753, and represents the year of manufacture. The letter A stands for 1753, B for 1754, and so on. The letter W was omitted. In 1778 the date letters were doubled, the first being AA. The system was discarded in 1793, finishing with PP. The letters A, B, and C refer to pieces made at Vincennes, the letter D onwards to those made at Sèvres. Letters and devices added outside the mark usually refer to artists who can, on some cases, be identified therefrom. Figures in soft biscuit porcelain were *never* marked.

R.F
Sevres.

Sèvres: Period of the first Republic.

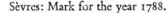

Sèvres: Period of Charles X. 1824–1828. The last two figures of the year were usually added.

Sèvres: Louis Phillipe. 1845–1848.

 Sèvres: Period of Napoleon III.

 Strasbourg: Paul Hannong. 1752–1755.

 Niderviller: 1770–1793

 Sceaux.

Paris (de la Courtille). In blue underglaze, and incised.

Paris (Rue Popincourt). For Nast of Paris. Nast is sometimes written in full.

Paris (Clignancourt).

Paris (Rue Thiroux). In underglaze blue.

Fontainebleau: Jacob Petit.

Tournai (Belgium). In various colours.

GERMAN PORCELAIN

GERMAN porcelain is usually well marked. Nevertheless, a mark is neither a safe nor satisfactory test of genuineness. At best it can only provide confirmatory evidence. This list includes all the more usual marks to be found, but, for the sake of brevity, it omits workmen's marks, and marks which are self-explanatory, e.g. "Gera", which is sometimes used in full under topographical paintings of this town. For a more detailed list the reader is referred to Honey (*Dictionary of European Ceramic Art*) or Chaffers (*Marks and Monograms*), where the various ancillary marks are recorded in full.

𝕏.𝓟𝓜   MEISSEN. 1723–1724. For Königliche Porzellan Manufaktur. Also "K.P.F." (Königliche Porzellan Fabrik) and "M.P.M." (Meissner Porzellan Manufaktur).

   MEISSEN. 1723 onwards. The caduceus (*Merkurstab*) used principally on coffee-cups for the Turkish market.

   MEISSEN. 1725 onwards. Date of cessation doubtful, but prior to 1763. The monogram of Augustus, for Augustus Rex. Used generally on pieces intended for royal gifts or for the Elector's personal use.

   MEISSEN. An early version, about 1725. The mark was introduced about 1724. The crossed swords from the Electoral Arms of Saxony.

   MEISSEN. The usual type of mark appearing in the 1740s.

   MEISSEN. 1763–1774. The Academic Period (*Die Punktzeit*).

   MEISSEN. 1774–1814. The Marcolini Period. The asterisk between the *points* at an earlier period on blue painted ware is a workman's mark.

VIENNA. Du Paquier Period. 1719–1744. An imitation Chinese seal-mark. Other imitations of Chinese marks have been recorded.

VIENNA. 1744–1749. Impressed. An early version.

VIENNA. 1749–1820. Painted in blue. The impressed shield was used again after 1820.

NYMPHENBURG. 1754–1765. The early variety.

NYMPHENBURG. *c.* 1765–1780.

 NYMPHENBURG. Used from 1763 to 1767 on some specimens. The hexagon mark. This was painted in underglaze blue.

HÖCHST. 1750–1796. In crimson or purple. Slight variations from time to time. The mark also occurs (rarely) in an impressed form.

HÖCHST. Probably between 1765–1774. The wheel surmounted by the Electoral Crown.

PH FRANKENTHAL. Impressed. Mark of Paul Hannong. Also to be found on Strasbourg porcelain.

FRANKENTHAL. 1756–1759. Lion from the Arms of the Palatinate. Sometimes found in conjunction with "IH" impressed, for Joseph Hannong, who owned the factory from 1759 to 1762.

FRANKENTHAL. *c.* 1756. In blue. From the Electoral Arms.

 FRANKENTHAL. With slight variations from 1762 to 1793. The commonest mark. The monogram of the Elector, Carl Theodor.

W BERLIN. Wegely's factory. Impressed and in blue.

Ç BERLIN. 1761–1763. Gotzkowsky's factory. In blue underglaze.

BERLIN. 1765–1770. The sceptre mark.

BERLIN. 1770–1800.

F Fürstenberg. In blue. This, and the following mark, are early. Later, it was added much more sketchily.

F Fürstenberg. In blue.

 Ludwigsburg. 1758–1793. The monogram of Carl Eugen, Duke of Württemberg. Usually in blue.

 Ludwigsburg. Another version of the mark listed above. Late marks are often crudely drawn.

Ludwigsburg. Late 18th century. Stag's antler from the Arms of Württemberg.

A Ansbach. The "A" is for the Markgraf Alexander. In blue.

Ansbach. Impressed.

 Ansbach. Sometimes found with the "A" beneath.

Kelsterbach. From 1768 to the end of the century. In blue or manganese. For Hesse-Darmstadt.

Kelsterbach. From 1766, but usually a late mark. In blue or impressed.

Fulda. From *c.* 1780. For Fürstlich Fuldaisch. The *Heinrichsmarke.*

Fulda. From *c.* 1765 to 1780. An early mark.

Hesse-Cassel. In blue.

T. Tettau. From 1794 onwards.

R Gotha. From at least 1783.

R.g Gotha. From 1783 to 1805.

 Gotha. From the end of the 18th century. A late mark.

WALLENDORF. *c.* 1778 onwards. This should not be confused with the mark of Wegely's Berlin factory.

WALLENDORF. An early mark imitating Meissen.

VOLKSTEDT. 1760–1799. A pseudo-Meissen mark.

VOLKSTEDT. 1799 onwards.

KLOSTER-VEILSDORF. 1760–1797. The commonest mark.

KLOSTER-VEILSDORF. Probably before 1765. Rare.

KLOSTER-VEILSDORF. From 1797 onwards. Also used at Limbach, Groszbreitenbach, and Ilmenau from about 1788.

LIMBACH. 1772–1788.

LIMBACH. An imitation Meissen mark.

LIMBACH. After 1788. Clover-leaf. Also used at Kloster-Veilsdorf, Groszbreitenbach, and Ilmenau.

ILMENAU. *c.* 1792.

GERA. The name is sometimes inscribed in full.

RAUENSTEIN. This, and the following mark, from about 1783 onwards.

RAUENSTEIN.

ITALIAN PORCELAIN

Florence. On Medici porcelain. Several variations known.

Capo–di–Monte. A similar mark was used at Buen Retiro.

Naples (Royal Factory), 1771–1806. In blue, red, and impressed.

Doccia: In blue, red, gold, or impressed.

Nove (Venice) in red, blue, or gold.

Venice (The Cozzi factory)·

Vinovo (Near Turin). In blue and incised. Some variations observed.

SPANISH PORCELAIN

Buen Retiro. Incised.

Buen Retiro. Incised. A late mark.

OTHER EUROPEAN FACTORIES

Copenhagen (Denmark). From 1775.

MB   Marieberg (Sweden). In several forms. From about 1766. Incised, in blue, and in red.

St. Petersburg (Leningrad) Russia. In blue. 1762–1796. The monogram represents Ekaterina (i.e. Catherine II).

The letter "P" representing the Emperor, Paul. 1796–1801.

Moscow (Russia). Impressed. Gardner's factory. Early 19th century.

"AP". Popoff's factory, Moscow. Early 19th century.

Zürich (Switzerland). In blue.

Nyon (Switzerland). In underglaze blue.

Weesp (Holland). In underglaze blue. 1759 onwards.

Oude Loosdrecht (Holland). Incised, enamel colours, and underglaze blue.

Oude Amstel (Holland). In blue and black.

The Hague (Holland). In underglaze blue. In overglaze blue the mark usually denotes Tournai porcelain decorated at The Hague.

APPENDIX III

Chinese Chronology

c. 3500–2000 B.C.	Neolithic culture. Decorated pottery recovered from graves.
c. 1766–1122 B.C.	Shang-Yin Dynasty. Period of finest ritual bronze vessels.
1122–255 B.C.	Chou Dynasty. Ritual bronzes and jades. Early pottery.
c. 481–205 B.C.	Period of the Warring States.
221–206 B.C.	Ch'in Dynasty. Great Wall of China constructed.
206 B.C.–A.D. 220	Han Dynasty. Pottery, stoneware, bronzes, jades.
220–589	The Six Dynasties.
	386–535: Period of the Northern Wei (pottery and tomb figures).
	506–556: Period of the Liang.
581–618	Sui Dynasty.
618–906	T'ang Dynasty. Fine pottery, tomb figures, metal-work, jades, etc.
960–1280	Sung Dynasty. Pottery, porcelain, stonewares with coloured glazes, jades, etc.
1280–1368	Yüan Dynasty. First blue-and-white porcelain.
1368–1644	Ming Dynasty.

1368–1398: Hung Wu.
1399–1402: Chien Wên.
1403–1424: Yung Lo.
1425: Hung Hsi.
1426–1435: Hsüan Tê.
1436–1449: Chêng T'ung.
1450–1456: Ching T'ai.
1457–1464: T'ien Shun.
1465–1487: Ch'êng Hua.
1488–1505: Hung Chih.
1506–1521: Chêng Tê.
1522–1566: Chia Ching.
1567–1572: Lung Ch'ing.
1573–1619: Wan Li.
1620: T'ai Ch'ang.
1621–1627: T'ien Ch'i
1628–1643: Ch'ung Chêng.

Decoration in coloured enamels. Fine blue-and-white porcelain. *San tsai* decoration. Jades. Enamels. Lacquer. Development of painting on porcelain.

1644-1912   Ch'ing Dynasty.
                 1644-1661: Shun Chih.
                 1662-1772: K'ang Hsi.
                 1723-1735: Yung Chêng.
                 1736-1795: Ch'ien Lung.
                 1796-1820: Chia Ch'ing.
                 1821-1850: Tao Kuang.
                 1851-1861: Hsien Fêng.
                 1862-1873: T'ung Chih.
                 1874-1908: Kuang Hsü.
                 1909-1912: Hsüan T'ung.
                 1912 onwards: The Chinese Republic.

CHINESE REIGN MARKS

THE following marks are found on Chinese works of art of all kinds, and record the dynasty and the name of the emperor. Great caution is necessary in accepting them at their face value, however, since the Chinese often add early reign marks to things made in the style of the period, and sometimes even without this much justification. Unless the other factors present are sufficient to justify an acceptance, such marks should not be used as evidence of age.

The marks given are in standard form. Slight differences in calligraphy will be observed between (say) marks drawn in the Ming period and those done later, but some acquaintance with Chinese calligraphy is necessary before this can be used as evidence of date.

It is possible to say, fairly definitely, that if the mark was done in the Ming period, then it will have been done in the reign of the emperor given. Examples of the later use of Ming reign marks usually occur in the following (Ch'ing) dynasty, not later in the Ming Dynasty.

Marks can be interpreted as follows:

(4)	Hua	Hua		(1)	Ta	Great
(5)	nien	} period made		(2)	Ming	Bright (dynasty)
(6)	chih			(3)	Ch'eng	Ch'êng

The characters are read from the top right, downwards.

MING DYNASTY

年 洪   Hung Wu   德 大   Hsüan Tê
製 武   (1368-1398)   年 明   (1426-1435)
                                製 宣

年 永   Yung Lo   化 大   Ch'êng Hua
製 樂   (1403-1424)   年 明   (1465-1487)
                                製 成

MING DYNASTY

年製	成化	Ch'êng Hua (1465–1487)
治年製	大明弘	Hung Chih (1488–1505)
德年製	大明正	Chêng Tê (1506–1521)
靖年製	大明嘉	Chia Ching (1522–1566)
慶年製	大明隆	Lung Ch'ing (1567–1572)
曆年製	大明萬	Wan Li (1573–1619)
啟年製	大明天	T'ien Ch'i (1621–1627)
年製	崇禎	Ch'ung Chêng (1628–1643)

MANCHU, OR CH'ING DYNASTY

治年製	大清順		Shun Chih (1644–1651)
熙年製	大清康		K'ang Hsi (1662–1722)
正年製	大清雍		Yung Chêng (1723–1735)
隆年製	大清乾		Ch'ien Lung (1736–1795)
年製	嘉慶		Chia Ch'ing (1796–1820)
光年製	大清道		Tao Kuang (1821–1850)
豐年製	大清咸		Hsien Fêng (1851–1861)
治年製	大清同		T'ung Chih (1862–1873)
緒年製	大清光		Kuang Hsü (1874–1908)

THE SQUARE SEAL MARKS SOMETIMES REPLACE THE MORE USUAL CHARACTERS.

LONDON

THE mark of the *Leopard's Head* was introduced in 1300, and the *maker's mark* in 1363.

A letter, changed annually to mark the year of manufacture, was first incorporated within the mark of the *Leopard's Head* from 1463 to 1478. Thereafter a separate *date letter* has always been punched. Thus from 1478 to 1544 three marks were used (viz., *Leopard's Head*, *maker's mark*, and *date letter*). In 1544 the *Lion passant* was added, making a total of four thenceforward, except for: (i) the temporary or optional changes made by the Acts of 1696 and 1719 respectively, and (ii) from 1784 until 1890, when a fifth mark, the *Sovereign's Head*, was punched.

In each of the tables below and on the next page, the twenty letters of the reduced alphabet used at Goldsmith's Hall are columnated on the left and against them in the following columns are placed the years which the letters signify. It should perhaps be repeated that the letter was changed on 19 May in the period covered by the upper table and 29 May in that by the lower; thus one letter served from, e.g., 19 May 1550 until 18 May 1551; in these tables (and in similar cases in the succeeding pages) only the prior of the two calendar years involved is placed against the appropriate letter.

In the table below, which embraces the eleven cycles from the introduction of the separate *date letter* until the break in sequence in 1696–1697, only the marks from 1558 onwards are included. The table of thirteen cycles (p. 264) brings the series up to date. In both tables the regularity of the London cycles has allowed two lines to be ruled across the tables at ten-year intervals to aid reference. The letter *A* of each alphabet with the *Leopard's Head* are shown: no *makers' marks* are shown, and information about them should be sought in Sir C. J. Jackson's *English Goldsmiths and their Marks*, 2nd edn., 1921 (or the 1949 edn.).

A	1478	1498	1518	1538	1558	1578	1598	1618	1638	1658	1678
B	1479	1499	1519	1539	1559	1579	1599	1619	1639	1659	1679
C	1480	1500	1520	1540	1560	1580	1600	1620	1640	1660	1680
D	1481	1501	1521	1541	1561	1581	1601	1621	1641	1661	1681
E	1482	1502	1522	1542	1562	1582	1602	1622	1642	1662	1682
F	1483	1503	1523	1543	1563	1583	1603	1623	1643	1663	1683
G	1484	1504	1524	1544[1]	1564	1584	1604	1624	1644	1664	1684
H	1485	1505	1525	1545	1565	1585	1605	1625	1645	1665	1685
I	1486	1506	1526	1546	1566	1586	1606	1626	1646	1666	1686
K	1487	1507	1527	1547	1567	1587	1607	1627	1647	1667	1687
L	1488	1508	1528	1548	1568	1588	1608	1628	1648	1668	1688
M	1489	1509	1529	1549	1569	1589	1609	1629	1649	1669	1689
N	1490	1510	1530	1550	1570	1590	1610	1630	1650	1670	1690
O	1491	1511	1531	1551	1571	1591	1611	1631	1651	1671	1691
P	1492	1512	1532	1552	1572	1592	1612	1632	1652	1672	1692
Q	1493	1513	1533	1553	1573	1593	1613	1633	1653	1573	1693
R	1494	1514	1534	1554	1574	1594	1614	1634	1654	1674	1694
S	1495	1515	1535	1555	1575	1595	1615	1635	1655	1675	1695
T	1496	1516	1536	1556	1576	1596	1616	1636	1656	1676	1696
U	1497	1517	1537	1557	1577	1597	1617	1637	1657	1677	——

1. The *Lion passant* introduced in 1544.

	A											
A	1697[1]	1716	1736	1756	1776	1796	1816	1836	1856	1876	1896	1916	1936
B	1697	1717	1737	1757	1777	1797	1817	1837	1857	1877	1897	1917	1937
C	1698	1718	1738	1758	1778	1798	1818	1838	1858	1878	1898	1918	1938
D	1699	1719	1739	1759	1779	1799	1819	1839	1859	1879	1899	1919	1939
E	1700	1720[2]	1740	1760	1780	1800	1820	1840	1860	1880	1900	1920	1940
F	1701	1721	1741	1761	1781	1801	1821[4]	1841	1861	1881	1901	1921	1941
G	1702	1722	1742	1762	1782	1802	1822	1842	1862	1882	1902	1922	1942
H	1703	1723	1743	1763	1783	1803	1823	1843	1863	1883	1903	1923	1943
I	1704	1724	1744	1764	1784[3]	1804	1824	1844	1864	1884	1904	1924	1944
K	1705	1725	1745	1765	1785	1805	1825	1845	1865	1885	1905	1925	1945
L	1706	1726	1746	1766	1786	1806	1826	1846	1866	1886	1906	1926	1946
M	1707	1727	1747	1767	1787	1807	1827	1847	1867	1887	1907	1927	1947
N	1708	1728	1748	1768	1788	1808	1828	1848	1868	1888	1908	1928	1948
O	1709	1729	1749	1769	1789	1809	1829	1849	1869	1889	1909	1929	1949
P	1710	1730	1750	1770	1790	1810	1830	1850	1870	1890[5]	1910	1930	1950
Q	1711	1731	1751	1771	1791	1811	1831	1851	1871	1891	1911	1931	1951
R	1712	1732	1752	1772	1792	1812	1832	1852	1872	1892	1912	1932	1952
S	1713	1733	1753	1773	1793	1813	1833	1853	1873	1893	1913	1933	1953
T	1714	1734	1754	1774	1794	1814	1834	1854	1874	1894	1914	1934	1954
U	1715	1735	1755	1775	1795	1815	1835	1855	1875	1895	1915	1935	1955

1. The *A* of the first sequence lasted only from 27 March till 29 May 1697.

2. After 1 June 1720 the marks of the old standard were resumed, as in the third column, while those of the new standard were used concurrently, with the same date letter, on such plate as was made of the higher standard required.

3. The *Sovereign's Head* mark was added on 1 December 1784 to show the payment of tax and continued until 30 April 1890.

4. The *Leopard's Head* is no longer crowned after 1821.

5. The *Sovereign's Head* mark was not used after 1890.

BIRMINGHAM

The Assay Office was established at Birmingham in 1773, with the *Anchor* as its distinguishing punch. When the duty was doubled in 1797, the *King's Head* was duplicated for a short time (†). The sequences are of twenty-five, omitting *J* or *I*, or twenty-six letters.

A	1773	1798	1824	1849	1875	1900	1925	1950
B	1774	1799	1825	1850	1876	1901	1926	1951
C	1775	1800	1826	1851	1877	1902	1927	1952
D	1776	1801	1827	1852	1878	1903	1928	1953
E	1777	1802	1828	1853	1879	1904	1929	1954
F	1778	1803	1829	1854	1880	1905	1930	etc.
G	1779	1804	1830	1855	1881	1906	1931	
H	1780	1805	1831	1856	1882	1907	1932	
I	1781	1806	1832	1857	1883	1908	——	
J	——	1807	——	1858	——	——	1933	
K	1782	1808	1833	1859	1884	1909	1934	
L	1783	1809	1834	1860	1885	1910	1935	
M	1784[1]	1810	1835	1861	1886	1911	1936	
N	1785	1811	1836	1862	1887	1912	1937	
O	1786	1812	1837	1863	1888	1913	1938	
P	1787	1813	1838	1864	1889	1914	1939	
Q	1788	1814	1839	1865	1890[1]	1915	1940	
R	1789	1815	1840	1866	1891	1916	1941	
S	1790	1816	1841	1867	1892	1917	1942	
T	1791	1817	1842	1868	1893	1918	1943	
U	1792	1818	1843	1869	1894	1919	1944	
V	1793	1819	1844	1870	1895	1920	1945	
W	1794	1820	1845	1871	1896	1921	1946	
X	1795	1821	1846	1872	1897	1922	1947	
Y	1796	1822	1847	1873	1898	1923	1948	
Z	1797†	1823	1848	1874	1899	1924	1949	

1. The *Sovereign's Head* mark was added on 1 December 1784 to show the payment of tax and continued until 30 April 1890.

CHESTER

There seems to have been a succession of moneyers at Chester from Saxon times and of goldsmiths from the 13th century. The omission of any mention of Chester in early Acts has been explained on the ground that both the city and country were under the Earl of Chester and not under the Crown until the time of Henry VIII. There were *makers' marks*, but no regular assay office marks until 1686; a sequence of date letters began in 1701 with cycles of irregular lengths.

	A	1701	1726	1751	1776	1797	1818	1839	1864	1884	1901	1926
	A	1701	1726	1751	1776	1797	1818	1839	1864	1884	1901	1926
	B	1702	1727	1752	1777	1798	1819	1840	1865	1885	1902	1927
	C	1703	1728	1753	1778	1799	1820	1841	1866	1886	1903	1928
	D	1704	1729	1754	1779	1800	1821–2	1842	1867	1887	1904	1929
	E	1705	1730	1755	1780	1801	1823	1843	1868	1888	1905	1930
	F	1706	1731	1756	1781	1802	1824	1844	1869	1889	1906	1931
	G	1707	1732	1757	1782	1803	1825	1845	1870	1890[1]	1907	1932
	H	1708	1733	1758	1783	1804	1826	1846	1871	1891	1908	1933
	I	1709	1734	1759	1784[1]	1805	1827	1847	1872	1892	1909	1934
	K	1710	1735	1760	1785	1806	1828	1848	1873	1893	1910	1935
	L	1711	1736	1761	1786	1807	1829	1849	1874	1894	1911	1936
	M	1712	1737	1762	1787	1808	1830	1850	1875	1895	1912	1937
	N	1713	1738	1763	1788	1809	1831	1851	1876	1896	1913	1938
	O	1714	1739	1764	1789	1810	1832	1852	1877	1897	1914	1939
	P	1715	1740	1765	1790	1811	1833	1853	1878	1898	1915	1940
	Q	1716	1741	1766	1791	1812	1834	1854	1879	1899	1916	1941
	R	1717	1742	1767	1792	1813	1835	1855	1880	1900	1917	1942
	S	1718	1743	1768	1793	1814	1836	1856	1881	——	1918	1943
	T	1719	1744	1769	1794	1815	1837	1857	1882	——	1919	1944
	U	1720	1745	1770	1795	1816	1838	1858	1883	——	1920	1945
	V	1721	1746	1771	1796	1817	——	1859	——	——	1921	1946
	W	1722	1747	1772	——	——	——	1860	——	——	1922	1947
	X	1723	1748	1773	——	——	——	1861	——	——	1923	1948
	Y	1724	1749	1774	——	——	——	1862	——	——	1924	1949
	Z	1725	1750	(1775)	——	——	——	1863	——	——	1925	1950

1. The *Sovereign's Head* mark was added on 1 December 1784 to show the payment of tax and continued until 30 April 1890.

DUBLIN

Goldsmiths were working in Dublin at least as early as the 13th century. In 1605 the City Council required that each maker strike his mark, and that three others, *Lion, Harp,* and *Castle,* be stamped, and in 1637 the goldsmiths were granted a charter. Three cycles of date letters are found from 1638 into the 18th century, but so little plate survives that the table below does not begin until 1720; the figure of *Hibernia* was added in 1731(†); the duty stamp of the *King's Head* was not punched till 1807(*).

A	1720	1747	1773	1797	1821	1846	1871	1896	1916	1942
B	1721	1748	1774	1798	1822	1847	1872	1897	1917	1943
C	1722	1749	1775	1799	1823	1848	1873	1898	1918	1944
D	1723	1750	1776	1800	1824	1849	1874	1899	1919	1945
E	1724	1751	1777	1801	1825	1850	1875	1900	1920	1946
F	1725	1752	1778	1802	1826	1851	1876	1901	1921	1947
G	1726	1753	1779	1803	1827	1852	1877	1902	1922	1948
H	1727	1754	1780	1804	1828	1853	1878	1903	1923	1949
I	1728	1757	1781	1805	1829	1854	1879	1904	1924	1950
K	1729	1758	1782	1806	1830	1855	1880	1905	1925	1951
L	1730–1†	1759	1783	1807*	1831	1856	1881	1906	1926	1952
M	1732	1760	1784	1808	1832	1857	1882	1907	1927	1953
N	1733	1761	1785	1809	1833	1858	1883	1908	1928	1954
O	1734	1762	1786	1810	1834	1859	1884	1909	1929	etc.
P	1735	1763	1787	1811	1835	1860	1885	1910	1930–1	
Q	1736	1764	1788	1812	1836	1861	1886	1911	1923	
R	1737	1765	1789	1813	1837	1862	1887	1912	1933	
S	1738	1766	1790	1814	1838	1863	1888	1913	1934	
T	1739	1767	1791	1815	1839	1864	1889	1914	1935	
U	1740	1768	1792	1816	1840	1865	1890[1]	1915	1936	
V	——	——	——	——	1841	1866	1891	——	1937	
W	1741–2	1769	1793	1817	1842	1867	1892	——	1938	
X	1743–4	1770	1794	1818	1843	1868	1893	——	1939	
Y	1745	1771	1795	1819	1844	1869	1894	——	1940	
Z	1746	1772	1796	1820	1845	1870	1895	——	1941	

1. *Sovereign's Head* discontinued.

EDINBURGH

The goldsmiths of Edinburgh were associated with the other hammer-men there and their records date from 1525. In 1457 a deacon and other officers were appointed by statute and the *deacon's mark* and the *maker's mark* had to be stamped. The town mark, a *Triple-towered Castle*, was added in 1485. In 1681 a variable *date letter*, changed in September, was adopted and the *Deacon's mark* was replaced by the *Assay-master's mark*; in 1759 this last was replaced by the *Thistle*.

A	1681	1705	1730	1755	1780	1806	1832	1857	1882	1906	1931
B	1682	1706	1731	1756	1781	1807	1833	1858	1883	1907	1932
C	1683	1707	1732	1757	1782	1808	1834	1859	1884	1908	1933
D	1684	1708	1733	1758	1783	1809	1835	1860	1885	1909	1934
E	1685	1709	1734	1759	1784[1]	1810	1836	1861	1886	1910	1935
F	1686	1710	1735	1760	1785	1811	1837	1862	1887	1911	1936
G	1687	1711	1736	1761	1786–7	1812	1838	1863	1888	1912	1937
H	1688	1712	1737	1762	1788	1813	1839	1864	1889	1913	1938
I	1689	1713	1738	1763	1789}	1814	1840	1865	1890[1]	1914	1939
J	—	—	—	—	1789}	1815	—	—	—	—	—
K	1690	1714	1739	1764	1790	1816	1841	1866	1891	1915	1940
L	1691	1715	1740	1765	1791	1817	1842	1867	1892	1916	1941
M	1692	1716	1741	1766	1792	1818	1843	1868	1893	1917	1942
N	1693	1717	1742	1767	1793	1819	1844	1869	1894	1918	1943
O	1694	1718	1743	1768	1794	1820	1845	1870	1895	1919	1944
P	1795	1719	1744	1769	1795	1821	1846	1871	1896	1920	1945
Q	1696	1720	1745	1770	1796	1822	1847	1872	1897	1921	1946
R	1697	1721	1746	1771	1797	1823	1848	1873	1898	1922	1947
S	1698	1722	1747	1772	1798	1824	1849	1874	1899	1923	1948
T	1699	1723	1748	1773	1799	1825	1850	1875	1900	1924	1949
U	—	1724	1749	1774	1800	1826	1851	1876	1901	1925	1950
V	1700	1725	1750	1775	1801	1827	1852	1877	1901	1926	1951
W	1701	1726	1751	—	1802	1828	1853	1878	1902	1927	1952
X	1702	1727	1752	1776	1803	1829	1854	1879	1903	1928	1953
Y	1703	1728	1753	1777	1804	1830	1855	1880	1904	1929	1954
Z	1704	1729	1754	1778 1779	1805	1831	1856	1881	1905	1930	1955

1. The *Sovereign's Head* mark was added on 1 December 1784 to show the payment of tax and continued until 30 April 1890.

EXETER

Goldsmiths were working at Exeter from the 14th century onwards, but it was not until the Act of 1701 that eleven of the small number of gold-smiths working there established a sequence of date letters. The amount of plate produced declined in the 19th century and little was assayed after 1850. The office was closed in 1883. The *Leopard's Head* was not used after 1777(*).

A	1701	1725	1749	1773	1797	1817	1837	1857	1877
B	1702	1726	1750	1774	1798	1818	1838	1858	1878
C	1703	1727	1751	1775	1799	1819	1839	1859	1879
D	1704	1728	1752	1776	1800	1820	1840	1860	1880
E	1705	1729	1753	1777*	1801	1821	1841	1861	1881
F	1706	1730	1754	1778	1802	1822	1842	1862	1882
G	1707	1731	1755	1779	1803	1823	1843	1863	
H	1708	1732	1756	1780	1804	1824	1844	1864	
I	1709	1733	1757	1781–2	1805	1825	1845	1865	
K	1710	1734	1758	1783	1806	1826	1846	1866	
L	1711	1735	1759	1784¹	1807	1827	1847	1867	
M	1712	1736	1760	1785	1808	1828	1848	1868	
N	1713	1737	1761	1786	1809	1829	1849	1869	
O	1714	1738	1762	1787	1810	1830	1850	1870	
P	1715	1739	1763	1788	1811	1831	1851	1871	
Q	1716	1740	1764	1789	1812	1832	1852	1872	
R	1717	1741	1765	1790	1813	1833	1853	1873	
S	1718	1742	1766	1791	1814	1834	1854	1874	
T	1719	1743	1767	1792	1815	1835	1855	1875	
U	—	1744	1768	1793	1816	1836	1856	1876	
V	1720	—	—	—	—	—	—	—	
W	1721	1745	1769	1794	—	—	—	—	
X	1722	1746	1770	1795	—	—	—	—	
Y	1723	1747	1771	1796	—	—	—	—	
Z	1724	1748	1772	—	—	—	—	—	

1. The *Sovereign's Head* mark was added on 1 December 1784 to show the payment of tax and continued until 30 April 1890.

GLASGOW

The Glasgow goldsmiths were incorporated with other metal-workers there as early as 1536, and a minute-book covering the period 1616–1717 survives. Although a cycle of date letters has been tentatively traced from 1681 to 1705, when the *Fish, Tree,* and *Bell* mark (from the burgh arms) was used, it was not until as late as the Act of 1819 that the Glasgow Gold-smiths' Company was constituted a body corporate and the *Lion Rampart* mark (from the Royal Standard of Scotland) was introduced. A regular sequence of date letters began in that year and the sixth cycle of twenty-six letters is now in progress.

A	1819¹	1845	1871	1897	1923	1949
B	1820	1846	1872	1898	1924	1950
C	1821	1847	1873	1899	1925	1951
D	1822	1848	1874	1900	1926	1952
E	1823	1849	1875	1901	1927	1953
F	1824	1850	1876	1902	1928	1954
G	1825	1851	1877	1903	1929	1955
H	1826	1852	1878	1904	1930	etc.
I	1827	1853	1879	1905	1931	
J	1828	1854	1880	1906	1932	
K	1829	1855	1881	1907	1933	
L	1830	1856	1882	1908	1934	
M	1831	1857	1883	1909	1935	
N	1832	1858	1884	1910	1936	
O	1833	1859	1885	1911	1937	
P	1834	1860	1886	1912	1938	
Q	1835	1861	1887	1913	1939	
R	1836	1862	1888	1914	1940	
S	1837	1863	1889	1915	1941	
T	1838	1864	1890²	1916	1942	
U	1839	1865	1891	1917	1943	
V	1840	1866	1892	1918	1944	
W	1841	1867	1893	1919	1945	
X	1842	1868	1894	1920	1946	
Y	1843	1869	1895	1921	1947	
Z	1844	1870	1896	1922	1948	

1. The *Sovereign's Head* indicates payment of tax.
2. The *Sovereign's Head* was discontinued in this year.

NEWCASTLE

Goldsmiths were working at Newcastle at least from the middle of the 13th century, although no extant plate made there seems to date from before the middle of the 17th century, when the mark of the *Three Castles* stood alone with that of the maker. The Newcastle Assay Office was re-established in 1702, with an erratic cycle in gothic capitals, and closed in 1884.

A	1721	1740	1759	1791	1815	1839	1864
B	1722	1741	1760–8	1792	1816	1840	1865
C	1723	1742	1769	1793	1817	1841	1866
D	1724	1743	1770	1794	1818	1842	1867
E	1725	1744	1771	1795	1819	1843	1868
F	1726	1745	1772	1796	1820	1844	1869
G	1727	1746	1773	1797	1821	1845	1870
H	1728	1747	1774	1798	1822	1846	1871
I	1729	1748	1775	1799	1823	1847	1872
J	—	—	—	—	—	1848	—
K	1730	1749	1776	1800	1824	1849	1873
L	1731	1750	1777	1801	1825	1850	1874
M	1732	1751	1778	1802	1826	1851	1875
N	1733	1752	1779	1803	1827	1852	1876
O	1734	1753	1780	1804	1828	1853	1877
P	1735	1754	1781	1805	1829	1854	1878
Q	1736	1755	1782	1806	1830	1855	1879
R	1737	1756	1783	1807	1831	1856	1880
S	1738	1757	1784[1]	1808	1832	1857	1881
T	1739	(1758)	1785	1809	1833	1858	1882
U	—	—	1786	1810	1834	1859	1883
W	—	—	1787	1811	1835	1860	
X	—	—	1788	1812	1836	1861	
Y	—	—	1789	1813	1837	1862	
Z	—	—	1790	1814	1838	1863	

1. The *Sovereign's Head* mark was added on 1 December 1784 to show the payment of tax and continued until 30 April 1890.

SHEFFIELD

The assay office was instituted at the same time as that at Birmingham, with the *Crown* as its town mark. The first two cycles are complicated because the letters are jumbled and not in sequence.

A	1779	1806	1824	1844	1868	1893	1918	1943
B	1783	1805	1825	1845	1869	1894	1919	1944
C	1780	1811	1826	1846	1870	1895	1920	1945
D	1781	1812	1827	1847	1871	1896	1921	1946
E	1773	1799	1828	1848	1872	1897	1922	1947
F	1774	1803	1829	1849	1873	1898	1923	1948
G	1782	1804	1830	1850	1874	1899	1924	1949
H	1777	1801	1831	1851	1875	1900	1925	1950
I	1784[1]	1818	——	1852	——	1901	1926	1951
J	——	——	——	——	1876	——	——	1952
K	1786	1809	1832	1853	1877	1902	1927	1953
L	1790	1810	1833	1854	1878	1903	1928	1954
M	1789–94	1802	1834	1855	1879	1904	1929	etc.
N	1775	1800	——	1856	1880	1905	1930	
O	1793	1815	——	1857	1881	1906	1931	
P	1791	1808	1835	1858	1882	1907	1932	
Q	1795	1820	1836	——	1883	1908	1933	
R	1776	1813	1837	1859	1884	1909	1934	
S	1778	1807	1838	1860	1885	1910	1935	
T	1787	1816	1839	1861	1886	1911	1936	
U	1792	1823	1840	1862	1887	1912	1937	
V	1798	1819	1841	1863	1888	1913	1938	
W	1788	1814	——	1864	1889	1914	1939	
X	1797	1817	1842	1865	1890[1]	1915	1940	
Y	1785	1821	——	1866	1891	1916	1941	
Z	1796	1822	1843	1867	1892	1917	1942	

1. The *Sovereign's Head* mark was added on 1 December 1784 to show the payment of tax and continued until 30 April 1890.

YORK

Being the second city in the land during the Middle Ages, York had a mark as early as 1411 and a cycle of date letters is thought to have begun in 1559, with the town mark – *"the halfe leopard head and half flowre-de-luyce"*; the former half may have been a half *rose* crowned from 1632–1698, but there seems to be no record of a change until the re-establishment of the office in 1700, when the *Cross charged with five Lions passant* (from the city arms) was introduced, with the *Leopard's Head erased* and *Britannia*, and a new but short-lived cycle. After an interval of seventy-three years another incomplete cycle has been noted, followed by two cycles, each of twenty-five letters, omitting *J*, and part of a third which brought the series to an end when the office was closed in 1857.

A	(1559)	1583	1607	1631	1657	1682	1700	(1776)	1787	1812	1837
B	(1560)	1584	1608	1632	1658	1683	1701	(1777)	1788	1813	1838
C	(1561)	(1585)	1609	1633	1659	1684	1702	1778	1789	1814	1839
D	(1562)	(1586)	1610	1634	1660	1685	1703	1779	1790	1815	1840
F	(1563)	1587	1611	1635	1661	1686	(1704)	1780	1791	1816	1841
E	1564	(1588)	1612	1636	1662	1687	1705	1781	1792	1817	1842
G	1565	(1589)	1613	1637	1663	1688	1706	1782	1793	1818	1843
H	1566	1590	1614	1638	1664	1689	——	1783	1794	1819	1844
I	(1567)	(1591)	1615	1639	1665	1690	——		1795	1820	1845
J	——	——	——	(1640)	——	——	——	1784	——	——	——
K	1568	1592	1616	1641	1666	1691	——	1785	1796	1821	1846
L	1569	1593	1617	1642	1667	1692	——	1786	1797	1822	1847
M	1570	1594	1618	1643	1668	1693	——	——	1798	1823	1848
N	(1571)	1595	1619	1644	1669	1694	——	——	1799	1824	1849
O	1572	1596	1620	1645	1670	1695	——	——	1800	1825	1850
P	1573	1597	1621	1646	1671	1696	——	——	1801	1826	1851
Q	1574	1598	1622	1647	1672	1697	——	——	1802	1827	1852
R	1575	1599	1623	1648	1673	1698	——	——	1803	1828	1853
S	1576	(1600)	1624	1649	1674	1699	——	——	1804	1829	1854
T	1577	1601	1625	1650	1675	——	——	——	1805	1830	1855
U	——	——	1626	1651	1676	——	——	——	1806	1831	——
V	(1578)	(1602)	——	1652	1677	——	——	——	1807	1832	1856
W	(1579)	(1603)	1627	1653	1678	——	——	——	1808	1833	
X	(1580)	1604	(1628)	1654	1679	——	——	——	1809	1834	
Y	(1581)	(1605)	1629	1655	1680	——	——	——	1810	1835	
Z	1582	(1606)	1630	1656	1681	——	——	——	1811	1836	

CLOCK CHARTS

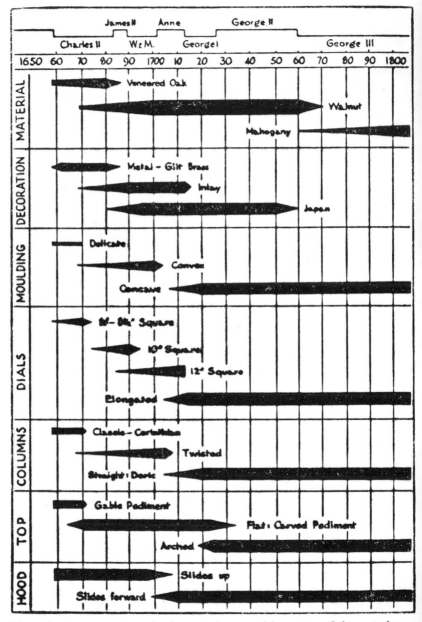

Chart showing approximately the periods covered by various fashions in horological materials, techniques, and styles from 1650 to 1800, for domestic clocks.

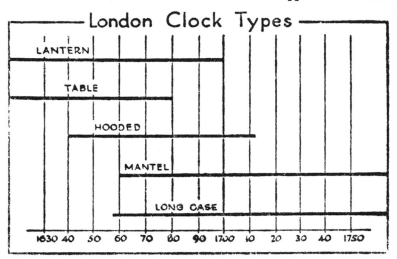

Chart showing the periods and progressions of popular clock types in demand
from London makers, *circa* 1630–1750. Provincial styles followed.

Bibliography

ARMS AND ARMOUR

Ashdown, C. H. *British & Foreign Arms & Armour*. London, 1909.

Burlington Fine Arts Club. *Illustrated Catalogue of an Exhibition of European Chased and Embossed Steel and Ironwork*. London, 1800.

Burton, Sir Richard F. *The Book of the Sword*. London, 1884.

ffoulkes, C. *The Armourer and his Craft*. Oxford, 1909.

Jackson, H. J. *European Hand Firearms*. London, 1923.

Laking, Sir Guy Francis. *A Record of Arms and Armour through Seven Centuries*. 5 vols. London, 1920–1922.

(This is the armour collectors' bible.)

Metropolitan Museum. *Handbook of Arms and Armour*. New York, 1915.

Pollard, H. B. C. *The Book of the Pistol and Revolver*. London, 1917.

Stone, G. C. *A Glossary of the Construction, Decoration and Use of Arms and Armour*. Portland (Maine), 1934.

Tower of London, The. *Inventory and Survey of the Armouries*. C. J. ffoulkes. London, 1916.

Wallace Collection, The. *European Arms and Armour*. 3 parts. Sir James G. Mann, 1924–1945.

CARPETS, RUGS, TAPESTRIES, ETC.

Ashton, Leigh. *Samplers*. London, 1926.

Edwards, A. Cecil. *The Persian Carpet*. London, 1953.

Erdmann, Kurt. *Der Orientalische Knapfteppiche*. Tübingen, 1955.

Flemming, H. *An Encyclopedia of Textiles*. Berlin, 1934.

Glazier. *Historic Textile Fabrics*. London, 1923.

Griffin, C. G. *The Practical Book of Oriental Rugs*. Philadelphia and London, 1911.

Haach, Hermann. *Oriental Rugs*. Eng. trans. London, 1960.

Hunton. *English Decorative Textiles*. London, 1930.

Kendrick, A. F. Tattersall C. E. *Handwoven Carpets, Oriental and European*. London, 1922

Palliser, Mrs. Bury. *History of Lace*.

Tattersall, C. *The Carpets of Persia*. London, 1931.

Thomson, W. *A History of Tapestry*. London 1930.

V & A Museum Catalogue. *Samplers*. R. C. Trendell, London, 1922.

V & A Museum Catalogue. *Tapestries*. Kendrick. London, 1924.

V & A Museum. *Notes on Carpet Knotting and Weaving*. Tattersall, 1939.

Wolfe. *How to Identify Oriental rugs*. London, 1927.

CERAMICS

GENERAL

Burton, W. *Porcelain: Its Nature, Art, and Manufacture.* London, 1906.
Cox, Warren E. *Pottery and Porcelain.* New York, 1944.
Danckert, Ludwig. *Handbuch des Europäischen Porzellans.* Munich, 1954.
Hannover, Emil. *Pottery and Porcelain.* London, 1925.
Hofmann, Friedrich H. *Das Porzellan der europäischen Manufakturen im 18. Jahrhundert.* Berlin, 1932.
Honey, W. B. *A Dictionary of European Ceramic Art.* London, 1952.
Honey, W. B. *The Art of the Potter.* London, 1940.
Leach, Bernard. *A Potter's Book.* London, 1940.
Rosenthal, Ernst. *Pottery and Ceramics.* Pelican Books, London, 1949.
Savage, George. *Porcelain through the Ages.* Pelican Books, London, 1954.
Savage, George. *Pottery through the Ages.* Pelican Books. London, 1959.
Schmidt, Robert. *Das Porzellan als Kunstwerk und Kulturspiegel.* Munich, 1925. Translated by W. A. Thorpe as *Porcelain as an Art and Mirror of Fashion.* London, 1932.

MARKS

Apart from the volumes mentioned below, which are primarily devoted to marks on pottery and porcelain, most of the books mentioned devote some space to marks. In the case of Honey's *Dictionary of European Ceramic Art*, this is particularly extensive.

Burton, W., and Hobson, R. L. *Handbook of Marks on Pottery and Porcelain.* London, 1928.
Chaffers, W. *Marks and Monograms on Pottery and Porcelain.* Various English and American editions from 1876 onwards.
This is a standard handbook of marks which has been revised from time to time. The later editions are, of course, the most useful, the earlier containing inaccuracies of attribution and fact. A shortened edition, containing only the marks, is also published.
Cushion, J. P., and Honey, W. B. *Handbook of Pottery and Porcelain Marks* London, 1956.
Rhead, G. W. *British Pottery Marks.* 1920.

JOURNALS

The following journals publish articles on antique pottery and porcelain, and other antiques and works of art, mentioned herein.

The Antique Collector.
The Antique Dealer and Collectors' Guide.
The Connoisseur.
Apollo.
The Burlington Magazine.
The Antiques Magazine. New York.

The following societies devoted to the study of pottery and porcelain publish transactions from time to time:

The English Ceramic Circle.

The Oriental Ceramic Society.
The Wedgwood Society.

SPECIALIZED PUBLICATIONS

Egyptian Faience

Wallis, Henry. *Egyptian Ceramic Art* (The MacGregor Collection). London, 1898.
Wallis, Henry. *Egyptian Ceramic Art*, London, 1900.

Greek and Roman Pottery

Charleston, R. J. *Roman Pottery.* London, 1954.
Hutton, C. A. *Greek Terra-cotta Statuettes.* London, 1899.
Lane, Arthur. *Greek Pottery.* London, 1948.
Walters, H. B. *History of Ancient Pottery, Greek, Etruscan, and Roman.* London, 1905.

Far Eastern Pottery and Porcelain

Gray, Basil. *Early Chinese Pottery and Porcelain.* London, 1953.
Hetherington, A. L. *Early Ceramic Wares of China.* London, 1922.
Hetherington, A. L. *Chinese Ceramic Glazes.* South Pasadena, 1947.
Hobson, R. L. *Chinese Pottery and Porcelain.* London, 1915.
Hobson, R. L. *Wares of the Ming Dynasty.* London, 1922.
Hobson, R. L., and Hetherington, A. L. *The Art of the Chinese Potter.* London, 1923.
Hobson, R. L. *The Later Ceramic Wares of China.* London, 1925.
Hobson, R. L. *The Catalogue of the George Eumorfopolous Collection.* London, 1925.
Hobson, R. L. *A Catalogue of Chinese Pottery and Porcelain in the Collection of Sir Percival David.* London, 1934.
Hobson, R. L. *British Museum Handbook of Pottery and Porcelain of the Far East.* London, 1937.
Hobson, R. L., Rackham, Bernard, and King, William. *Chinese Ceramics in Private Collections.* London, 1931.
Honey, W. B. *The Ceramic Art of China and Other Countries of the Far East.* London, 1937.
Honey, W. B. *Corean Pottery.* London, 1947.
Honey, W. B. *Chinese Porcelain, K'ang Hsi, Yung Chêng, and Ch'ien Lung.* London, 1927.
Jenyns, Soame. *Later Chinese Porcelain.* London, 1952.
Jenyns, Soame. *Ming Pottery and Porcelain.* London, 1955.
Wu, G. D. *Prehistoric Pottery in China.* London, 1938.
Zimmermann, Ernst. *Chinesisches Porzellan.* Leipzig, 1923.

Chinese and Japanese Export Porcelain

Crisp, F. A. *Armorial China.* London, 1907.
Hyde, J. A. Lloyd, *Oriental Lowestoft.* Newport, 1954.
Jourdain, Margaret, and Jenyns, Soame. *Chinese Export Art in the 18th Century.* London, 1950.
Phillips, J. G. *China Trade Porcelain.* London, 1957.
Tudor-Craig, Sir A. *Armorial Porcelain of the 18th Century.* London, 1925.
Volker, T. *Porcelain and the Dutch East India Company.* Leiden, 1954.

Persia and the Middle East

Hobson, R. L. *Guide to Islamic Pottery of the Near East.* London, 1932.
Lane, Arthur. *Early Islamic Pottery.* London, 1947.

Turkish Pottery

Hobson, R. L. *Guide to Islamic Pottery of the Near East.* London, 1932.
Victoria and Albert Museum. *Turkish Pottery* (A Picture Book). London, 1955.

Spain (Hispano-Moresque and Tin-enamelled Ware)

Frothingham, A. W. *Catalogue of Hispano-Moresque Ware in the Collection of the Hispanic Society of America.* New York, 1936.
Frothingham, A. W. *Talavera Pottery.* New York, 1944.
van der Put, A. *Hispano-Moresque Ware of the Fifteenth Century.* London, 1904.

Italy

Chompret, Dr. J. *Répertoire de la majolique italienne.* Paris, 1949.
Eisner Eisenhof, Baron A. de. *Le Porcellana di Capo-di-Monte.* Milan, 1925.
Lane, Arthur. *Italian Porcelain.* London, 1954.
Morazzoni, G. *Le Porcellane italiane.* Milan, 1935.
Rackham, Bernard. *Catalogue of Italian Maiolica in the Victoria and Albert Museum.* London, 1940.
Rackham, Bernard. *Italian Maiolica.* London, 1952.

Germany and the Austrian Empire

POTTERY

Bayer, A. *Die Ansbacher Fayence Fabriken.* Ansbach, 1928.
Falke, O. von. *Das Rheinische Steinzeug.* Berlin, 1908.
Feulner, A. *Frankfurter Fayencen.* Berlin, 1935.
Hofmann, F. H. *Geschichte der bayreuther Fayencefabrik.* Augsburg, 1928.
Hüseler, K. *Die Hamburger Fayencen des 17. Jahrhunderts.* Flensberg, 1925.
Kolschau, K. *Rheinisches Steinzeug.* Munich, 1924.
Meyer, A. *Böhmisches Porzellan und Steingut.* Leipzig, 1927.
Pazaurek, G. E. *Steingut: Formgebung und Geschichte.* Stuttgart, 1927.
Riesebieter, O. *Die deutschen Fayencen der 17. und 18. Jahrhundert.* Leipzig, 1921.

Books on German pottery in English are very scarce. A brief account is given by Savage (*Pottery through the Ages*). The subject is covered in various entries by Honey (*Dictionary of European Ceramic Art*). Hannover, whose work is now very scarce and expensive, devotes space to it. The best general work in German on faience is that of Riesbieter, which discusses all the important factories with many illustrations, and long lists of marks.

PORCELAIN

Bayer, A. *Ansbacher Porzellan.* Ansbach, 1933.
Berling, K. *Meissner Porzellan und seine Geschichte.* Leipzig, 1900.

Berling, K. *Festschrift der königlichen sächsischen Porzellanmanufaktur Meissen, 1710–1910.* Leipzig, 1910.
> A very rare English translation is entitled *Publication to Commemorate the 200th Jubilee of the Oldest European Porcelain Factory.*

Braun, E. W., and Folnesics, J. *Geschichte der k.k. Wiener Porzellanmanufaktur.* Vienna, 1907.

Christ, Hans. *Ludwigsburger Porzellanfiguren.* Berlin, 1921.

Graul, R., and Kurzwelly, A. *Alt-Thüringer Porzellan.* Leipzig, 1909.

Handt and Rakebrand. *Meissner Porzellan der Achzehnten Jahrhundert, 1710–1750.* Dresden, 1957.

Hayward, J. F. *Vienna Porcelain of the du Paquier Period.* London, 1952.

Hofmann, Friedrich H. *Frankenthaler Porzellan.* Munich, 1911.

Hofmann, Friedrich H. *Geschichte der bayerischen Porzellanmanufaktur Nymphenburg.* Leipzig, 1921–1923.

Hofmann, Friedrich H. *Das Porzellan der europäischen Manufacturen im 18. Jahrhundert.* Berlin, 1932.

Honey, W. B. *Dresden China.* London, 1947.

Honey, W. B. *German Porcelain.* London, 1947.

Lenz, G. *Berliner Porzellan: Die Manufaktur Friedrichs des Grossen, 1763–86.* Berlin, 1913.
> This enormous jubilee publication in two volumes is extremely scarce, but it the main source of detailed information on the work of this factory.

Meyer, H. *Böhmisches Porzellan und Steingut.* Leipzig, 1927.

Pazaurek, Gustav E. *Deutsche Fayence- und Porzellan-Hausmaler.* Leipzig, 1928.
> This is the standard work on the subject.

Pazaurek, Gustav E. *Meissner Porzellanmalerei des 18. Jahrhunderts.* Stuttgart, 1929.

Poche, E. *Bohemian Porcelain.* London, Post-war.

Röder, K., and Oppenheim, M. *Das Höchster Porzellan.* Mainz, 1930.

Sauerland, Max. *Deutsche Porzellanfiguren des 18. Jahrhunderts.* Cologne, 1923.

Savage, George. *18th-century German Porcelain.* London, 1958.

Scherer, C. *Das Fürstenberg Porzellan.* Berlin, 1909.

Schnorr von Carolsfeld, L. *Porzellan der europäischen Fabriken des 18. Jahrhunderts.* Berlin, 1912.

Schönberger, Arno. *Meissener Porzellan mit Höroldt-Malerei.* Darmstadt, Post-war.

Zimmermann, Ernst. *Die Erfinduhg und Frühzeit des Meissner Porzellans.* Berlin, 1908.

Zimmermann, Ernst. *Meissner Porzellan.* Leipzig, 1926.

France and Belgium

POTTERY

Chompret, Dr. J. *Les Faïences françaises primitives d'après les apothicaireries hospitalières.* Paris, 1946.

Damiron, C. *La Faïence artistique de Moustiers.* Lyons, 1919.

Damiron, C. *La Faïence de Lyon.* Paris, 1926.

Devaux, J. *Les Faïences d'Aprey.* Paris, 1908.
Gauthier, J. *Faïences et poteries rustiques.* Paris 1929.
Haug, H. *Les Faïences et porcelaines de Strasbourg.* Strasbourg, 1922.
Lane, Arthur. *French Faïence.* London, 1948.
Poncettin, F. and Salles, G. *Les Poteries françaises.* Paris, 1929.
Solon, M. L. *A History of Old French Faïence.* London, 1903.

PORCELAIN
Alfassa et Guérin. *Porcelaine Française.* Paris, 1932.
Auscher, A. S. *A History and Description of French Porcelain.* London, 1905.
Bourgeois, E. *Le biscuit de Sèvres au XVIIIe Siècle.* Paris 1909.
Chavagnac, Comte X. de, and Grollier, Marquis A. de. *Histoire des manufactures françaises de porcelaine.* Paris, 1906.
Haug, H. *Les faïences et porcelaines de Strasbourg.* Strasbourg, 1922.
Honey, W. B. *French Porcelain of the 18th Century.* London, 1950.
Soil de Moriame, E. J., and Desplace de Formanoir, L. *Les Porcelaines de Tournay.* Tournai, 1937.
Verlet, Grandjean, and Brunet. *Sèvres.* Paris, 1953.

Holland
Havard, H. *La Ceramique Hollandais.* Amsterdam, 1909.
Hudig, F. W. *Delfter Fayence.* Berlin, 1909.
de Jonge, C. H. *Oud-Nederlandsche Majolika en Delftsch Aardewerk.* Amsterdam, 1947.
Neurdenberg, E. (trans. Rackham). *Old Dutch Pottery and Tiles.* London, 1923.
Rackham, Bernard. *Netherlands Maiolica.* London, 1926.

Scandinavia
Hayden, A. *Royal Copenhagen Porcelain.* London, 1911.
Hüseler, K. *Geschichte der Schleswig-Holsteinischen Fayencen im 18. Jahrhundert.* Breslau, 1929.
Hüseler, K. *Die Kieler Fayence-Manufakturen.* Flensberg, 1923.

Russia
Lukomsky, G. *Russisches Porzellan, 1744–1923.* Berlin, 1924.
  This book, which is very rare, provides the best account of Russian porcelain. It is well illustrated, and has a comprehensive list of marks.

Switzerland
Ducret, S. *Zürcher Porzellan des 18. Jahrhunderts.* Zürich, 1944.
Molin, A. de. *Histoire documentaire de la manufacture de Nyon, 1781–1813.* Lausanne, 1924.

English Pottery and Porcelain
POTTERY
Barnard, H. *Chats on Wedgwood Ware.* London, 1924.
Burlington Fine Arts Club. *Illustrated Catalogue of Early English Earthenware.* London, 1914.
Burton, W. *A History and Description of English Earthenware and Stoneware.* London, 1904.

Church, Sir A. H. *English Earthenware*. London, 1911.
Garner, F. H. *English Delftware*. London, 1948.
Hodgkin, J. E. and E. *Examples of English Pottery Named, Dated, and Inscribed.* London, 1891.
Honey, W. B. *English Pottery and Porcelain*. London, 1933.
Honey, W. B. *Wedgwood Ware*. London, 1948.
Jewitt, Llewellyn, *The Ceramic Art of Great Britain*. London, 1878.
Lomax, C. J. *Quaint Old English Pottery*. Manchester, 1909.
Nance, E. Morton. *The Pottery and Porcelain of Swansea and Nantgarw.* London, 1942.
Poutney, W. J. *The Old Bristol Potteries*. Bristol, 1920.
Rackham, Bernard. *Medieval English Pottery*. London, 1948.
Rackham, Bernard. *Early Staffordshire Pottery*. London.
Rackham, B. *Catalogue of the Schreiber Collection of English Earthenware in the Victoria and Albert Museum.*
Rackham, Bernard, and Read, H. *English Pottery*. London, 1924.
Rhead, G. W. *The Earthenware Collector*. London, 1920.

PORCELAIN

General

Bemrose, Geoffrey. *Nineteenth-century English Pottery and Porcelain*. London, 1952.
Church, Sir A. H. *English Porcelain*. London, 1911.
Dixon, J. L. *English Porcelain of the Eighteenth Century*. London, 1952.
Eccles, Herbert, and Rackham, Bernard. *Analysed Specimens of English Porcelain*. London, 1922.
English Ceramic Circle. *The Commemorative Catalogue of an Exhibition of English Pottery and Porcelain at the V. and A. Museum*. London, 1949.
Fisher, Stanley W. *The Decoration of English Porcelain*. London, 1956.
Fisher, Stanley W. *English Blue-and-white Porcelain of the Eighteenth Century.* London, 1950.
Hobson, R. L. *Catalogue of English Porcelain in the British Museum*. 1905.
Honey, W. B. *Old English Porcelain*. London, 1948.
King, William. *English Porcelain Figures of the Eighteenth Century*. London, 1925.
Norman, Harold. *Veilleuses*. London, 1967.
Rackham, Bernard. *Catalogue of the Herbert Allen Collection*. London, 1923.
Rackham, Bernard. *Catalogue of the Schreiber Collection of English Porcelain, Enamels, and Glass*. London, 1930.
Savage, George. *Eighteenth-century English Porcelain*. London, 1952.

Biographical

Cook, Cyril. *The Life and Work of Robert Hancock*. London, 1948.
MacAlister, Mrs. D. *William Duesbury's London Account Book*. London, 1931.
Tapp, Major W. H. *Jeffryes Hamett O'Neale*. London, 1938.

Chelsea

Bemrose, William. *Bow, Chelsea, and Derby Porcelain*. London, 1898.
Blunt, R. (Ed.). *Cheyne Book of Chelsea Porcelain*. London, 1924.
Bryant, G. F. *Chelsea Porcelain Toys*. London, 1925.

Hurlbutt, Frank. *Chelsea China.* London, 1937.
King, William. *Chelsea Porcelain.* London, 1922.
MacKenna, F. Severne. *Chelsea Porcelain: The Triangle and Raised Anchor Wares.* Leigh-on-Sea, 1948.
MacKenna, F. Severne. *Chelsea Porcelain: The Red Anchor Wares.* Leigh-on-Sea, 1951.
MacKenna, F. Severne. *Chelsea Porcelain: The Gold Anchor Wares.* Leigh-on-Sea, 1952.

Bow
Hurlbutt, Frank. *Bow Porcelain.* London, 1926.
Tiffin, F. W. *A Chronograph of the Bow, Chelsea, and Derby China Factories.* Salisbury, 1957.

Derby
Gilhespy, F. Brayshaw. *Derby Porcelain.* Leigh-on-Sea, 1950.
Haslem, J. *The Old Derby China Factory.* London, 1875.
Hurlbutt, F. *Old Derby Porcelain and Its Artist-workmen.* London, 1925.
Hyam, E. E. *The English Period of Derby Porcelain.* London, 1926.

Worcester
Barrett, F. A. *Worcester Porcelain.* London, 1953.
Hobson, R. L. *Worcester Porcelain.* London, 1910.
Hobson, R. L. *Catalogue of the Frank Lloyd Collection of Worcester Porcelain in the British Museum.* London, 1923.
MacKenna, F. Severne. *Worcester Porcelain.* Leigh-on-Sea, 1950.

Longton Hall
Bemrose, W. *Longton Hall Porcelain.* London, 1898.
Warney, Dr. Bernard. *Longton Hall Porcelain.* London, 1957.

Lowestoft
Murton, A. E. *Lowestoft China.* Lowestoft, 1932.
Spelman, W. W. R. *Lowestoft China.* London and Norwich, 1905.

Liverpool
Boney, Dr. Knowles. *Liverpool Porcelain.* London, 1957.
Gatty, C. T. *The Liverpool Potteries.* Liverpool, 1882.
Mayer, Joseph. *History of the Art of Pottery in Liverpool.* 1885.

Plymouth, Bristol, and New Hall
Hurlbutt, F. *Bristol Porcelain.* London, 1928.
MacKenna, F. Severne. *Cookworthy's Plymouth and Bristol Porcelain.* Leigh-on-Sea, 1946.
MacKenna, F. Severne. *Champion's Bristol Porcelain.* Leigh-on-Sea, 1947.
Owen, Hugh. *Two Centuries of Ceramic Art in Bristol.* London, 1873.
Stringer, George Eyre. *New Hall Porcelain.* London, 1949.
Trapnell, Alfred E. *A Catalogue of a collection of Plymouth and Bristol Porcelain made by.* London, 1912.

Welsh Porcelain
John, W. D. *Nantgarw Porcelain.* London, 1948.
Meager, Kildare S. *Swansea and Nantgarw Potteries.* Swansea, 1949.

Nance, Morton. *The Pottery and Porcelain of Swansea and Nantgarw*. London, 1943.

Williams, I. J. *Guide to the Collection of Welsh Porcelain in the National Museum of Wales*. 1931.

CLOCKS

Baillie, G. H. *Watches: Their History, Decoration and Mechanism*. London, 1929.

Britten, F. H. *Old Clocks and Watches and Their Makers*. London. Various editions.

(This is the clock collectors' bible.)

Cecinsky, Herbert, and Webster, Malcolm. *English Domestic Clocks*. London, 1913.

Cecinsky, Herbert. *The Old English Master Clock-makers and Their Clocks*. London, 1938.

Hayden, Arthur. *Chats on Old English Clocks*. London, 1917.

Symonds, R. W. *A History of English Clocks*. Penguin Books, 1947.

Symonds, R. W. *Thomas Tompion*. London, 1951.

Ullyett, Kenneth R. *British Clocks and Clock-makers*. London, 1947.

Ullyett, Kenneth R. *In Quest of Clocks*. London, 1950.

ENAMELS

Cunynghame, H. *European Enamels*. London, 1906.

Mew, Egan. *Battersea Enamels*. London, 1926.

Victoria & Albert Museum. *Catalogue of the Schreiber Collection*. Vol. III.
also

Cook, Cyril. *The Life and Works of Robert Hancock*. London, 1948.

This refers to the work of Hancock on enamels as well as on porcelain.

FORGERIES

Savage, George. *Fakes, Forgeries and Reproductions*. London, 1963.

FURNITURE, ENGLISH

Allsop, Bruce. *Decoration and Furniture*. London, 1952.

Bell, J. Munro. *The Furniture Designs of Chippendale, Hepplewhite, and Sheraton*. London, 1938.

Brackett, Oliver. *English Furniture Illustrated*. London, 1950.

Brackett, Oliver. *Thomas Chippendale*. London, 1924.

Cecinsky, Herbert. *English Furniture of the 18th Century*. London, 1909.

Cecinsky, H. *The Gentle Art of Faking Furniture*. London, 1931.

Edwards, Ralph. *Dictionary of English Furniture*. London, 1954.

Edwards, Ralph and Jourdain, Margaret. *Georgian Cabinet Makers*. London, 1948.

Fastnedge, Ralph. *English Furniture Styles from 1500 to 1830*. Pelican Books, London, 1956.

Kendrick, A. F. *English Decorative Fabrics of the 16th to 18th Centuries*. London, 1934.

MacQuiod, Percy. *History of English Furniture*. London, 1938.

Marillier, H. C. *English Tapestries of the 18th Century*. London, 1930.

Roe, F. Gordon. *English Cottage Furniture*. London, 1950.
Sugden, A. V., and Edmondson, J. L. *A History of English Wallpaper, 1500–1914*. London, 1925.
Symonds, R. W. *Veneered Walnut Furniture, 1660–1700*. London, 1946.
Symonds, R. W. *Masterpieces of English Furniture and Clocks*. London, 1940.
Symonds, R. W. *The Present State of Old English Furniture*. London, 1921.
Symonds, R. W. *Old English walnut and lacquer furniture, and the Methods of the Furniture Faker, etc.* London, 1923.
Truman, Nevil. *Historic Furnishing*. London, 1950.
Wenham, Edward. *Old Furniture for Modern Rooms*. London, 1939.

FURNITURE, FOREIGN

Bode, W. von. *Italian Renaissance Furniture*. New York, 1921.
Dilke, Lady. *French Furniture and Decoration of the XVIIIth Century*. London, 1901.
Downs, Joseph. *American Furniture: Queen Anne and Chippendale Periods*. New York, 1952.
Graul, R. *Das Achtzehnten Jahrhundert, Dekoration und Mobiliar*. Berlin, 1905.
Morazzoni, G. *Il Mobilo Italiano*. Florence, 1940.
Molinier, E. *La Mobilier aux XVIIe et XVIIIe siècles*. Paris, 1899.
Nagel, Charles. *American Furniture: 1650–1850*. New York, 1949.
V & A Museum. *Catalogue of the Jones Collection. Furniture*. 1922.
Wallace Collection Catalogue. Furniture (F. J. B. Watson). London, 1956.

GLASS

Bergstrom. *Old Glass Paperweights*. London, 1948.
Bles, Joseph. *Rare English Glasses of the 17th and 18th Centuries*. London, 1925.
Buckley, Francis. *A History of Old English Glass*. London, 1925.
Buckley, W. *European Glass*. London, 1926.
Buckley, W. *Diamond Engraved Glass of the 16th Century*. London, 1929.
Buckley, W. *The Art of Glass*. London, 1939.
Dillon, E. *Glass*. London, 1907.
Frémy, E. *Histoire de la Manufacture Royale des Glaces de France aux XVIIe et au XVIIIe siècles*. Paris, 1909.
Frothingham, A. *Hispanic Glass*. New York, 1941.
Hartshorne, A. *Old English Glasses*. London, 1897.
Haynes, E. Barrington. *Glass*. Pelican Books, London, 1948.
Honey, W. B. *Glass* (Victoria and Albert Museum Handbook). London, 1946.
Hudig, F. W. *Das Glas*. Vienna, 1925.
Kisa, A. *Das Glas im Altertums*. Leipzig, 1908.
Lamm, C. J. *Mittelalterliche Gläser und Steinschnittarbeiten aus dem nahen Osten*. Berlin, 1929.
Lorenzetti, G. *Vetri di Murano*. Rome, 1931.
Neuberg, Frederic. *Glass in Antiquity*. London, 1948.
Pazaurek, G. E. *Gläser der Empire – und Biedermeiezeit*. Leipzig, 1923.
Pazaurek, G. E. *Kunstgläser der Gegenwart*. Leipzig, 1925.

286   *The Antique Collector's Handbook*

Savage, George. *Glass.* London, 1964.
Schmidt, Robert. *Das Glas.* Berlin, 1922.
Thorpe, W. A. *A History of English and Irish Glass.* London, 1929.
Thorpe, W. A. *English Glass.* London, 1935.

HERALDRY

Fox-Davies, A. C. *The Art of Heraldry.* London, 1905.
Fox-Davies, A. C. *Complete Guide to Heraldry.* London, 1925.
Debrett, *Peerage of the United Kingdom.*

IVORIES

Maskell, Alfred. *Ivories.* London, 1905.
V & A Museum. *Catalogues of Carvings in Ivory.* 1927–1929.

JADE AND HARDSTONES

Davis, F. *Chinese Jade.* London, 1944.
Hansford, S. Howard. *Chinese Jade Carving.* London, 1950.
Laufer, B. *Jade.* Chicago, 1912.
Savage, George. *Chinese Jade.* London, 1964.
Various authors. *Chinese Art.* London, 1935.
Willetts, W. *Chinese Art.* Pelican Books, London, 1958.

LACQUER

Huish, Marcus B. *Japan and Its Art.* London, 1912.
Strange, E. F. *Catalogue of Chinese Lacquer in the Victoria and Albert Museum.* London, 1925.
Strange, E. F. *Chinese Lacquer.* 1926.
Strange, E. F. *Catalogue of Japanese Lacquer.* V & A Museum. London, 1924.
Various authors. *Chinese Art.* London, 1935.
Willetts, W. *Chinese Art.* Pelican Books, London, 1958.

METAL-WORK
(a) Bronze

Bode, Wilhelm von. *Italian Bronze Statuettes of the Renaissance.* London, 1907–1908.
Huish, M. B. *Japan and Its Art.* London, 1912.
Karlgren. *New Studies in Chinese Bronzes.* Stockholm, 1937.
Koop, A. J. *Early Chinese Bronzes.* London, 1924.
Museum of Far Eastern Antiquities, Stockholm. *Bulletin No. 8.* 1936.
Museum of Far Eastern Antiquities. *Bulletin No. 24.* 1952.
Willetts, W. *Chinese Art.* Pelican Books, London, 1958.
Yetts, W. P. *Chinese Bronzes.* London, 1924.
And the part of the Catalogue of the Eumorfopolous Collection devoted to bronzes by the same authority.

(b) Other Metal-work

Ayrton, M., and Silcox, A. *Wrought Iron and Its Decorative Use.* London, 1929.
Burgess, F. W. *Chats on Old Copper and Brass.* London, 1954.

Cotterell, H. H. *Old Pewter – Its Makers and Marks*. London, 1929.
Graeme, A. V. S. *Old British Pewter, 1500–1800*. London, 1952.
Hoever, Otto. *An Encyclopedia of Ironwork*. London, 1927.
Laughlin, L. I. *Pewter in America*. Boston, 1940.
Weaver, Sir Lawrence. *English Leadwork*. London, 1909.

PRICES

Reitlinger, Gerald. *The Economics of Taste*. Vols. I and II. London, 1961 and 1963.

RESTORATION

Lucas, A. *Antiques: Their Restoration and Preservation*. London, 1932.
Plenderleith, Dr. H. J. *The Preservation of Antiquities*. London, 1934 and 1956.
Plenderleith, Dr. H. J. *The Preservation of Leather Bookbindings*. London, 1946.
Scott, Dr. Alexander. *The Cleaning and Restoration of Museum Exhibits*. London, 1921, 1923, and 1926.
Savage, George. *The Art and Antique Restorers' Handbook*. London, 1954.

SILVER

Avery, C. Louise. *Early American Silver*. New York, 1930.
Bradbury, Fredk. *Collectors' Guide to Marks of Origin on Silver Plate made in Great Britain and Ireland*. Sheffield. 1933.
Bradbury, Fredk. *History of Old Sheffield Plate*. London, 1912.
Castro, J. P. de. *Law and Practice of Hall-marking Gold and Silver Wares*. London, 1935.
Cripps, W. J. *Old English Plate*. London, 1878.
Cripps, W. J. *Old French Plate*. London, 1880.
Dent, H. C. *Wine, Spirit, and Sauce Labels of the 18th and 19th Centuries*. Norwich, 1933.
Graham, J. *Early American Silver Marks*. New York, 1936.
Heal, Sir Ambrose. *The London Goldsmiths, 1200–1800*. Cambridge, 1935.
How, G. E. P. and J. P. *English and Scottish Spoons*. London, 1952.
Jackson, Sir Charles J. *English Goldsmiths and Their Marks*. London, 1949.
Jackson, Sir Charles J. *The Illustrated History of English Plate*. London, 1911.
Jones, E. A. *Old Silver of Europe and America*. London, 1928.
Norton, R. M. *History of Gold Snuff-boxes*. London, 1938.
Oman, Sir Charles. *English Domestic Silver*. London, 1947.
Penzer, N. M. *Paul Storr*. London, 1955.
Phillips, P. A. S. *Paul de Lamerie*. London, 1935.
Taylor, Gerald. *Silver*. Pelican Books. London, 1955.
Veitch, H. N. *Sheffield Plate*. London, 1908.

ULTRA-VIOLET RADIATION

Rorimer, James J. *Ultra-violet Rays and Their Use in the Examination of Works of Art*. New York, 1931.

WOOD-CARVING

Maskell, A. *Wood Sculpture*. London, 1911.

Index

288